Reading, Writing, and Revolution

Reading, Writing, and Revolution

ESCUELITAS AND THE EMERGENCE OF A MEXICAN AMERICAN IDENTITY IN TEXAS

PHILIS M. BARRAGÁN GOETZ

University of Texas Press

AUSTIN

Requests for permission to reproduce material from this work should be sent to:
Permissions
University of Texas Press
P.O. Box 7819
Austin, TX 78713–7819
utpress.utexas.edu/rp-form

♾ The paper used in this book meets the minimum requirements of ANSI/NISO
Z39.48–1992 (R1997) (Permanence of Paper).

Library of Congress Cataloging-in-Publication Data

Names: Barragán Goetz, Philis M. author.
Title: Reading, writing, and revolution : escuelitas and the emergence of a Mexican
American identity in Texas / Philis M. Barragán Goetz.
Description: First edition. | Austin : University of Texas Press, 2020. | Includes
bibliographical references and index.
Identifiers: LCCN 2019040637
ISBN 978-1-4773-2092-1 (paperback)
ISBN 978-1-4773-2093-8 (ebook)
ISBN 978-1-4773-2094-5 (ebook other)
Subjects: LCSH: Mexicans—Education—Texas—History. | Mexican American chil-
dren—Education—Texas—History. | Public schools—Texas—History. | Educational
equalization—Texas—History. | Education and state—Texas—History.
Classification: LCC LC2687.T4 B37 2020 | DDC 371.829/680764—dc23
LC record available at https://lccn.loc.gov/2019040637

doi:10.7560/320914

For all the Davids, Lucianas, and Adelinas
in the world,
but most especially
for mine.

CONTENTS

Reading, Writing, and Revolution

ESCUELITAS, LITERACY, AND IMAGINARY DUAL CITIZENSHIP

"To this day I cannot repeat the eight times table in English, only in Spanish," Rico Vásquez says about the lifelong influence of having attended Doña Albinita García de León's summer escuelita in his hometown of Mercedes, Texas.[1] Wistfully remembering his escuelita days, he recalls "laying down on a towel close to the torn screen door so I could feel the breeze over my sweaty brow when we took our naps."[2] He was seven when his family left Mercedes for San Antonio, where he enrolled in the "English only" public school "and began the new adventure into being the American in a Mexican American."[3] Although Doña Albinita taught reading, writing, poetry, and arithmetic—subjects common to any public school curriculum then and now—she did so from an ethnic Mexican perspective, an approach common to any escuelita in the first half of the twentieth century. Reading assignments were drawn from Spanish newspapers, writing was focused on Spanish literacy, poetry meant Mexican poetry, and Spanish was always the language of instruction.

Escuelita is a generic term, as literary and cultural critic José Limón noted, for a broad base of community schools that were both informal (those that individuals, usually women, started in their own living rooms) and formal (those that had their own schoolhouse to which an entire community contributed).[4] They truly were a grassroots phenomenon in that there was never a governmental or communal body overseeing their development. Instead, they arose from ethnic Mexicans' attempts to educate their children in response to various obstacles that were time- and place-specific, and they did so while keeping the ethnic Mexican experience at the center. Since different circumstances surrounded the founding of each school, and as their trajectories were tied to the ways in which their local communities responded to national and transnational developments, they had varying degrees of longevity while being both reactionary and progressive.

In the early days of this project, when I was a doctoral student thinking about how to put together a method for studying a topic that is simultaneously everywhere and nowhere in the historical record, Elaine Ayala, a columnist for the *San Antonio Express-News*, wrote an article about my research. Her last paragraph asked readers to reach out to me if they had ever attended one of these little schools.[5] Answering Ayala's call—and assuaging my own desperate hope for a response—Rico Vásquez shared his escuelita escapades, noting, "A rush of memories came over me [reading Ayala's article]. . . . I have fond memories of that time in my life but my memory is fading fast."[6] His recollection serves as a microcosm for a much larger history of ethnic Mexican education and the debates surrounding it. Like many others, his experience illustrates the historical tension between escuelitas and the public school system—an example of the ways in which education on the US-Mexico border is both a hegemonic tool of domination and a subaltern tool of survival.[7]

Within the historiographical narrative of Mexican American education in Texas, the role of escuelitas has been impacted greatly by the politics surrounding ethnic Mexican schooling. From the mid-nineteenth century to the present, the widespread interpretation of the relationship between ethnic Mexicans and education is that they simply do not value it. Before and after the turn of the twentieth century, superintendents throughout Texas who oversaw large student populations of ethnic Mexicans unequivocally made this claim year after year. Well over a century later, scholars of ethnic Mexican education are still laboring to debunk this allegation in the hope of contributing a usable past through which the larger American culture will interpret ethnic Mexicans' educational plight in the present.

The first work to make an intervention was Guadalupe San Miguel's *"Let All of Them Take Heed"* (1987), which documents the organized struggles that the League of United Latin American Citizens (LULAC), the American GI Forum, and the Mexican American Legal Defense and Education Fund undertook on behalf of school integration, examining both how law and policy enabled education inequality and how Mexican Americans fought against it. As the first full-length text on the subject, San Miguel focused attention on Mexican Americans as active agents rather than passive victims of Anglo oppression. Carlos K. Blanton's *The Strange Career of Bilingual Education in Texas* (2004) is a comparative study of language policy in Texas using bilingual educational history as a lens for analyzing how ethnic

Mexicans—as well as German, Czech, and Polish people—responded to top-down structures such as state legislation and public school curriculum. San Miguel's and Blanton's emphasis on policy and legal activism focused their scholarship on the public school system within US borders.

Amid the evidence collected in their efforts to build a historiography disproving these pervasive stereotypes sit the escuelitas. For San Miguel and Blanton, who were intent on staying away from a lens of victimization in favor of one focused on agency, the proliferation of these little schools from the late nineteenth century to the onset of World War II provided the perfect example of ethnic Mexicans resisting Anglo hegemony in the name of education.[8] Many other scholars have also made this argument skillfully and effectively.[9]

A cultural resistance paradigm, however, does not always fit the complexity and nuance of escuelita history. Unlike New Mexico, and to some extent California, the government of Texas always conducted its state affairs in English. The Anglo population of the Republic of Texas worked to keep Spanish from becoming a language of political importance well before annexation in 1845.[10] In Texas, as in other places across the nation, language functioned as a signifier for power, and the escuelitas operated as a vehicle for communities to negotiate that power. As such, the grassroots nature of these little schools makes them a gauge for the extent to which ethnic Mexicans incorporated themselves into US society. Their proliferation during various time periods points to an unfulfilled demand, and likewise, their decline signals their growing irrelevance among the ethnic Mexican population. Essentially, their existence, their vicissitudes—when placed within both the national and transnational contexts of modernization, progressivism, the expansion of the public school system, Mexican immigration, and the Mexican Revolution—point to junctures of ethnic Mexican cultural negotiation.

The history of escuelitas is more than one of cultural resistance in the face of Anglo hegemony. It is a history of how small neighborhoods, whose needs and intentions fluctuated over several decades, negotiated their constant engagement with the two nations surrounding them. It is a story about empowered and educated women assuming leadership roles in historically patriarchal communities, and a tale of the ways in which adults look to their children's education to manage the problems of their own lives. But above all, it is a forgotten narrative of how ethnic Mexicans—whose daily experiences, for generations, unfolded at the crossroads of language and education, race and identity, and survival and conquest—reacted and progressed as they settled into the idea of becoming Mexican Americans.

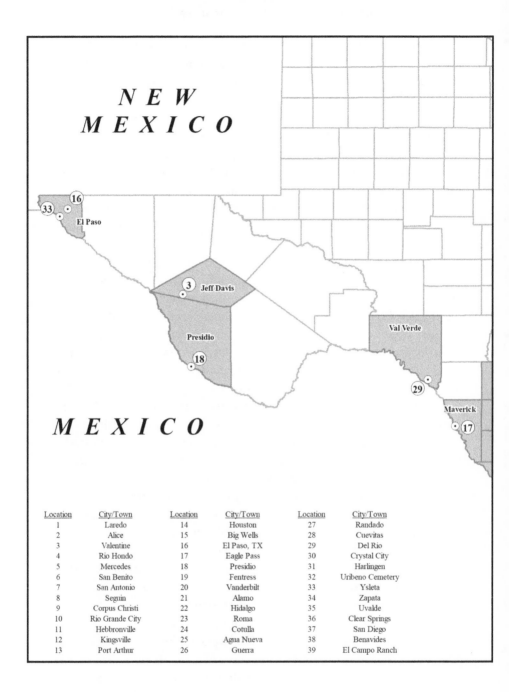

NEW MEXICO

16
33
El Paso

3 Jeff Davis

Presidio

18

Val Verde

29

MEXICO

Maverick

17

Location	City/Town	Location	City/Town	Location	City/Town
1	Laredo	14	Houston	27	Randado
2	Alice	15	Big Wells	28	Cuevitas
3	Valentine	16	El Paso, TX	29	Del Rio
4	Rio Hondo	17	Eagle Pass	30	Crystal City
5	Mercedes	18	Presidio	31	Harlingen
6	San Benito	19	Fentress	32	Uribeno Cemetery
7	San Antonio	20	Vanderbilt	33	Ysleta
8	Seguin	21	Alamo	34	Zapata
9	Corpus Christi	22	Hidalgo	35	Uvalde
10	Rio Grande City	23	Roma	36	Clear Springs
11	Hebbronville	24	Cotulla	37	San Diego
12	Kingsville	25	Agua Nueva	38	Benavides
13	Port Arthur	26	Guerra	39	El Campo Ranch

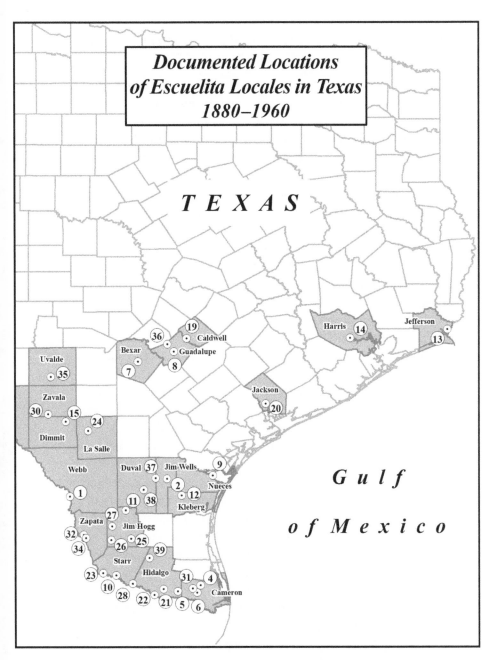

**Documented Locations
of Escuelita Locales in Texas
1880–1960**

TEXAS

Uvalde
35

Zavala
30   15
24
Dimmit
La Salle

Webb
1
11   38
27
Zapata
32   Jim Hogg
34   26   25
39
Starr
23   Hidalgo
10   31   4
28   22   21   5   6   Cameron

Bexar
7   8   Guadalupe
36   19   Caldwell

Jackson
20

Duval 37   Jim Wells   9
2   Nueces
12
Kleberg

Harris 14   Jefferson
13

Gulf

of Mexico

This map reflects the compiled information on documented escuelita locations from archival records, oral history interviews conducted by the author and other scholars, and historical newspapers.

MODERN PROGRESSIVES AND PROGRESSIVE MODERNISTS: AN OVERVIEW OF ESCUELITA HISTORY IN SOUTH TEXAS

The Texas public school system began with the Common School Law of 1854, but the Civil War and the tumultuous politics that followed stunted its growth dramatically in the subsequent three decades.[11] In 1870, the National Bureau of Education referred to Texas as "the darkest field educationally in the United States" because of its dearth of state-supported schools. In fact, the bureau found there to be no state-supported schools at all and only one public school building.[12] In this early period, escuelitas represented one of the few opportunities for education that many Texas Mexican children had, and as superintendents reported, they existed in just about every rural settlement throughout south Texas.[13]

Two of the most salient paradigms for understanding the trajectory of escuelita history and the history of the Texas public school system in the late nineteenth and early twentieth centuries are modernization and progressivism. Scholars of modernization typically characterize it as being closely tied to the social and economic changes brought about by the complex development of capitalism and the innovation and constant change on which it depends. Typically, modernity is understood as a phenomenon that unfurled in urban areas and was created by men, who, unfettered by community and family, used the emotional toll from these economic transformations as their muse.[14]

Modernity had a different narrative on the US-Mexico border—a phenomenon called borderland modernity—because ethnic Mexicans' modern experience was so closely tied to their community and to Anglo hegemony.[15] Modernization in south Texas enabled the dominant industry of the arid landscape—ranching—to shift to agribusiness as the rise of irrigation technology and the expansion of the railroads restructured the economy around the burgeoning corporate farming industry, transforming political and social relationships in the process. Associations between employers and employees became more impersonal, and the new agribusinesses required a large pool of unskilled, low-wage workers to pick crops.[16] Modernization dovetailed with progressivism and a fierce nativism, enabling the public school system to expand under the auspices of progressive educators, while ethnic Mexican children filled this need for unskilled laborers. The Progressive Era—more of a "spirit" than an organized movement, as one scholar notes—sought to implement reforms that these capitalist developments necessitated, reforms concerned with democracy, efficiency, corporate regulation, social justice, and public service.[17] Women's suffrage, Prohibition, child labor, and educational reform were key issues for progressives in the early part of the twentieth century.

Nationally, the Progressive Era is thought to have begun in the late nineteenth century and gone into decline by 1920. This age of reform, however, took on a different trajectory with distinct consequences in the South, a region struggling to reconcile the needs of the agribusiness industry while still encouraging a growing level of industrialization. In the midst of this transition, urban middle-class reformers often found it difficult to wrest political power from local interests because southerners interpreted the new bureaucratic agencies created to carry out social reform as what one Progressive Era historian has called "the expansion of coercive state intervention" determined to undermine local autonomy.[18] Therein lies the paradox of southern progressivism: if southerners wanted to benefit from the new policies, they needed to sacrifice control over their own communities. The paradox of southern progressivism was more complicated for minorities. Ethnic Mexicans were expected not only to set aside what little voice they had in local affairs in order to experience some of the benefits of social reforms intended for Whites only, but also to undergo complete and unequivocal assimilation in an era of intense nativism and xenophobia.[19]

The year 1884 saw the arrival of the progressive education movement in Texas with the passage of the school reform bill, which attempted to create a centralized educational apparatus that prized the district system over the older community system—a system that granted a measure of autonomy to local and minority communities. Despite the community system's drawbacks, it allowed parents to have control over how their public schools functioned.[20] Other reforms that were part of the 1884 bill included school consolidation, teacher certification, and English-only instruction. These reforms, however, had a negative impact on bilingual education for ethnic Mexican, German, and Czech children, who were taught that a Hyphenated American is no American at all. The change in the relationship in 1884 between ethnic Mexicans and the public school system politicized escuelitas, whose curriculum of Spanish literacy and Mexican history and cultural traditions were subjects that Texas public school superintendents vehemently worked to ban from their course of study.

In 1910, escuelita history took another turn. First, in that year the state superintendent of public instruction, F. M. Bralley, announced in the seventeenth biennial report on the state of education in Texas that the community system finally was dead.[21] As the community system disappeared, education officials implemented an Americanization curriculum in segregated public schools across the state. These schools relied on subtractive

Americanization—expecting students to leave their families' language and culture behind permanently—rather than additive, which allows students to keep them.[22] Social scientists of the era believed the newly invented IQ test was a reliable assessment of intelligence. Ethnic Mexicans' under-achievement on these highly biased exams justified the perpetuation of a subtractive Americanization curriculum within the confines of vocational, segregated schools. Subsequent reforms, such as Texas's compulsory school law passed in 1915, also negatively impacted ethnic Mexicans because they were not enforced. Many superintendents failed to report ethnic Mexican children's absences for a number of reasons: continuing to collect state funds for students who were not there, minimizing the ethnic Mexican presence by not requiring them to attend school, and supporting the corporate farming industry by permitting students to be a source of cheap, unskilled labor.[23] Southern progressive educators believed these tactics constituted a modern approach to the business of public education. The IQ test, subtractive Amer-icanization, segregation, and vocational training provided the best return on the state's investment, and the public school system became a reliable source of low-wage ethnic Mexican labor.[24]

There is a tragic irony in the relationship between ethnic Mexican education, progressivism, and modernization. Ethnic Mexicans' desire to become part of the emerging capitalist economy made English-language education increasingly important, and larger numbers of them enrolled their children in the public school system. The development of the capitalist economy, however, encouraged the Anglo power structure to use segregated and vocational schooling as a tool for preventing upward socioeconomic mobility. Essentially, the expansion of capitalism influenced ethnic Mex-icans to participate in the public education system while simultaneously hindering their very admittance. At the center of these intersections of nativism, progressivism, and modernization stood ethnic Mexican children who attended segregated, vocational schools that did not go beyond the fourth grade.

The political consequences of these new policies were not lost on escuelita advocates such as Jovita Idar, who argued from Laredo in 1911, amidst the backdrop of the Mexican Revolution, that their communities needed these alternative institutions to keep Mexico alive within the colonia mexicana (the colony of ethnic Mexicans living in the United States) and to provide Texas Mexican children with a path to socioeconomic mobility. In fact, many ethnic Mexican journalists, in addition to Idar, participated in heated debates about the role of escuelitas in a modernizing, progressive, English-only American society.

The second development to influence escuelita history around 1910 was the change in the structure of the ethnic Mexican community, which occurred just as progressives gained more influence and the public schools' commitment to English-only instruction within an Anglo-centric curriculum intensified. Before 1900, Mexican immigrants accounted for 1 percent of the population in south Texas, but by 1930, they accounted for 15 percent.[25] The onset of the Mexican Revolution's violent uprisings throughout the country engendered the influx of about a million Mexican refugees and political exiles to the American Southwest. Between 1910 and 1920, as the revolution took more vicious turns, and as various coups d'etat forced federal power to change hands, the Mexican government watched as hundreds of thousands of its citizens fled for the United States. The large influx of Mexican immigrants greatly impacted the composition of the ethnic Mexican population in the United States, leading to long-lasting, complex tensions between Mexican immigrants and Texas Mexicans that are embedded in escuelita history.[26]

Previously, the Mexican government had shown little interest in the well-being of its citizens living north of the Río Grande, but after 1920, those expatriates became an integral part of Mexico's postrevolutionary plan. After 1920, Mexico struggled to construct its own national identity both at home and to the colonia mexicana because (1) Mexico's diverse population made constructing a stable and more unified culture difficult and complicated; (2) the United States' colonial domination extended far beyond its own ethnic Mexican population to the people of Mexico, exerting much influence in shaping the younger country's development; and (3) in the years after the revolution, the Mexican Consulate aggressively sought to create a Mexican national identity while hundreds of thousands of its citizens were crossing the northern border. After the revolution ended in 1920, Álvaro Obregón, Mexico's president from 1920 to 1924, looked to the legions of Mexican citizens living in the United States, who he believed had gained years of experience as diligent and skilled laborers, as the vital element needed to rebuild the nation if only they could be persuaded to return.[27]

Obregón differentiated his policies from those of his predecessor, Venustiano Carranza, by encouraging the Mexican Consulate to offer services to those living in the United States who had resisted assimilation and maintained their Mexican citizenship.[28] The Department of Protection, which the consulate founded in 1920, not only mitigated employment issues between Mexican laborers and American business owners, but also offered support to escuelitas.[29] The consulate never fully funded the construction of an escuelita in Texas—with Mexico's finances already stretched thin to rebuild its own public school system, as well as the rest of the nation, it did not have the money—but it did offer moral support and provide books and materials whenever it could. Beginning in 1920, then, the consulate almost immediately began exerting great effort to ensure that Mexican citizens living in the United States held on to their native language and culture, hoping that it would encourage them to return to Mexico—or in the case of those born in the United States, it hoped they would move to Mexico to take part in the effort to unite the nation. The consulate's efforts to support escuelitas in Texas, however, arose just as the state superintendents' decades-long complaints that escuelitas undermined the Americanizing work they were doing in the public schools took on a greater sense of urgency.

American public school officials were not the only obstacle the consulate needed to overcome. The 1920s saw the emergence of a politically active Mexican American middle class that concerned itself with the fight for full integration—socially, politically, and educationally. These men and women spent the 1920s forming civil rights coalitions, eventually uniting them in 1929 to create LULAC. The organization's message of educational equality resonated with the immigrant and Texas Mexican masses. When the Mexican government needed its citizens to return home or needed the descendants of its citizens to relocate to the motherland, these people chose instead to remain in the United States and enroll their children in the Texas public school system. The effects of this decision, and of the emergence of the Mexican American civil rights movement, marked the beginning of the escuelitas' decline. For example, Mercedes, a small town in the Río Grande Valley with a predominantly ethnic Mexican population, had several escuelitas as late as the mid-1930s, but by 1940, most of them had closed.[30] Unquestionably, the history of escuelitas is tied to the history of public schooling and the limited opportunities it presented for ethnic Mexican children, but it is also tied to the economic and nationalistic developments of the United States' rapid growth and Mexico's postwar trauma.

CHILDHOOD LITERACY AS A GATEWAY TO CITIZENSHIP

In the years before, during, and after the Mexican Revolution (1910–1920), politically influential Mexican nationals, refugees, and government officials often immigrated to the United States, arguing that their sojourn was only temporary; so too, they tended to make the case that no ethnic Mexican should submit to any aspect of US culture and should never settle there permanently. On the other hand, politically powerful Americans made no secret of their belief that ethnic Mexicans needed to succumb to complete, unequivocal assimilation. Each group courted ethnic Mexicans only when it was in their interest to do so. Often, both sides disregarded the needs of their communities.[31]

Adults' choices about their children's education, in addition to the way they chose to report their own citizenship on the US census, reflected their feelings about these hegemonic messages Mexican and American officials sent them.[32] Childhood education was a vehicle for parents' cultural and political negotiation because ideas about childhood have the ability to both naturalize and oppose power structures.[33] Literary critic Courtney Weikle-Mills's *Imaginary Citizens* examines the "profound notion that children can ratify national narratives," a concept not lost on the public school superintendents and teachers who tried to convince ethnic Mexican parents that their children needed to be literate in English.[34] Nor was it lost on the Mexican Consulate, whose consuls desperately tried to convince ethnic Mexicans living in the United States that their children needed to attain Spanish literacy, as well as learn Mexican customs and traditions. Each side saw the ethnic Mexican child as a tool for ratifying their own respective national narrative because children both justify the past and influence the future.

"Imaginary citizenship," to use Weikle-Mills's phrase, provides a framework for understanding the different meanings books and literacy had for children, parents, teachers, and the nation-state. The concept of imaginary citizenship encompasses the ways in which literate children used the act of reading to understand themselves as citizens, despite the fact that they lacked the ability to exercise any political rights. It also encompasses the ways in which both adults and the nation-state oversaw children's civic, cultural, and linguistic education. Books and literacy were the mechanism through which children could assert their agency; parents and teachers could control children; and the nation-state could naturalize the restrictions it placed on its citizens.[35] Ethnic Mexican children who were students of both escuelitas and the public school system—as many escuelita students also attended local public schools after the turn of the twentieth century—possessed an imaginary dual citizenship that encouraged them to exercise their own agency while being subject to the dichotomous cultural and linguistic demands of their parents, teachers, and nation-states.

IMAGINING ETHNIC MEXICAN CHILDREN AND THEIR (LACK OF) BOOKS

To apply the notion of "imaginary citizenship" to ethnic Mexican children, it is necessary to understand the two reasons why they had a very different relationship to books as compared to middle-class Anglo American children. First, everyone I interviewed stated that their families, as well as their escuelitas, could not afford to purchase books, the scarcity of which meant that when they were available, they were treated as objects of reverence rather than doctrinal signs of controlling adults or a hegemonic nation-state. Many escuelitas, both before and after the Mexican Revolution, used Spanish-language newspapers for their reading material in place of books, meaning that these newspapers, functioning as a form of children's literature, became an instantiation for the Mexican nation-state. Spanish-language newspapers published articles about their audience's civic duty to Mexico and the United States, as well as about their rights as US citizens. Some newspapers, notably *El Continental* in El Paso and *El Defensor* in Edinburg, included sections specifically for children. Each article relied on didactic methods to teach them about education, patriotism, and moral behavior.[36]

Second, ethnic Mexican children, historically, have had a different relationship with the English language more generally. Debates about how much of Mexico the United States should conquer abounded during the US-Mexico War, and Americans' belief in manifest destiny was tempered only by their stronger belief in Mexican inferiority. Many American politicians advocated taking only Mexico's northern territories, with the expectation that the scattered inhabitants would leave their language and traditions behind and assimilate into the larger US culture as greater numbers of White Americans moved west.[37]

At the war's end in 1848, the Treaty of Guadalupe Hidalgo granted ethnic Mexicans in the ceded territories protection as naturalized citizens, or "treaty citizens," as one scholar calls those who lived in New Mexico and California.[38] In practice, and especially in Texas, they were "alien citizens"—citizens whom the larger American culture and the state still consider foreign.[39] As the phrase implies, they lived their lives largely in the socioeconomic and educational margins of US society despite the efforts of multiple generations to use the treaty as the basis for claiming their rights. Additionally, granting them citizenship could not overcome the entrenched racism and prejudice of many Anglo Americans.[40] And the fact that Mexico had failed to win the war only exacerbated Anglos' feelings about Mexican inferiority.[41]

For several decades after 1848, when the racist rhetoric surrounding their inclusion during the US-Mexico War still lingered, ethnic Mexicans in the Southwest were not yet willing to attain English-language literacy skills, and their reasons might have varied depending on where they lived. While Spanish may have served as a "language of politics" in New Mexico during the latter half of the nineteenth century—meaning it was used as a basis for conducting government business—it was never a basis for state affairs in Texas after its independence from Mexico in 1836.[42] Nonetheless, in ethnic Mexican communities in south Texas—largely isolated until the turn of the twentieth century, when the railroad connected the Río Grande Valley to the rest of the nation—people continued to speak Spanish in every facet of daily life, laying the foundation for what one linguist calls "Mexican Spanish in the United States."[43]

These various developments throughout the Southwest facilitated ethnic Mexican children's different relationship to language and literacy. Childhood education played a role in the subsequent assimilation of Mexican Americans more generally because the literacy of ethnic Mexican children determines their ability to contribute to the formation and evolution of not only the social, political, and economic developments of their region, state, and country, but also the historical narratives that frame interpretations of them. The notion of imaginary citizenship, therefore, bears significant implications for ethnic Mexican children, whose very incorporation into the United States, particularly their acquisition of English literacy, signaled both the emergence of a new American population—Mexican Americans—and the conquest of the West.[44] The proliferation of escuelitas between 1848 and 1940 functioned as an obstacle to the conquest's completion and a vehicle for Mexican American cultural creation because they encouraged the next generation to speak, read, and write Spanish as a way to negotiate their experience as cultural and political subjects of Mexico and the United States. Escuelitas enabled their student populations to retain their families' language and culture, providing a stronger foundation from which to endure Anglo hegemony in the coming decades.

At the turn of the twentieth century, as the public school system expanded, escuelitas showed few signs of decline, and ethnic Mexican children living in the United States continued to be subjects of two languages. Between 1890 and 1940, although it is impossible to say for certain, it is extremely unlikely that any escuelitas founded by ethnic Mexicans were not tied to Mexico in some way, regardless of the Mexican Consulate's role. The Anglocentric curriculum of the public schools and the Mexican-centric curriculum of the escuelitas were the means through which each nation-state represented itself to the people.

We will never know exactly how many ethnic Mexican children attended escuelitas either exclusively or in addition to public schools. Despite the lack of concrete numbers, the available evidence—Spanish-language press articles on escuelitas, superintendents' reports, and oral histories—indicates that escuelita enrollment threatened the public school system for several decades. For example, in 1893, F. A. Parker, the superintendent of the Laredo Independent School District, reported that there were 958 White students, the majority of which were ethnic Mexicans, enrolled in his district. He also reported that there were "many hundreds [of Mexican children]" who were not enrolled in the public school system; instead, they "attend[ed] small schools where they are taught in the Mexican or Spanish language."[45] He estimated there were at least forty escuelitas in Laredo. If each one had twenty-five students—a conservative estimate for this era—then it is possible that the escuelita enrollment for Laredo in 1893 equaled, or even surpassed, public school enrollment. Between 1880 and 1910, superintendents stated again and again that ethnic Mexican children would not attend public school until the state passed a compulsory school law.[46]

As the twentieth century progressed, the intersections of literacy, nation-states, and citizenship became more complex with the rise of the Mexican American civil rights movement. English-language textbooks, initially objects of subjection by the Anglo power structure that imposed segregated and vocational schooling, became a sign of inclusion for the young activists—even in the midst of segregation. In 1929, when Mexican American men founded LULAC, they required all their members to be US citizens, declared that English was the official language of the organization, and worked for public school integration.

Ethnic Mexican children, then, had a dual citizenship that was both imagined and literal. The curriculum of public schools and escuelitas facilitated children's ability to understand themselves as citizens of the United States and Mexico, as well as what the expectations would be for them when they came of age to exercise their political rights. The emergence of Mexican American scholars from the 1930s to the present—whether they self-identify as Mexican American, Chicanx, and/or Latinx—participating in debates about ethnic Mexican educational history, and doing so in English, illustrates that after generations of cultural resistance, a new form of opposition has emerged, embedded in linguistic assimilation. Their post-escuelita scholarship demonstrates that the United States' conquest of the West is complete, but also that its completion will always be questioned and contested by the very population the conquest helped create.

A NOTE ON TERMINOLOGY

In referring to the various subgroups within the Mexican-origin population living in the United States, I attempt to use the same terms that the subgroups use (or used) to refer to themselves, which are time- and place-specific. I use the term *Texas Mexican* to refer to the Mexican-origin people living in Texas from the late nineteenth century to the mid-twentieth century. Often these individuals were US citizens, but referred to themselves as "Texas Mexicans" rather than "Mexican Americans." The generation of the 1920s and 1930s that founded civil rights organizations, including LULAC and the Order of the Sons of America, referred to themselves as "Mexican American," and I use that term to refer to these groups. *Mexican American* refers to a person of Mexican descent who is a US citizen. When referring to Mexican citizens living in the United States, I use the terms *Mexican, Mexican immigrants,* or *Mexican nationals.* I refer to those who immigrated to the United States during the Mexican Revolution as *Mexican refugees* or *political exiles. Chicano* is a politicized term embraced by activists of the 1960s and 1970s, who used it to refer to themselves as well as the historical actors at the center of their scholarship.

The phrase *ethnic Mexican* refers to the Mexican-origin population in the United States without regard to their status as citizen or alien. David G. Gutiérrez coined the phrase in *Walls and Mirrors* (1995), and since then, many scholars have adopted it as a way to emphasize the connection between Mexican immigrants and Mexican Americans, particularly in regard to the similarities of their lived experiences in the United States. As Raúl Ramos states, the term has encouraged scholars to "mov[e] away from labels and toward markers of difference."[47] I use *ethnic Mexican* for the same reasons; however, I do so with caution. While at times it is necessary to de-emphasize citizenship status, we must also remember that it was not the only factor influencing ethnic Mexicans' lived experiences. Members of these communities created many divisions themselves along the lines of gender, class, skin tone, and educational background, and they maintained their own socioeconomic hierarchies. Use of the term *ethnic Mexican,* while a practical analytical tool, tends to mask these internal divisions.

CHAPTER BREAKDOWN

Chapter 1 examines two eras in escuelita history, one from 1865 to 1884 and the other from 1884 to 1910, analyzing these time periods within the context of the expansion of the Texas public school system and its adoption of segregation, as well as superintendents' views of ethnic Mexican students. In the first era, from 1865 to 1884, I argue that though escuelitas provided a strong foundation for a later generation to counter Anglo hegemony in the public schools, they did not exist necessarily to counter it in that time. In the first two decades after the Civil War, there were so few public schools throughout the state that escuelitas filled a need to provide children with educational opportunities. After 1884, when southern progressives gained a stronger foothold on the public school curriculum, many of them claimed that escuelitas were in decline, a sign that the ethnic Mexican population of

Texas would be assimilated within a generation. In the midst of the public schools' progress, however, ethnic Mexican intellectuals debated the escuelitas' role in the new modern society, and el Colegio Altamirano, the most well-known escuelita, began its sixty-year existence.

Chapter 2 examines how in the latter half of 1910, just as the revolutionaries in Chihuahua began their armed uprisings, the Mexican Consulate began an investigation into the treatment of ethnic Mexican children in the Texas public schools. In response to the consulate's investigation, a Spanish weekly newspaper in Laredo, *La Crónica*, published articles calling for an end to educational segregation. The Idar family, who published and wrote for *La Crónica*, had a social relationship with the Mexican consul in Laredo, and the nature of their campaign—asking the consulate to help ethnic Mexicans negotiate their present and future existence in the United States—illustrates the role education played in the burgeoning Mexican American identity. Chapter 2 argues that the paradoxical nature of *La Crónica's* campaign manifests how childhood education served as a vehicle for cultural negotiation as ethnic Mexicans began demanding public school inclusion while still sending their children to escuelitas. Additionally, the Idar family provides a useful prism. In 1910 they identified with Mexico, which their campaign indicated, but by the 1920s, they had helped found LULAC, which prioritized US citizenship and English literacy.

Chapter 3, set from 1910 to 1920, focuses on the labor of four teachers—Jovita Idar, Leonor Villegas de Magnón, María Villarreal, and María Rentería—who started their own escuelitas in Laredo. Too involved in dealing with the revolution to offer any aid to ethnic Mexicans living in the United States, the Mexican Consulate hastily ended the investigation discussed in chapter 2 in early 1911 and remained silent about any issues pertaining to ethnic Mexicans living north of the border. These women, acknowledging the lack of help their children were receiving from either country, labored to create their own educational spaces for ethnic Mexican children living in Laredo, prioritizing Spanish literacy in the face of public school Americanization. Chapter 3 argues that these women and children, whose lives were impacted by both the Mexican Revolution and modernization in Texas, used children and escuelitas to negotiate and contest the dislocating phenomena taking place on both sides of the border.

Chapter 4 investigates the fate of escuelitas in the 1920s and 1930s. Analyzing the Mexican government's motives for encouraging cultural programs in the United States in the wake of the revolution, chapter 4 examines the consulate's work in ethnic Mexican education, including support of escuelitas and their diplomatic criticism of the public school system. It also examines the escuelitas' decline, which was prompted by the rise of the Mexican American Generation's campaign for educational integration. This chapter draws from oral history interviews of teachers and students of 1930s–1950s escuelitas, arguing that though the Mexican government's intention was for these little schools to carry out a hegemonic purpose, many students used them to negotiate their lives in the United States.

Chapter 5 examines the influence that escuelitas had on the Mexican American Generation's activism. Many of these early activists attended escuelitas as children, and excavating their educational history complicates our understanding of them. Chapter 5 argues that these advocates drew from their escuelita experiences in one of two ways. One group sought to integrate the escuelita curriculum into that of the public school, making the educational experience more inclusive. Another group used the escuelita model to teach children English. The escuelitas bolstered the Mexican American Generation's activism, but at the same time facilitated their own decline.

From 1880 to 1940, ethnic Mexicans enrolled their children in both public schools and escuelitas—two contradictory educational traditions with mutually exclusive messages. Texas public school administrators believed that you could not live in the United States and be a citizen—regardless of birthright—if you did not speak English and were not familiar with US laws. Mexican consuls and countless upper-class Mexican nationals believed that the residents of the Mexican colony had a responsibility to keep the true Mexico alive in the United States while Mexico moved past the violent chaos of the revolution. Each side demanded that ethnic Mexicans choose to which country they would belong. Both nation-states scoffed at the idea that they would choose something in between. But for many decades, numerous ethnic Mexicans did choose something in between, and eventually the escuelita model transformed to meet the needs of Mexican Americans. The escuelitas were the first place where an alternative narrative that was focused on ethnic Mexicans' experiences emerged, and where that narrative belongs—in its own space or integrated into the dominant one—is a question we have yet to answer today.

CHAPTER 1

ESCUELITAS AND THE EXPANSION OF THE TEXAS PUBLIC SCHOOL SYSTEM, 1865–1910

Each year between 1880 and 1910, Texas school superintendents filled out their annual reports and sent them to the state superintendent of public instruction, chronicling their plight in trying to stabilize a nascent school system during a period of upheaval and transformation. Perhaps adding to the instability of a progressive education system on the rise, these superintendents typically did not have any pedagogical training. They were elected county judges expected to carry out an additional duty of overseeing the local schools, which entailed keeping track of the scholastic census and teacher rosters, tax assessments and expenditures, and itemized lists of facilities and materials. The position also required them to travel great distances across the county to conduct personal inspections of each school multiple times. Many superintendents found these additional responsibilities to be a great burden, disclosing such in the "General Remarks" portion of these annual statements. In fact, many of these reports appear to be hastily written, and often divulged the judges' personal, usually pessimistic and prejudicial, perceptions of not only their superintendent responsibilities, but also public education legislation and immigrant student populations, saying much about the tenuousness of ethnic Mexicans' relationship to public education in Texas in this era. The private and official nature of these reports, coupled with the provisional and amateur state of the superintendents themselves, bolsters the sincerity and significance of their racism, while telling a story about how modernization and progressivism on the Texas-Mexico border influenced the expansion of the public school system.

These reports also hint at the vicissitudes of the escuelitas' history. As socioeconomic transformations gained a stronger foothold at the turn of the twentieth century, superintendents recounted the decline of escuelitas, stating that fewer and fewer of them remained open as their public school scholastic population expanded instead. Remaining true to their role as progressive educators, they interpreted this development as a sign that ethnic Mexicans were embracing the modern era. But just as these superintendents were celebrating the escuelitas' decline, what would become one of the most famous escuelitas, el Colegio Altamirano, opened in Hebbronville, Texas, in 1897 and remained open until 1958.

Historiographically, scholars have pointed to the existence of escuelitas in the Southwest as evidence that (1) though the dominant culture thought otherwise, ethnic Mexicans cared rather profoundly about educating their children, and (2) that ethnic Mexicans asserted agency in resisting Anglo hegemony, segregated schooling, and Americanization policies. The former is unequivocally true, but applying the latter to this earlier period before the turn of the twentieth century is more difficult to prove.

In the period before 1884, the scarcity of public schools throughout the state, particularly in rural areas where a ranching economy dominated, meant that escuelitas existed to fill a need of educating local children. (Churches and charities also built their own schools to fill this need.) To be clear, it is not that racism against ethnic Mexicans in Texas did not prevail during this period, but that segregation and Americanization policies did not become part of the public school system until the 1880s or 1890s, when more schools existed throughout the state. Therefore, it is hard to argue that in this early period escuelitas existed as a way to defy segregation and Americanization because those policies did not come into their own until after 1884. And while these reports capture the progressive ideology that dominated the public school system, it is likely that we can attribute the escuelitas they discuss—at least those that existed before 1890—to the fact that they were already there before progressive education reformers undertook their work to transform and expand the public education system. Those that appeared after 1890, and certainly after 1900, most likely were a response to the progressive educational methodologies—segregated schooling, English-only instruction, and an Anglocentric curriculum—that disparaged ethnic Mexicans' language and culture.

As the twentieth century approached, more and more superintendents claimed in their reports that enrollment of ethnic Mexican children in the public schools was increasing and the number of escuelitas—or Spanish-language schools, as they called them—was dwindling. And as superintendents described these changes in their constituents' relationship with public education, they also revealed the role of language as a defining characteristic of citizenship, as they sought to instill English-only pedagogical methodologies into their curriculum to turn immigrant children into good Americans. When placed in the appropriate historical context and read against the grain, these records reveal the complexity of the changing roles of escuelitas and public schools in ethnic Mexicans' cultural and political negotiation with dominant American society. Additionally, their discussions of language, citizenship, and socioeconomic development elucidate how school superintendents interpreted the role of the ethnic Mexican child in the burgeoning public education system and the new modern economy.

TEXAS PUBLIC SCHOOL EDUCATION IN THE ANTEBELLUM AND POSTBELLUM ERAS

Between 1836 and 1870, political leaders were unable to figure out a way to pay for a public school system without imposing a tax, or how to incorporate public education into the daily lives of a citizenry extremely wary of their government becoming a tyrannical state. Texas, during its days as a republic and for decades after statehood, was not able to reconcile the situation, and it is possible that the populace did not think this reconciliation necessary in the first place. Frederick Eby, a historian of Texas education at the University of Texas at Austin from 1909 to 1957, evaluated the situation as follows:

> There is no hint that the state can justly impose taxation upon all the property of the state for the education of all the children. By a "system" [Texans] understood that the state, from out of its vast unsettled domain, should gratuitously make provision for the establishment and equipment of schools. The maintenance and control of schools devolved wholly upon the parents who sent their children. It must be noted that the lands given for the schools [by the state] were handed over unconditionally to the counties. Congress reserved no supervisory role, and it did not set up any machinery for the purpose of directing the schools. . . . General gratuitous instruction furnished by the state for all children was not thought of. To control the training of their children was one of the inalienable rights of a free people.[1]

This system of giving public lands to counties for educational purposes failed to yield any schools. The Common School Law of 1854 was the first to establish a school system, requiring the state to organize and pay for the construction of common schools and cover the tuition of orphans and impoverished children. It also required the state to use one-fifth of the $10 million it received when the United States purchased public lands (as a result of the Compromise of 1850) to create a school fund; however, it did not allow cities to levy taxes to maintain their public schools unless they had special permission from the legislature. The main source of income for these schools was tuition.[2]

In 1856, the people of New Braunfels established the New Braunfels Academy, the first public school building in the state, and two years later, the state legislature granted a twenty-year charter that allowed the school to operate under the authority of a six-member board of trustees and—at the request of the citizens of New Braunfels—receive funding from a city-imposed tax. The school also sustained itself by charging tuition.[3] The state's approach to public education during the antebellum era was called the community system, which did not break counties up into school districts. Rather, as Eby states, parents "were permitted to unite and organize themselves into school communities, embracing such population as might agree to take advantage of the benefits of the available free school fund."[4]

When the Civil War began in 1861, the New Braunfels Academy was still the only public school building in the entire state of Texas, and it remained so until 1869. The Civil War's "immediate effects on the schools were destructive and caused Texas to flounder in chaos for twenty years."[5] Much of the destruction stemmed from the war itself, but the subsequent floundering stemmed from a series of bad investments before the war and bitter partisan politics afterward.

Between 1856 and 1862, the state legislature used $1.8 million from the school fund to make a series of loans to the railroad companies, which they were unable to pay back. After the war began, the governor reallocated the remaining balance of the school fund, almost $1.3 million, to the Confederate war effort. It would be more than a decade before the permanent school fund was functional again. Following the Congressional Reconstruction Acts of 1867, the Texas legislature passed the Constitution of 1869, which founded a system of free schools for all children between ages six and eighteen; mandated compulsory attendance for four months of the year; brought a brief and limited acceptance of bilingualism to the curriculum; and defined a state board of education, consisting of the governor, the attorney general, and the state superintendent of public instruction. It also stipulated that 25 percent of the state's annual taxes, as well as all funds stemming from the sale of public lands, be put into the school fund, which would no longer be allowed to pay for anything other than the state's educational system. Though this document ushered in a foundation for public education, many Texans believed that it was the evil work of northern carpetbaggers who only wanted free education for all so that they could educate African Americans to help them stay in power.[6]

The year 1869 also saw the election of a Republican majority in the state house and senate, as well as of pro-Reconstruction Republican governor Edmund J. Davis, a former Union general. Following the Constitution of 1869, the Republicans passed the school laws of 1870 and 1871, both of which outlined regulations for school reform, including fixed teacher salaries and teacher certification, state-mandated courses of study and textbooks, and board of directors' responsibilities for school districts. Texas Democrats, profoundly bitter about having lost their political power in 1869, saw the new school system as an oppressive directive from a tyrannical national party, and they organized vehemently to oppose it. Many school officials across the state refused to carry out their responsibilities—such as collecting information on their counties' scholastic census, tax information, and number of school buildings—and therefore impeded the superintendent of public instruction's ability to do his job.[7]

Reconstruction Republicans remained in power only until 1875, and when Democrats took back the executive and legislative branches of government, they immediately repealed Republican legislation. The Constitution of 1876 rescinded all the school system regulations of the Constitution of 1869, including terminating the office of the state superintendent of public instruction, terminating compulsory attendance, and reducing the school age from six to eighteen years to eight to fourteen years. It also illegalized levying local taxes to construct and maintain schools. The Constitution of 1876 returned public education in Texas to the community system of the antebellum era.[8]

Though it had numerous drawbacks, the community system provided a haven for bilingual schooling because local communities—parents—had almost complete control over the teachers hired and the curriculum taught. Historian Carlos Kevin Blanton states, "The lack of centralized supervision over curriculum or the employment of teachers inherent in the community system meant that language minorities were able to do what they wanted. Schools instructed students entirely in German or Spanish or bilingually if they so desired."[9]

The progressive education movement made its way to Texas in 1884 and eventually brought an end to the community system and concomitantly to bilingual education. Progressives believed that the high degree of localism hindered the development of public education in Texas, so they restructured the system in a way that undermined the autonomy of local communities. The newly centralized system's negative effects for bilingual pedagogical practices were not lost on progressive educators, as a strict adherence to English-only in all facets of public education was central to their ideology.[10] The rise of progressive education and its English-only pedagogy dovetailed with the rise of nativism across the United States, which heightened the importance of the relationship between language and citizenship—the link between English and Americanization.[11] When they passed the school reform bill of 1884 to convert the community system to a district system within the confines of English-only pedagogy, progressive educators sought to redefine the relationship many inhabitants of Texas had with education, a feat that proved much more complicated, and certainly took much longer, than they expected.

In his 1884–1885 biennial report, Benjamin M. Baker, the state superintendent of public instruction, stated that he had received

> many complaints . . . to the effect that some of the schools are conducted in the German and some of them in the Spanish languages. Investigation disclosed the truth of some of the charges, but the Superintendent in a majority of instances found himself powerless to remedy the evil. . . . I do not hold it objectionable to teach other languages than the English in the schools, but they should be pursued as studies, while the language of the school should be the English.[12]

Baker was talking not about escuelitas or schools affiliated with churches or charities, but about the schools set up through the public school community system that gave parents and their local public officials complete control over how they ran them, including the hiring of teachers and the curriculum they taught. Baker continues, "I have myself conversed with teachers who could not speak the English sufficiently well to be understood."[13] One of the ways progressive educators undermined the community system was by instituting teacher certification requirements, which the state administered in English. Many of these teachers would not be eligible to continue working in the newly structured public school system because they would not be able to pass an oral and written exam in English.[14]

The superintendents' annual reports from the 1880s to 1910 elucidate progressive educators' preoccupation with terminating the community system, particularly its loophole for sustaining bilingual schools. Concomitantly, they also elucidate their use of the ethnic Mexican child as a vehicle for assimilating the large ethnic Mexican population into US society and as the basis for constructing an acculturated citizenry. On the other hand, these reports also hint at how modernity and progressivism engendered changes in the relationship between language and citizenship and how ethnic Mexicans responded to these changes—indicating that for ethnic Mexicans, education was a form of cultural negotiation. As the public school system emerged, many chose to keep their children in the escuelita or parochial school they already attended, but many also chose to enroll their children in the public school. And many enrolled them in both. In educating their children, they were negotiating with the multiple cultural worlds that surrounded them in establishing not only who they were, but also who they wanted their progeny to become—where they saw their own future in the United States.

ETHNIC MEXICANS, POVERTY, AND EDUCATION IN MAVERICK AND ZAPATA COUNTIES

The superintendents in counties along the Texas-Mexico border obsessed over ethnic Mexicans' relationship to public education, and with differentiating that relationship from those that Anglo American children had with education. The "Summary of Scholastic Census" report required superintendents to classify students by race, and they were categorized as either "white" or "colored." Mexicans, as a condition of the Treaty of Guadalupe Hidalgo that ended the US-Mexico War in 1848, were legally considered White.[15] The scholastic census may have had to classify them as White, but it did not have to classify them as American. The bottom portion of the "Summary of Scholastic Census" also included a section that counted the children by "nationality," which meant that Mexicans, as well as Italians, Germans, and Bohemians, could be identified as such. Grouping children by nationality makes it impossible to know how many of the Mexican children were actually US citizens. The "American" category included only "white" and "colored." For example, in the "Summary of Scholastic Census" for the Eagle Pass Independent School District (in Maverick County) for the 1910–1911 academic year, the top portion that categorizes the children by race states that between the ages of seven and seventeen, there were 1,181 White children and 29 Black children. Below the race portion, the census also categorized the children based on nationality, and there were 1,015 Mexican children and 183 American children—154 White and 29 Black—enrolled in the Eagle Pass Independent School District.[16] Officially documenting the size of the ethnic Mexican scholastic population, particularly when it was a large majority, made it easier for superintendents to attribute the slow development of the county schools to the large number of "immigrants."

A key example is in the 1897 annual report J. A. Bonnet, county superintendent for public instruction and county judge in Maverick County, wrote:

The people [of Maverick County] are mostly Mexicans who do not put any great value in the education of their children, mostly being very poor are unable to buy books for them, also a number keep their children away from school because it is sometimes eight or ten, and often 20 miles to the nearest school . . . the Legislature had an eye to patriotism when they formulated the present school laws and regulations—I beg to differ with you when it comes down to patriotism with these people who take all the benefits of our free school system and shout "Viva Mexico."[17]

Though Bonnet acknowledged the existence of poverty and distance as obstacles, he still reported that the vast majority of his constituents did not believe education was an essential part of being a citizen because they did not see themselves as citizens at all. Ironically, his remarks dwell on the reasons why Mexican children did not attend school, and then argue that the state was wasting funds on people reaping the benefits of a state-funded education system while steadfastly remaining patriotic Mexicans rather than becoming loyal Americans.

Bonnet's report indicates two salient points regarding education in Maverick County. First, it is likely that the county had its own network of escuelitas, especially since there were so few schools in the area; in 1908, Maverick County's superintendent of public instruction, A. L. Wallace, reported that two schools forty miles apart were the only schools in Maverick County other than in the Eagle Pass Independent School District.[18] When Bonnet states that the nearest school might be twenty miles away, he meant that literally, but the fact that the county's public school system consisted of two schools forty miles apart did not stop ethnic Mexicans from pursuing an education.

In 1910, thirteen-year-old Guadalupe Hernández, who was born in Eagle Pass, lived with Josefa Calderón Hernández, her adopted mother, and attended school rather than work for wages. Orphaned before the age of three, Hernández was adopted by Calderón, a woman she referred to as her grandmother, though it is unlikely the two were related in that way.[19] Hernández attended various escuelitas in Maverick County, where she learned how to read and write in Spanish, sew, play the guitar and mandolin, and sing. She could not speak, read, or write English.[20] Calderón spoke only Spanish, could read but not write, and worked as a cook, probably selling her food to the miners of the Olmos Coal Company.[21] These two women were both born in Texas—Calderón was born in Texas around 1861, though both of her parents were born in Louisiana—and neither of them ever learned

English, ever attended a public school, or ever assimilated into the dominant American culture. In fact, Hernández was at least a second-generation American citizen (her mother was born in Texas), and if she was truly related to Calderón, she was a third-generation Texas Mexican and a fourth-generation American citizen.[22] They represent the generations of American citizens of Mexican origin who lived their entire lives as members of the Mexican colony rather than members of US society. As tuition-paying parent and student, they participated in the network of escuelitas that educated Maverick County children—many of them American citizens—in Spanish literacy, Mexican history, and arts and crafts.

Taking into account the remote nature of the public schools and the fact that many ethnic Mexicans in the area were literate in Spanish but not English, escuelitas probably thrived in Maverick County at least until 1910, when the county began to build more public schools. In 1909, county superintendent A. L. Wallace reported that some of the "very large landowners" were beginning to divide their properties and sell tracts to farmers, bringing more settlers who demanded public education, an indication of the strong link between capitalist development and education.[23]

Additionally, Bonnet's report signals a turn in the way Texans viewed public education. Twenty years before, the majority of public officials believed that the Bible endowed parents with the right to choose how they educated their children, which is why the Constitution of 1876 reverted to the community system. Rather than seeing a state-funded education system as a sign of tyranny, as many did before and after the Civil War, Bonnet interpreted it as a manifestation of the state's desire to nurture a romantic nationalist feeling, but he argues that ethnic Mexicans' relationship to Mexico, despite their resident and/or citizenship status in the United States, undermined that very patriotic sentiment.

Three years later, the 1900 report of W. A. Bonnet—a bank president who most likely was J. A. Bonnet's son—placed his argument regarding ethnic Mexicans and education within the context of Texas's tri-ethnic population of Anglos, ethnic Mexicans, and African Americans.[24] He argued that Mexican children were less intelligent and more indolent than Anglo and African Americans. Unlike many superintendents who wrote one or two paragraphs, if they wrote anything at all, Bonnet wrote two pages of remarks, and much of it is worth quoting at length. He stated:

> The scholastic population of our county is composed of about 80 percent Mexicans, 10 percent Colored and 10 percent White Americans. The colored children attend school very well and were

making excellent progress when their teacher suddenly became insane. Quite a number of White American children live too far from school to attend. Those that live within a reasonable distance all attend. The Mexican part of our population is a sore trial for our teachers. The Mexicans are of the laboring class and do not believe in education. About ³/₄ of the Mexican scholastic population are children of coal miners. As soon as a boy gets to be 10 or 12 years old he is put to work in the mines as "water boy," "driver" or some other work he can do. The few months schooling is soon forgotten. Mexicans do not believe girls should be educated at all. Of the Mexican scholastic population only about 15% are enrolled and not 10% are regular attendants. A compulsory school law is badly needed. A law prohibiting child labor in mines might be some benefit. . . . What can we do with this class of people if there is no way of compelling them to attend schools paid for by the state. It really would be a good thing to divide the school money according to *attendance* and not according to scholastic population. We would not get more than ¼ of what we are now drawing from the state fund, but it would give other counties better and more schools where people take an interest in school matters. I have driven from house to house urging these people (Mexicans) to give their children an education, the teachers have done all they could do, and yet we cannot fill our school houses.[25]

Bonnet states that African American children in Maverick County were good students, and any drawbacks they encountered were not through any fault of their own, but because their teacher experienced some mental and/or emotional breakdown. In creating a tri-ethnic hierarchy based on intelligence and diligence, Bonnet ranks African Americans above ethnic Mexicans, a telling assertion in light of the fact that by 1900, Reconstruction had long been over. The rise of the Democratic Party in the South ushered in a wave of oppression that manifested in violence, voter intimidation, and Jim Crow, which, along with a general acceptance among White Americans of the intellectual inferiority of African Americans, frustrated African American socioeconomic advancement. Texas was no exception; however, according to the superintendent records for the counties on the Texas-Mexico border, where the African American communities were either extremely small or nonexistent, African American children were becoming educated more quickly than Mexican children. Undoubtedly, their small numbers meant they were less of a social threat.[26]

Bonnet also states that White American children often lived too far away from school to make commuting possible, but those that lived close enough attended without any problem. The implication here is that White American children and their families did value education, so if they were not attending, it was because there was an outside barrier preventing them from doing so. However, Mexican children, who, we know from J. A. Bonnet's report from the same county just three years earlier, lived between eight and twenty miles from school. W. A. Bonnet never mentions this fact because using it as an excuse for White American children's low attendance would automatically give Mexican children the opportunity to do the same, undermining the notion that their apathy, even disdain, for education was at the center of their low attendance, regardless of other outside factors.

Instead, he focuses on Mexican children's poor attendance as a corollary of their socioeconomic status as impoverished miners, which Bonnet equated with carelessness and ignorance. His statement that "the Mexicans are of the laboring class and do not believe in education" indicates that there is a direct link between their work as laborers and the desire for their children to avoid school. Roberto R. Calderón states that in the coal mining industry of Maverick County from 1900 to 1910, about 27 percent of the ethnic Mexican school-aged population attended school, and that "young males were much more likely than their female counterparts to be employed . . . 28.7 percent of young males were employed, compared to 1.6 percent for young females . . . school-age males were expected to secure employment more often than females in order to contribute to their parents' household income."[27] Young men worked to help support their parents and siblings, often not marrying until they were older, and contrary to what Bonnet claims, Calderón states that girls were more likely to attend school than boys. Young women often married older men who had already established themselves enough to support a family. Though young men found employment early in life, it is unlikely that Mexicans sent their ten- and twelve-year-old sons down into the mines rather than sending them to school. Calderón states, "The [1900–1910] census schedules did record the presence of coal miners in their early teens working in the region's mines, although it was uncommon. Perhaps only the most economically desperate families sent their young sons into the pits."[28]

In addition to callous neglect of issues such as poverty and distance, there were exclusionary factors built into the public school system that directly impeded ethnic Mexican children from attending. Though the Texas public school system was founded on the principle of free education, there were other fees that students' families had to pay. Since many areas of the

state did not levy property taxes to help support the local public schools—
Maverick County was only one of many such examples—and the state
funding was not enough to support a full term, the schools needed to charge
tuition for part or all of the year to be able to sustain a nine-month term.
Many public schools throughout the state, then, were free for only a portion
of the year and operated as a private school the rest of the year, collecting
tuition for four to five months. For example, in the 1905–1906 academic year,
Floresville Independent School District had two terms: a private school term
from September to January during which students paid tuition as well as for
their books, and a public school term from January to early June.[29]

Additionally, the state did not provide free textbooks until voters passed
the free textbook law in 1918.[30] Before then, parents had to buy the books
and necessary supplies that the school assigned, and Bonnet was not alone
in pointing out the exclusionary impact this fee had on students. Public
school superintendents from the county schools and the independent school
districts from all over Texas wrote in their annual reports that if the state
paid for the textbooks and possibly even for stationery, attendance would
increase dramatically, as many families could not afford such expenses.[31]

Ethnic Mexican superintendents also made note in their reports of
the widespread poverty of many families, but they interpreted it as an obstacle rather than an indication of negligence and laziness, unlike most of
their White counterparts. One such example is Zapata County judge and
superintendent of public instruction from 1888 to 1894 José Antonio George
Navarro, the oldest son of José Antonio Navarro, one of three Mexicans to
sign the Texas Declaration of Independence.[32] Navarro's 1894 report stated,
"The great drawback to a further advancement of pupils is the poverty among
them which does not enable them to buy the necessary books, if these could
be procured for them their interest would be doubled and advancement
certain."[33] Navarro was not making a general statement about poverty among
ethnic Mexican populations, but speaking to an environmental catastrophe
in his county. By 1894, Zapata County was six years into a drought. Navarro,
along with A. P. Spohn, who would succeed him as county superintendent
in 1895, publicized the poverty and starvation that those living in Zapata
County were experiencing.[34]

In March 1894, just six months before Navarro completed his annual
report, the *Houston Post* published an article entitled "Destitution Reigns:
Citizens of Zapata County Ask the World for Assistance," which details
the creation of the committee on resolutions, of which Navarro was a
prominent member. The committee sought to find ways of helping those
in the county who were starving, and according to the article, there were

many. They stated that though Zapata County residents were willing to work, there were no jobs available. The financially fortunate residents had been giving as much as they could to aid the poor for the last six years, but they could not give anymore, so the committee was turning to the citizens of the world to send whatever materials they could to Zapata County. Their plea for help was published in newspapers throughout Texas, Oklahoma, and Kansas.[35]

HIDALGO COUNTY JUDGE JUAN MANUEL DE LA VIÑA: A CASE STUDY IN BECOMING

The year after Navarro filed his 1894 report, Juan M. de la Viña became the first ethnic Mexican elected as county judge in Hidalgo County, farther south along the Río Grande. He served as the county superintendent of public instruction from 1894 to 1902.[36] In his 1896 annual report to the state superintendent, he also identified widespread poverty as the most significant obstacle to public school enrollment and regular attendance.

It is a well-known fact that the reason for having had very little improvements in our public schools in this county until now, is the irregularity in attending the children to school. But this irregularity does not consist nearly in the negligence and indolence of the parents, as some have thought. The truth of such failure is the poverty of most all the parents. There being some who are not even able to support their families with necessities of life. Therefore, I think that, if from the general appropriation made to the schools, there could be set apart a little amount of money to furnish those children (entirely destituted of means) with books and a slight garment, so as to be able to attend school would give a very good result, as to improvements, and at the same time it would be a great help to those families, whose children could not be educated otherwise.[37]

When de la Viña stated, "But this irregularity does not consist nearly in the negligence and indolence of the parents, as some have thought," he was speaking directly to his colleagues—his fellow superintendents from other counties on the border who believed that ethnic Mexicans were too irresponsible and shiftless to care about education. Identifying poverty as the biggest barrier to regular attendance, de la Viña argued that while socioeconomic transformations modernized the region's school system and economy, they

Hidalgo County judge Juan Manuel de la Viña was one of the few ethnic Mexicans to be a county superintendent of public instruction in Texas, a position he held from 1894 to 1902. COURTESY OF MARGARET H. MCALLEN MEMORIAL ARCHIVES, MUSEUM OF SOUTH TEXAS HISTORY.

also limited ethnic Mexican involvement. Ultimately, he argued that his colleagues' interpretation was wholly inaccurate.

De la Viña came from an elite ranching family and became Hidalgo County's first ethnic Mexican judge by working with the Anglo political machine run first by John Closner and subsequently by A. Y. Baker.[38] Despite the fact that his position as a county judge depended on his being in good favor with the local political bosses, de la Viña used the annual report that he sent directly to James M. Carlisle, the state superintendent of public instruction, to counter pervasive ideas about ethnic Mexicans and education, indicating his own ambivalence toward embracing all the dominant views of the Hidalgo County political machine that enabled him to wield a certain amount of governmental power.

Two years later, his 1898 report to the state superintendent complicated the situation in Hidalgo County even further, as well as his perspective on it, in arguing that because the county was over 90 percent Mexican, his constituents "have race prejudice to overcome."

It has been only a few years that outside the town of Hidalgo and one or two other localities where there are a few English speaking people that the natives would patronize the public schools. We are now gradually overcoming this prejudice by employing teachers who are thoroughly familiar with the people, and I impress it upon the teachers that not only the children but the parents must be instructed—if not in the language—in the laws of the country as far as possible, and the more intelligent Mexicans are realizing the necessity of English education for the rising generation. In fact our schools are really doing missionary work.[39]

Ignoring the role of poverty altogether, de la Viña pointed out that ethnic Mexicans' lack of trust in the public school system stemmed from the large number of Anglo teachers who did not speak Spanish. Fifteen years earlier, the state had only a handful of schools, and the children living in rural south Texas most likely attended an escuelita on a ranch or elsewhere. Why would ethnic Mexican parents pull their children from an educational tradition that they understood and enroll them in a school several miles away with a teacher who was of a different culture and spoke a different language? Referring to their distrust as "racial prejudice," de la Viña argued that hiring teachers familiar with the Spanish language and Mexican culture was what persuaded these parents to enroll their children in a largely Anglo institution. Many other county schools along the border, in an effort to convince more ethnic Mexicans to send their children, also hired Spanish-speaking teachers, but many superintendents complained that they could not find enough bilingual teachers who could pass the certification tests in English and converse with Mexican families in Spanish.

De la Viña's 1898 report emphasized his own belief in the strong link between enrolling children in the public school system and self-identifying as an American citizen, arguing that children and parents needed to learn English *and* the law of the United States. As the county superintendent making the argument, he included himself among those who understood the link between the English language and US citizenship, personally identifying with the public school system's power structure. He stated, "*We* are now gradually overcoming this prejudice," and "*our* schools are really doing missionary work." He considered himself to be the overseer of his county's missionary work in educating "the more intelligent Mexicans."[40] Like many other superintendents, de la Viña assessed ethnic Mexican intelligence by how willing the parents were to learn English and US laws, and to encourage their children to do the same. Essentially, superintendents measured ethnic Mexicans' intelligence by how willing they were to put the futures of their children in the hands of the state.

De la Viña himself embodied the ways in which ethnic Mexicans' changing relationship to education, language, and citizenship transformed their identities. He was born in 1835, either on his father's ranch in Reynosa, Tamaulipas, Mexico, or on his family's property on El Sal del Rey, Texas, about twenty miles northeast of Edinburg.[41] He went to grade school in Monterrey but attended a Catholic university in St. Louis, Missouri.[42] After he and Genoveva Muguerza married, around 1859, they most likely traveled between de la Viña's landholdings in Hidalgo, Texas, and Reynosa. (Though these cities are on opposite sides of the Texas-Mexico border, they are only five miles apart.)

Before he became county commissioner and later county judge in Hidalgo, de la Viña contributed to Reynosa's social and political life between 1860 and 1884. While he worked as a farmer in the 1860s, by 1884 he was working for the city of Reynosa in some capacity, possibly as a public official. He registered the deaths of his infant sons, Leopoldo and Manuel—in 1860 and 1863, respectively—the birth of his daughter, Manuela, in 1868, and her subsequent marriage in 1884 with the Registro Civil del Estado de Tamaulipas (the Civil Registration of the State of Tamaulipas). These official documents from Tamaulipas note that he was a Mexican citizen and a native of Reynosa. Finally, in 1880 he reported on the US census that he had been born in Mexico, embracing his Mexican citizenship on an official American document.[43]

However, at some point during the 1880s and 1890s, coinciding with his role as a Hidalgo County public official, de la Viña claimed US citizenship.[44] In the 1880 census, he identified himself as a Mexican citizen, but in the 1900 census, he stated that he was born in Texas.[45] His daughter, Manuela, whose birth he registered in Reynosa in 1868, died in Edinburg in 1953. Her death certificate states that her father had been born in Texas, so he passed down the story of his place of birth to his daughter and daughter-in-law, the informant upon Manuela's death.[46]

There seems to be some question about where de la Viña was born. Some scholars have stated that he was born at El Sal del Rey Ranch in Texas; documents from the city of Reynosa state that he was born there. But because of the contested history of the location of the border between Texas and Mexico, he could make a justifiable and legal claim to citizenship-by-birth for either country regardless of whether he was born at El Sal del Rey or in Reynosa.[47] De la Viña was born in the midst of the Texas Revolution, a war that ended at the Battle of San Jacinto in April 1836, a year after his birth. But Mexico, the new republic, and later the United States, claimed the part of Texas south of the Nueces River, the area where he was born, and the issue was not settled until after the US-Mexico War ended in 1848. De la Viña's answers to the 1880 and 1900 censuses question of "Place of Birth" were political ones, reflecting through which nationalist lens he saw himself, and the changes in his self-reflection are closely tied to his work as an Hidalgo county judge and superintendent for public instruction.

In addition to marking a long period of transition in de la Viña's identity, the period between 1880 and 1900 also marks a transition within the public school system. De la Viña owned El Capote Ranch in Hidalgo County, which had its own escuelita called El Capote School.[48] Ranch schools were common throughout south Texas, and the large ranch populations lived in close proximity to one another but at great distances from public schools. The children who attended El Capote School were instructed in English, and two of the school's teachers were sisters from an Anglo American family in east Texas, Josephine and Rosa Hooks, who taught there in 1905–1906 and 1908–1909, respectively.[49] The Hooks family, all of whom could read and write, moved sometime between 1900 and 1910 to Hidalgo County, where the sisters' father, Thomas Hooks, was vice president of the Donna Canal Company.[50] But despite the inclination toward a more Americanized curriculum, the Capote School still functioned outside the domain of the public school system and operated on the estate of the county superintendent of public instruction. The Capote School is not listed as a county public school in de la Viña's annual reports to the state superintendent. He was thus overseeing two institutions that drew from contradictory educational traditions, and shifts in his own identity aligning with his role as county school superintendent point to the emergence of the public school system influence on Mexican American consciousness.

R. A. MARSH AND THE MODERN IRRELEVANCE OF ESCUELITAS

R. A. Marsh succeeded de la Viña as Hidalgo County judge and superintendent in 1902, and he remained in that position until 1914. Whereas de la Viña's reports and life mark the early stages of transformations in ethnic Mexicans' relationship to education—shifting from one reliant solely on escuelitas and parochial institutions to one that began to patronize the public schools—Marsh's reports unequivocally tie ethnic Mexican education to the economic development that was occurring in Hidalgo County after 1900. Indeed, Marsh interpreted the economic development taking place in the Río Grande Valley as a boon to the entire population, and he was one of the most well-known boosters for the area. From 1903 to 1907, during his tenure as county judge and superintendent, Marsh edited the *Hidalgo Advance*, a weekly newspaper whose sole purpose was to promote economic development in the county.[51] In one of his editorials, which he wrote in 1903 during the beginning of his second term as superintendent, he stated,

The outlook for coming prosperous and happy times on the lower Rio Grande were never better or brighter than they are at the present time. With the certainty of one railroad being constructed, and running trains before the middle of next year, and probably two ere that time; with an influx of new settlers with money, and who are spending it with a lavish hand in development: fat cattle, horses, hogs, sheep and goats on every hand; grass a plenty and waterholes all full, with corn and beans in abundance, why should we not smile and feel thankful for the present blessings, and the future so bright?[52]

The same flowery discourse that filled Marsh's editorials filled the "General Report" section of his annual reports, and he closely associated public school expansion and economic development with the influx of "new settlers with money"—that is, Anglo Americans—to the Río Grande Valley. For example, in his 1908 and 1909 reports, he stated that an "intelligent class of farmers" whose "first demand is good school facilities for their children" were moving down to Hidalgo County.[53] According to Marsh, the migration of Anglo farmers was what drove the expansion of the public school system, not the "better class of Mexicans" who already lived in the county and had enrolled their children.

While the influx of Anglo farmers signaled progress, the manpower behind that very progress was a cheap, but Americanized, labor supply. An article in the *Hidalgo Advance* stated, "Mexican labor, which is abundant down here is coming to be appreciated, and is found to be more reliable than negro labor when properly handled."[54] Each year, Marsh claimed that enrollment and attendance among the Mexican students was up and English-language illiteracy rates were down. The public schools, he argued, were "allowing [the Mexican children] to become Americanized"—and the opportunity to become Americanized within a curriculum that stressed English literacy and vocational training enabled them to become a dependable—but controllable—source of labor.[55]

Like de la Viña before him, Marsh assessed ethnic Mexican intelligence by how willing the Mexicans were to integrate themselves into the socioeconomic transformations that Anglo American capitalists, boosters, and politicians supported. And in this new modern economy, there was no longer a place for escuelitas because these little Spanish schools, stuck in the past, hindered progress. In his 1902–1903 school year report, Marsh stated:

Within the last few months there has been considerable of an interest awakened in matters educational in this county, and I am pleased to state that our local school system has taken on new life.

Our population, which is about 90% Mexican, is becoming alive to the fact that it is to their vital interest to educate their children in the language of the country, and the Spanish schools which a short while back were maintained in nearly every settlement, are fast disappearing. It has never been deemed expedient to discourage Spanish schools here, as they certainly accomplish much good, and many have learned to read and write in them that would have remained illiterate without them; but their existence has always been a drawback to our public schools. During the past twelve months quite a change in conditions has come to this section, which promises developement [*sic*] along all lines, and the better element of the Mexican population are alive to the fact that to keep pace with the new order of things, that the rising generation must be encouraged to acquire the English language.[56]

He continued, stating that he had spent a significant portion of his time traveling to all the county schools "to urge upon the intelligent Mexicans the great necessity of their children acquiring the English language."[57] Giving his efforts much credit, Marsh interpreted 1903 as a turning point in ethnic Mexicans' relationship to education specifically, and in economic development in Hidalgo County generally. As noted earlier, in 1870 there were about three public schools in all of Texas, and the proliferation of escuelitas most likely arose out of necessity. Without them, ethnic Mexican children would never have been able to learn to read or write in any language. While he praised the escuelitas' past role, Marsh argued that they had outlived their usefulness and, in this modern time, had become an impediment to the social and economic advancement of Hidalgo County. Whereas the expansion and development of the public school system signified modernization and economic growth, the escuelitas signified ethnic Mexican enclaves clinging to a dark past.

THE ETHNIC MEXICAN PRESS DEBATES THE BENEFITS OF A MEXICAN EDUCATION IN TEXAS

Marsh's sense that the expansion of the public school system had caused a level of disruption for the escuelitas was accurate—though his readiness to take credit for such disruption was unfounded. A couple of years after he proclaimed escuelitas nearly extinct, Mexican journalists and teachers debated the benefits and drawbacks of these little schools in the Spanish-language press. The heated discussion began after an article in *El Sol* of Alice stated that education "by Mexican teachers could only be effective in Mexico," as these schools in the United States discouraged children from pursuing "positions of great importance in Texas" when they reached adulthood.[58] Referring to this article as "intellectual gibberish," *El Democrata Fronterizo* of Laredo responded that a firm grounding in one's native language facilitated the learning of a second language. The paper also noted that the public schools in Texas were not free, and that they required families to purchase textbooks that were "excessively expensive."[59]

Within a brief period of time, *El Mensajero* of Del Río entered the fray on the side of *El Sol*, and *El Cosmopolita* of Alice, printed by Eulalio Velázquez, who maintained an escuelita there, entered on the side of *El Democrata Fronterizo*. *El Democrata Fronterizo* issued a powerful rebuttal to *El Mensajero*, providing insight into the curriculum of these Spanish-language schools. The author stated that public school teachers regarded Mexican children as "idiots" because they did not speak English. As such, the entire public school curriculum structured itself around teaching children the English language. "[A]t the age of eight," the author noted, "the student comes to find out that he has come to learn to understand the English language, but he has not even reached the threshold of science, and is barely able to begin his studies."[60] He pointed out that once Mexican children completed their studies in the Spanish-language escuelita, they could attend night school English classes, "of which there are millions in Texas, and where for two to three pesos, you can in a year learn more English than a child without knowledge could learn in ten years in a public school."[61] They stated that they, too, believed learning English was beneficial for those living in the United States—and for those who lived outside of the United States—and attending a Mexican school did not prevent these children from learning English and attaining upward socioeconomic mobility. Without using the terminology of education scholars, what these journalists and teachers were arguing about was the efficacy of additive and subtractive Americanization. *Additive Americanization* refers to the process of learning English and American customs while maintaining your own language and traditions. *El Democrata Fronterizo* and *El Cosmopolita* advocated for just that, ethnic Mexicans integrating themselves into American society, while building on their own linguistic and cultural practices. *El Sol* and *El Mensajero* believed that the only way for ethnic Mexican children to have any future in the United States was to permit themselves to undergo the public school's requirement for subtractive Americanization, which required students to strip themselves from their native language and cultural traditions.[62]

The author also rebutted the insinuation that Mexican schools' agenda was to spread a "ridiculous patriotism." They contended that the purpose of these escuelitas was

> to provide the children with the greatest facilities for instruction, to arm them for the struggles of existence, in the least time, with the least expense, with the least inconvenience. Children are not citizens of any nation, but of the world. . . . Let us try to form men, they will choose their homeland.[63]

Whereas Marsh and the journalists of *El Sol* and *El Mensajero* argued that the exigencies of modernization made escuelitas irrelevant and pernicious, the journalists of *El Democrata Fronterizo* and *El Cosmopolita* contended that the exigencies of modernization were the very reasons why a Spanish-language education was necessary. The public schools, treating ethnic Mexican children like "idiots," would always funnel them into the low-wage jobs—reducing their intellectual potential to "simple braceros, day laborers without any intervention in public affairs." Additionally, *El Democrata Fronterizo* argued, *El Sol*'s perspective provided a justification for educational segregation.[64]

The imaginary citizenship of ethnic Mexican children did not belong to Mexico or to the United States. Once each child grew into an educated adult, they would make that decision themselves. Unlike the public school curriculum, the curriculum of Spanish-language escuelitas was an instantiation not for any country, *El Democrata Fronterizo* and *El Cosmopolita* argued, but for knowledge itself, for the beauty of learning. Education and instruction were about learning how to make one's way in the world, a skill entirely lost on those responsible for running the public school system. Essentially, *El Sol* and *El Mensajero* argued that these Mexican schools were a detrimental reaction to the English-only, subtractive Americanization approach of the public school system. *El Democrata Fronterizo* and *El Cosmopolita* counterargued that these schools were not a misguided reaction, but a progressive alternative that opened up many pathways for ethnic Mexican children's future in the United States.[65]

EL COLEGIO ALTAMIRANO

In Hebbronville, Duval County, around 1897, almost a decade before Marsh enthusiastically expounded on the decline of escuelitas in south Texas, and ethnic Mexican journalists debated their utility in the United States, el Colegio Altamirano, one of the most well known escuelitas, opened.[66] In 1895, Duval County, with more than 1,800 square miles of land, only had eighteen public schools—all of them ungraded with the exception of the one high school.[67] C. L. Coyner, county superintendent in 1894–1895, spoke to the quality of these schools, stating, "Our county needs more school-houses and better school houses—more books and better books. . . . Merchants in our county who buy school books seem to buy the cheapest class, and in order to get good books, parties have to send off and get them."[68] Additionally, Jim Hogg County—which Hebbronville became a part of in 1913—did not open a public school until 1921.[69]

No doubt motivated by the lack of public schools and the poor quality of those that existed, members of the ethnic Mexican community in Hebbronville—Ascencio Martínez, Tomás Barrera, Dionisio and Severo Peña, Francisco Barrera Guerra, and José Ángel Garza—donated money to open their own escuelita, el Colegio Altamirano. The school was named after the towering figure Ignacio Manuel Altamirano (1834–1893), an Aztec Indian from Tixtla de Guerrero, Mexico, who became a Supreme Court justice, novelist, and pedagogical theorist. El Colegio enrolled students from kindergarten to sixth grade and imported its materials and textbooks from Mexico.[70] Initially, it operated on the grounds of the Sociedad "Melchor Ocampo," but at the beginning of the twentieth century, Ascencio Martínez donated the property where a new building was constructed.[71] In 1929, Colegio Altamirano teacher Augustina Dávila, along with other prominent ethnic Mexican women of the community, founded the Sociedad "Josefa Ortiz de Domínguez," whose most important task was to raise money to keep el Colegio open.[72] The school property consisted of a large outdoor play area and a single building with one large room that had a small stage, a piano, and blackboards hanging on multiple walls.[73] When it first opened, decades before a public school did, the average attendance was at least a hundred students. After the public schools reached Hebbronville, the attendance remained between thirty-five and fifty students.[74]

The first teacher was Rosendo Barrera Guerra, who taught there until his death in 1907.[75] Mexican historian Bazant de Saldaña states that during the Porfiriato, the era from 1884 to 1911 when Porfirio Díaz was president of Mexico, Mexican intellectuals believed that every student who wanted to work in a professional field, including teaching, needed to be able to read, write, and speak Spanish, English, and French.[76] Barrera Guerra was trained at a university in Mexico during the Porfiriato, so he came from a specific Mexican pedagogical tradition that sought to teach the bourgeoisie

Students of el Colegio Altamirano, 1900. Rosendo Barrera Guerra, the school's first headmaster, is seated at the table. AG2008.0005, DEGOLYER LIBRARY, SOUTHERN METHODIST UNIVERSITY, LAWRENCE T. JONES III TEXAS PHOTOGRAPHS.

these three languages, and his descendants have stated that as headmaster of el Colegio, he did so.[77] It is unlikely that el Colegio Altamirano maintained this curricular commitment. In 1906, *El Democrata Fronterizo* referred to el Colegio Altamirano as a school that had been "established, sustained, and administered by a group of Mexicans to teach children in the Spanish language," not as a school that taught multilingual literacy.[78] Many students who attended afterward remember receiving their lessons only in Spanish.

Despite the fact that el Colegio remained open for more than six decades, it had a surprisingly small number of teachers. Following Barrera Guerra were Don Lauro Díaz; two sisters, Adelina and Ernestina Carmona, who taught there together; Ángela Ramírez; Augustina Dávila; and Emilia Dávila, who taught there for thirty-one years, from 1910 to 1916 and 1930 to 1955. Emilia Dávila was born in 1885 in Saltillo, Coahuila, and she was a graduate of the Normal School (teacher's college) there. Her approach to teaching throughout her life drew from her pedagogical training in Saltillo.[79] In her role as the sole teacher at el Colegio Altamirano for multiple decades,

Colegio Altamirano students, circa 1916. Sisters Ernestina (far left) and Adelina Carmona (far right) taught at el Colegio Altamirano between 1916 and 1919. Delia Vela is in the front row, sixth from left. COURTESY OF ROSA LIDIA VÁSQUEZ PEÑA.

she became known, as one parent stated, as "a true intellectual mother" of the children of Hebbronville.[80] Without an assistant, she directed six different grades in multiple subjects, structuring her classroom in such a way as to engage all levels in her pedagogical process. Part of the responsibilities of the older children was to help give lessons to the younger children.[81] She did not use textbooks, with the exception of a small book of poems, many of which the students studied, memorized, and recited in front of large crowds at school festivals and end-of-semester oral exams.[82]

Throughout the 1940s, tuition was two dollars per month per child.[83] School began every morning at eight, and children went home for lunch at noon. Class resumed again at one, and school ended at 3 or 4 p.m. for the younger students. Older children, however, stayed until 6 p.m. every day, using the extra hours of instruction to work on their sewing, drawing, and mapmaking.[84] First- and second-graders studied and received grades for the following subjects: the "lengua nacional" (Spanish), math, natural science, history, drawing, calligraphy, singing, manual trades, and physical exercise. Third-graders took all of the above but added geography, and fourth-graders added science.[85] Rosa Lidia Vásquez Peña, who attended el Colegio in

Students of el Colegio Altamirano, 1911. Emilia Dávila, who taught at el Colegio for thirty-one years, is sitting in front of the chalkboard (center left). Delia Vela is in the front row, second from left. COURTESY OF ROSA LIDIA VÁSQUEZ PEÑA.

the early 1940s, remembers Dávila's passionate lectures on Cortés and the Aztecs, La Malinche and Cuauhtémoc, and Father Miguel Hidalgo y Costilla and Josefa Ortiz de Domínguez. Students took their notes and practiced their drawings in composition books Dávila made out of cut-up pieces of paper that were sewn along the edge on one side.[86] And she looked to the community for other teaching materials. For example, in lecturing on the anatomy of the eye, she used a cow's eye that the local butcher, Don Dionicio, donated to the class.[87] Throughout the school year, she used oral exams to assess students' knowledge and abilities.[88]

Dávila regularly scheduled "días del campo," field days, when she would take her students for long walks to the end of town, toward Benavides, where they studied local plant life. She and the students had lunch by a large hill, a point they called el Puente Grande. The children spent the afternoon playing in the countryside and then walked back to the school before the day ended.[89] Delia Vela, Vásquez Peña's mother, attended el Colegio between 1911 and 1916, and studied under Dávila and the sisters Ernestina and Adelina Carmona. Vela's daughter, Rosa Lidia Vásquez Peña, attended the school from 1940 to 1944. Both Vela and Vásquez Peña participated in these días del campo with Dávila, so she began this activity with her students when she was a young teacher in her twenties and continued with it when she was a more experienced teacher in her fifties and sixties.

Widely known for her dedication to teaching, Dávila was noted for saying, "My children, before learning the sciences and the letters, I want to teach you to direct your tender heart, to train your character to govern your will."[90] She regularly led the children in physical exercise, including moments of silence in which they took deep breathes as they calmly stretched their arms above their heads.[91] Dávila was not a permissive teacher, though. Sergio Garza, grandson of founder José Ángel Garza, attended el Colegio from the first to the fifth grade from 1949 to 1953. Dávila lived in the house directly across the street from the school, which his grandparents owned. He remembers her versatility as a teacher and her sternness. "Stern to the ultimate," Garza recalled, smiling as he shared the memory of Dávila walking around the classroom with her small stick, which she used to hit the calves of students who were not focused on their work.[92] In spite of, or perhaps because of, her firmness, she developed close relationships with her students and their families. Eighty years after she studied under her, Vásquez Peña still visits Dávila's grave every time she visits Hebbronville.[93]

At the end of each school year, Colegio Altamirano students were required to participate in oral exams, and the Spanish-language press usually reported on the event. In fact, the end-of-semester exams were presented to the public as part of a festival filled with poetry recitations, plays, displayed art and sewing work, and musical presentations, in addition to the grueling academic questions students answered in front of the crowd. These end-of-year academic and literary celebrations, as they were called, charged admission, so they also functioned as fundraisers for the school.[94] Jovita González stated in her 1930 master's thesis that students' oral exams lasted between two and five days, and argued that escuelitas such as el Colegio Altamirano were much more academically demanding than the local public schools.[95]

It became rather common for students of el Colegio Altamirano to transfer to the public school system for junior high school. Harvey Edds, president of the Hebbronville Independent School District, wrote to the board of trustees that the students who transferred from el Colegio Altamirano were "more regular in their attendance, more obedient, and more capable of grasping the English language than those who have not had this training."[96] By the time Rosa Lidia Vásquez Peña left el Colegio in 1944, after she completed the fourth grade, she had already finished algebra and had begun learning geometry. When she began in the public school, the administrators placed her in third grade because she did not speak English, and she remembers

1897 EL 1948
COLEGIO ALTAMIRANO

CELEBRARA LA TERMINACION DEL AÑO ESCOLAR
CON UN

FESTIVAL ARTISTICO · LITERARIO
EN EL "TEATRO CASINO"
EL 1o. DE JULIO PROXIMO, PRINCIPIANDO A LAS
6:30 P. M. EL DESARROLLO DE SIGUIENTE

PROGRAMA:

1. Recitaciones, por alumnos del Colegio.
   La gota de agua — La Perla.
2. Coros — por varios alumnos.
   a—La Puesta del Sol.
   b—El pajarillo.
3. El Pais de los Holgazanes — Paso de comedia.
   El papá . . . . Roberto Vásquez
   La mamá . . . . Berta Hinojosa
   Perico . . . . Raimundo Hernández
   Tres y holgazanes — varios alumnos.
4. Chilena Guerverense.
   Bailable por las niñas Judith Vásquez y Diana D. Martínez
5. Recitaciones:
   Si tienes una madre.
   Dar.
   Una lágrima.
6. Bailes españoles, por la niña Judith Vásquez.
   a—España Cañí.
   b—Alegrías.
7. Coros, por varios alumnos.
   a—Torna a Sorrento.
   b—La Perla.
8. Las aceitunas, Pasillo cómico.
   José . . . . Alberto Carrión
   Luisa . . . . Ma. Luisa Garza
   Jacinta . . . . Olga Salinas
   Vecino . . . . Manuel Salinas
9. Chiapanecas — Bailable por varias alumnas.
10. Hilos de plata, canción por la Sra. Isaura M. Black.
11. Mosaico — Bailable por las niñas
    Judith Vásquez y Diana D. Martínez—
12. Cuando vuelvas, canción por la Sra. Isaura M. Black.
13. Bailes españoles por la niña Judith Vásquez.
    a—Los cuatro muleros.
    b—Silverio.
14. Noche azul — Canción por la Sra. Isaura M. Black.
15. Jarabe tapatío.

ENTRADA GENERAL 30c

The program for the 1948 end-of-the-year artistic and literary festival, for which students recited poetry and performed plays. Local businesses had begun supporting these festivals by the late 1940s, and all admission fees went toward supporting the school. COURTESY OF ROSA LIDIA VÁSQUEZ PEÑA.

that students in this class were learning multiplication. As she learned the language, her teachers moved her up the grades quickly until she was at the appropriate level for her age. When she graduated from Hebbronville High School, she was valedictorian, and her sister was salutatorian.[97] But there are many examples of alumni of el Colegio attaining some measure of success as doctors, lawyers, professors, engineers, and teachers. The founding director of the Bilingual and Bicultural Studies Department at the University of Texas at San Antonio, Albar Peña, was a graduate of el Colegio.[98]

In many ways, el Colegio was similar to other escuelitas in that the language of instruction was Spanish with a focus on conduct, Mexican civics, Mexican history, and practical life skills, such as public speaking, sewing, and manual trades. But it was different because of its longevity, lasting over sixty years with full community support. Vásquez Peña quipped, "El Colegio wasn't an escuelita, it was an escuelota [a very big school]."[99] She noted that Catariña Saldaña, who lived on Hickory, had an escuelita in her home. She taught Hebbronville children Spanish literacy and Mexican civics and history in her living room a few blocks from el Colegio.[100]

Undoubtedly, the standard escuelita curriculum was more academically challenging than that of the public school. Repeatedly, superintendents stated in their reports that the most important part of the curriculum for ethnic Mexican children was teaching them English, rather than any focus on other subjects such as math or the sciences. Superintendents also stated that many of the Mexican children did not learn as quickly as the Anglo children, so neither group would benefit if they were in the same classroom. These same issues would frame the relationship between ethnic Mexicans and education for decades, engendering multiple civil rights groups and court cases throughout the Southwest.

During the earliest decades of the Texas public school system, a specific ideology shaped the state's approach to education: the state provided money and land to build schoolhouses, but each community was responsible for sustaining the facility on its own. Predictably, this approach yielded very few schools. By 1884, this ideology had given way to the progressive education movement in Texas, which centralized and expanded the public school system, while using ethnic Mexican children as a vehicle for assimilating the ethnic Mexican population. By the early 1900s, county superintendents saw increased enrollment rates for ethnic Mexicans and proclaimed that fewer of them patronized the escuelitas, interpreting this as a sign of progress. In the midst of their premature optimism, el Colegio Altamirano, the most famous escuelita, opened. Unequivocally, ethnic Mexicans used education as a means for asserting agency in constructing their lives in the United States before and after the rise of the progressive education movement.

The year 1910 was a watershed for the history of escuelitas, and for the history of ethnic Mexican education in the United States. By then, though many escuelitas still existed on ranches or as summer and after-school programs, their numbers may have diminished slightly as the public school system developed. At this same moment, however, segregation spread throughout Texas so quickly that the press in Mexico and the Spanish-language press in Texas began publishing stories about Mexican children's exclusion north of the Río Grande. Responding to these articles, the Mexican Consulate opened an investigation into the matter. But to the consternation of prominent Texas Mexican journalists of Laredo, just as the investigation began picking up steam, the Mexican Revolution began, essentially ending the Mexican government's concern about the treatment of Mexicans in the United States for the next ten years.

Students of el Colegio Altamirano, circa 1915. Emilia Dávila is standing on the far left.
COURTESY OF ROSA LIDIA VÁSQUEZ PEÑA.

CHAPTER 2

IMAGINARY CITIZENS AND THE LIMITS OF THE TREATY OF GUADALUPE HIDALGO

Educational Exclusion and the Mexican Consulate Investigation of 1910

The year 1910 was pivotal in ethnic Mexicans' relationship to education and in their relationship to the United States. First, that year F. M. Bralley, the state superintendent of public instruction, reported that the community system had been shut down completely. Though the state department of education attempted to do away with the community system as early as 1884, it lingered in several counties until 1910.[1] Second, by then, more and more ethnic Mexicans were enrolling their children in the public school system, while at the same time a significant number of schools throughout Texas were segregating them.[2] In the midst of this crucial period, in August 1910, the Mexican Consulate began an investigation of issues regarding the education of Mexican children in Texas, and in their initial estimation, the public school system treated Mexican children well, spending adequate resources trying to teach them English in a respectful manner. Members of the Texas Mexican middle class with firsthand knowledge of the actual situation rejected these findings.

The Idars were one of the most educated families in south Texas and were unquestionably part of the area's ethnic Mexican cultural elite. Nicasio Idar, the family's patriarch, published Laredo's widely read Spanish-language weekly, *La Crónica*, from 1910 to 1914. In late 1910 and early 1911, Clemente Idar, Nicasio's son, wrote several articles on the exclusion and segregation of Mexican children in the Texas public school system. Many scholars have written about these articles and about the Idars' subsequent political activism; however, a key element missing from this scholarship is that they were a response to the investigation conducted by the Mexican Consulate during that period.

Upon hearing that the Mexican Consulate was ready to end its perfunctory inquiry on such a positive note, the Idars launched a campaign to refute these findings in the hope of reopening the investigation and ending educational segregation in Texas. Clemente Idar's articles, an exposé of the horrible treatment ethnic Mexican children received, were meant to convince the consulate to take up their cause. To be clear, the Idars were not speaking to the Texas state government, calling to its attention the public school system's false promises of democracy for Texas Mexicans; nor were they speaking to the US government, calling to its attention the failings of the Treaty of Guadalupe Hidalgo. The very nature of their campaign was a contradiction in and of itself: they were writing to the Mexican government, hoping that it would resume its investigation so that it would somehow make it possible for ethnic Mexican children to receive an equal opportunity for an education in the American public school system.

The contradictory nature of their campaign had significant implications for the ethnic Mexican child whose imaginary citizenship, in the minds of adults, still belonged to Mexico, but who had a future in the United States. The educational history of ethnic Mexican children in 1910 Texas manifests this liminal state of children's imaginary citizenship. The year 1910 marked a turning point for ethnic Mexicans and their relationship to education because throughout the investigation, neither the Idars nor any of their readers ever discussed escuelitas as the answer to the segregation issue. As education and literacy reflect children's imaginary citizenship, the omission of escuelitas is a telling part of the narrative. The Idars appealed to the Mexican Consulate for help in claiming a place for ethnic Mexican children in the Texas public school system; they were not appealing to the consulate to help the Mexican colony found more escuelitas, as many refugees of the Mexican Revolution would do throughout the 1920s and 1930s (discussed in chapter 4).

Within a few months of its beginning in November 1910, the revolution quickly overwhelmed every facet of the Mexican government's attention and resources, and the consulate suddenly broke off its investigation. Realizing that Mexico was in no position to offer any support, the Idars decided to take action themselves and began organizing El Primer Congreso Mexicanista (The First Mexican Congress), which included delegates from Texas and northern Mexico who met to create and mobilize multiple community organizations that would work to improve the status of Mexicans in Texas.[3] The conference took place during the Mexican Independence Day celebrations in September 1911, seven months after the consulate ended its investigation.

Throughout his campaign in 1910, Clemente Idar wrote about the close ties between Mexican immigrants and Texas Mexicans, but by the 1920s he advocated excluding Mexican immigrants from membership in the various Mexican American civil rights organizations of which he was a member—an indication of the growing importance of US citizenship among the young cohort of Mexican American activists.[4] Ten years after the investigation ended, in 1921, eight Texas Mexican men founded the Order of the Sons of America, the first formal Mexican American civil rights organization, and within eight years, three other groups emerged.[5] By 1929, these four civil rights groups united to create the League of United Latin American Citizens (LULAC), whose goal was to combat racism against Mexican Americans in public schools, jury selection, housing, and public accommodations, and create a larger Mexican American middle class.[6] Eduardo Idar, Clemente's brother, had to have been aware of *La Crónica*'s appeal to the Mexican Consulate in 1910, but in 1929 he was one of the principal writers of the LULAC constitution, which identified English as the league's official language and required its members to be United States citizens.[7]

Before the Idars' turn to embracing US citizenship, the consulate's abrupt end to its investigation made it clear that Mexico would not be able to lend any financial, political, or moral support to the Texas Mexican plight. Attempts to remedy public school segregation took place as early as 1910, when the Idars and their readers demanded inclusion in the public schools, albeit with an important caveat—they were requesting the help of the Mexican Consulate.

THE MEXICAN CONSULATE'S INVESTIGATION OF 1910

In August 1910, the Mexican ambassador to the United States, Francisco de la Barra, sent a letter from his office in Washington to Miguel E. Diébold, the Mexican consul in Laredo, which quite simply stated, "Please inform me, as soon as possible, about the accuracy of the published news by some newspapers in Mexico of the exclusion of Mexican children in the schools of the state of Texas."[8] Though de la Barra did not explicitly state why he instructed his consul members to fact-check the allegations of the Mexican newspapers, it is likely he was influenced by the large amount of American investment in the Mexican economy.[9] After he completed his investigations in November 1910, Diébold sent de la Barra a report on his findings, revealing that he could not locate any evidence of exclusion of Mexican children in Webb, Zapata, or Duval Counties, which formed the district under his charge. If Mexican children were segregated into separate schools, he explained, it was only because they did not speak English, "and therefore cannot, with benefit,

attend the ordinary schools."[10] He visited four of the six public schools in
Laredo, and as he stated, "with great satisfaction I learned of the attention
that they give the Mexican children that do not speak English."[11]

To conduct his inquiry, Diébold enlisted the help of John A. Valls, who
had been the district attorney of Laredo since 1902.[12] They contacted the
superintendents in the three counties, asking if they could, in writing, detail
the nature of their schools' treatment of Mexican children, particularly as
to whether or not they were excluded or segregated. He received responses
from B. Richardson, the county judge and superintendent for Webb County;
S. H. Woods, the county judge and superintendent for Duval County; L. J.
Christen, the superintendent of Laredo Public Schools; and Pedro Flores,
owner of the Union Saloon in Falfurrias, who wrote his response for J. M.
Garcia, a prominent landowner in Laredo. Flores was the only one to speak
harshly of the relations between Anglos and Mexicans, stating that the
"Americans maintain a terrible hatred" toward Mexicans.[13]

Richardson, Woods, and Christen, on the other hand, all wrote of the
ridiculousness of such a rumor. Richardson's pithy response merely stated,
"With respect to the assertion that Mexican children are in any way dis-
criminated against in the schools of Webb Co., the statement is made by one
who is either absolutely ignorant or an abominable liar."[14] Richardson, who
began his tenure as county superintendent in 1902, wrote in his 1903 report
that he instructed the teachers to make teaching English their number
one priority, adding, "There are thousands of children in the county, born
American citizens and not understanding a word of the language of their
country. It is a significant fact that 98 percent of the crime of this county
(as per court records) is among the ignorant Mexican population."[15] It is
unlikely that Richardson considered his own statements discriminatory, but
nonetheless, similar to the opinions of many other county superintendents
of his time, he linked ethnic Mexicans' lack of English proficiency to his
county's downfall.[16]

Prejudiced views of ethnic Mexicans aside, Webb County was not without problems that negatively impacted public education. Between 1902,
when Richardson first took office, and 1910, Webb County went through a
drought during which the food that teachers bought for their students was,
in many cases, the only food they had to eat. Multiple epidemics of malig-
nant mumps followed the drought, killing as many as ten children and one
board trustee. In the 1905–1906 academic year, all the papers, books, and
records of the affected schools were burned to avoid spreading the disease.[17]
Additionally, Webb County, with very few country roads, comprised about
4,500 square miles and, outside of the Laredo Independent School District,

had between twenty-one and twenty-three schools for the entire county.[18] Between the drought, high poverty rates, mumps epidemics, and isolation of schools, low student attendance was a pressing issue.

S. H. Woods's response to Diébold was less of a contrast to the remarks he made in his annual reports to the state superintendent.

Our Mexican and American children receive the same treatment . . . they attend the same school, play in the same yard, sit in the same rooms, study the same subjects and in many instances they are taught by Mexican teachers, in fact there is no distinction made between the races. The Mexican and American people of our County work hand in hand for the best interest of our people regardless of nationality, I am sorry that such rumors have been circulated for there is not a county on the border that has as little prejudice between the races as Duval.[19]

His statement to Diébold emphasizes the equality between Whites and Mexicans: not only did the children of the two groups have the same experiences in the public school system, but the adults also worked together equally to elevate all citizens of Duval County. It should be noted, however, that by 1906, *El Democrata Fronterizo* claimed that school segregation had already taken root in Duval County. Additionally, that 1910 academic year, 2,173 White children were enrolled in the Duval County schools. Of that population, seventy-five were American (Anglo) and 2,098 were Mexican.[20] As only 3.5 percent of the scholastic population were "Anglo," it was not financially feasible to build them their own school, especially since it is unlikely that all seventy-five of them lived close to each other.

Woods's 1893 annual report, however, illustrates his ambivalence about ethnic Mexicans and education. He stated that 90 percent of the student population of Duval was Mexican,

and [they] manifest but little interest in school affairs as is shown by the low enrollment. The Mexicans, however, are beginning to take more interest in education. Some splendid work is being done by these Mexican scholars and the children of the best families are rank[ed] well with those of any nationality of the same age and opportunity.[21]

Woods attributed low enrollment to the belief that Mexicans did not value education rather than to issues of poverty, isolation from schools, and cultural differences. And like other superintendents, when he acknowledged Mexican students' intelligence, he did so by distinguishing between the "best families" and everyone else, the implication being that "everyone else" was from the larger majority of impoverished Mexicans who did not value education. He referred to the children from the "best families" as "Mexican scholars" rather than as children, students, or, as was more common, just "Mexicans." These scholars were doing "splendid work," and he even stated they had the same level of intelligence and potential as "those of any nationality"—that is, Whites—as long as they came from the same age group and class. The implication is that Mexican children from a less privileged background do not have the potential to do as well in their educational endeavors—assuming they cared about school enough to attend—because poverty had a tendency to diminish intelligence.

L. J. Christen's letter also provides insight into how superintendents interpreted ethnic Mexicans' relationship to education. First, Christen also stated that the Laredo Independent School District made "no distinction whatever in enrolling pupils all we ask is age and place of residence," adding, "In the primary grades all our teachers speak the Spanish Language which we find absolutely necessary."[22] He also stated that the Laredo Independent School District's scholastic population had 1,201 students, of which 267 were American, 904 were Mexican, and 30 were "colored." Despite the fact that Mexican children accounted for 75 percent of the entire scholastic population of the Laredo Independent School District, Anglo American children accounted for 91 percent of the student body from the fourth grade through high school.[23] Numerous other counties could claim the exact situation: the majority of students in the primary grades were ethnic Mexican, while the majority in the fifth grade through high school were Anglo American. In some cases, superintendents stated that many of the Mexican families worked as migratory farm laborers, and the children often traveled from farm to farm throughout the year. In other cases, such as Eagle Pass in the early 1890s, Mexican children were not allowed to move forward to the next grade because they did not speak English.[24]

In early November of 1910, Diébold forwarded these letters, along with his report, to de la Barra in Washington. He concluded that the public schools of Webb, Duval, and Zapata Counties held the Mexican children in high regard, writing:

> The Mexican children of the rural districts to the south of the state
> of Texas do not speak the English language, and for this reason,
> they cannot, with benefit, attend an ordinary school; and given this

circumstance, in almost all the counties of the south of the state of Texas, the directors, in the majority also are of Mexican origin, have established schools directed by Mexican professors in which they teach to the children both languages, English and Spanish.[25]

The following week, de la Barra forwarded Diébold's report and the additional letters to Enrique C. Creel—the minister of foreign affairs, whose office was in Mexico City—and recommended that if he found the outcome of Diébold's investigation suitable, he publish the findings as soon as possible to put an end to the rumors about which the press in Mexico and Texas were publishing articles more frequently.[26] According to his letter, de la Barra hoped this would be the end of the investigation.

A month later, however, on December 14, de la Barra sent letters to consuls in ten different cities, and he received responses from six of them, all of which claimed that the public schools in their districts did not exclude Mexican children.[27] The consul in Eagle Pass, specifically, made the same assertion regarding his own district, but he also mentioned that he had heard rumors that the public schools in Webb County excluded Mexican children. This allegation prompted de la Barra to write to Diébold again, a month after receiving his initial report, bluntly informing him of what the consul in Eagle Pass had said and asking whether or not it was true. In his response, dated January 17, 1911, Diébold continued to assert that there was not any exclusion of Mexican children in the public schools of Webb, Duval, or Zapata Counties. He suggested, however, that perhaps the consul in Eagle Pass had read recent editions of *La Crónica* and interpreted the exposé articles to mean that Webb County was guilty of exclusion. While Idar, the author of the articles, admitted that exclusion did not exist in Webb County, he wrote of it occurring in other counties in central and southern Texas. From then on, Diébold sent a copy of *La Crónica* to the Mexican Consulate each time Idar published an article about the exclusion of Mexican children in the public schools.

LA CRÓNICA'S CAMPAIGN TO REOPEN THE INVESTIGATION

Clemente Idar and his father, Nicasio, ran in the same social circles as many of the men involved in the investigation. In August 1910, he, his father, Christen, and García were in the International Club together. The following month, Mexican president Porfirio Díaz appointed Diébold as a special representative to supervise and work closely with the group to plan the itinerary for Mexico's centennial celebration, a four-day festival

Nicasio Idar (top) published La Crónica *from 1910 until his death in 1914. His sons, Clemente (left) and Eduardo, worked as journalists for the paper along with their sister, Jovita.* NO. 084-0589, GENERAL PHOTOGRAPH COLLECTION, UNIVERSITY OF TEXAS AT SAN ANTONIO, SPECIAL COLLECTIONS—INSTITUTE OF TEXAN CULTURES. COURTESY OF A. IKE IDAR.

that would open with 150 escuelita students singing the Mexican national anthem as the First Battalion band played.[28] Since they knew each other socially, the men must have discussed the consulate's investigation, and Diébold likely provided Idar access to all the correspondence between de la Barra, Creel, and himself. Beginning in December 1910, Idar wrote several articles critiquing the Mexican Consulate's investigation, but he did not just criticize the perfunctory nature of the inquiry. He quoted extensively from the consuls' correspondence to each other—often citing an entire letter—and followed each quote with scathing commentary and analysis.

Initially, Idar had two issues with Diébold's report to de la Barra. First, he argued that segregating children because of language was not a valid practice, noting that the Texas Department of Public Instruction did not require children to know English before enrolling.[29] Second, he repudiated the notion that the majority of school directors and teachers were people of Mexican origin, arguing that neither he nor anyone he knew had ever heard that this was the case. Idar compared the bilingual nature of the public schools to the curriculum of Laredo's escuelitas to highlight the absurdity of Diébold's findings and of the Mexican Consulate's gullibility in accepting them. The individuals who founded escuelitas were "Professors" because their extensive pedagogical training and education gave them the credentials and experience to do their job professionally, as opposed to the public school teachers who—supposedly administering bilingual instruction—were not trained to teach Spanish literacy.

Idar's most scathing commentary, however, was for Esteva Ruiz, head of the Department of America, Asia, and Oceana Affairs. He argued that Diébold was given the job of investigating exclusion in the three counties included in his district, but Ruiz was responsible for taking Diébold's findings and applying them to the state of Texas as a whole, thinking that, as Idar states, he could "resolve the whole problem with a signature."[30] In a letter responding to Diébold's report, Ruiz outlined reasons why he felt compelled to extrapolate Diébold's conclusions to the rest of Texas, namely that Mexicans or individuals of Mexican origin held all the power in just about every county in Texas and constituted the majority of the state's population.[31] Idar declared that particular part of the letter "the most absurd that Mr. Esteva has said in all his life; but it is not possible that a person who has never lived in Texas can appreciate the truthful state of things." He continued,

> Texas is composed of 248 counties; Mexicans have complete political representation in 5 or 6 frontier counties to the south of the state, where we have concentrated during the last years; the power that he says we have "in almost all the counties of the state of Texas," is probably referring to the epoch when Texas was a Mexican territory.[32]

Conducting an investigation of whether or not the public schools of Texas were excluding Mexican children but focusing on only three counties—in which a significant majority of the students were Mexican—would undoubtedly yield favorable results. For example, in Zapata County in 1909, of the 944 White children who attended the county schools, 941 were Mexican and three were American (Anglo Saxon).[33] The crux of Idar's argument is that, of course, it is easy to state that public school officials treat Mexican and American children equally when there are only three American children in a scholastic population of 944.

Idar compared the consulate's response to educational matters in Texas to its response to the beginning of the revolution, stating,

> Because in Webb, Zapata, and Duval distinction [between the races] does not exist, then they do not believe exclusion is accurate? Then because in the offices of Foreign Relations they do not

hear the detonations from the rifles of the revolutionaries from Chihuahua, then there was not a revolution in Mexico.[34]

In mid-November 1910, a month before Idar published this first article critiquing the Mexican Consulate's investigation, Toribio Ortega, an organizer for Francisco Madero's Anti-Reelection Party and a spokesman for the community of Cuchillo Parado in the eastern part of the state of Chihuahua, became the first of many to take up arms against the government, and it did not take long before other parts of Chihuahua followed.[35] By late November, Enrique C. Creel, Mexico's minister of foreign affairs, and Mexican ambassador Francisco de la Barra were issuing statements to the US press that all was quiet in Mexico with the exception of the small town of Guerrero in western Chihuahua. They insisted it would not be long before the federal government was able to crush the small insurrection that still existed there.[36] However, the revolution quickly spilled over Chihuahua's borders into all other parts of Mexico and continued for ten years.

But in December 1910, Idar knew that the statements Creel and de la Barra were issuing to the American press were more indicative of what Mexican officials wanted to believe was true than what was actually true. If the Mexican Consulate was serious about conducting a thorough investigation, it would look at other counties in Texas where ethnic Mexicans were not a significant majority. Idar, however, did not limit his criticism to the consulate. He also implicated the state superintendent of public instruction, F. M. Bralley, in preferring to idealize the school system as the epitome of democracy rather than confront the institution's undemocratic tendencies.

ADDRESSING THE STATE SUPERINTENDENT OF PUBLIC INSTRUCTION

On December 28, 1910, two weeks after *La Crónica* launched its campaign, the Texas State Teachers Association held its thirty-second annual session in Abilene. Bralley gave an address on the conference's opening night entitled "Texas' Educational Outlook," in which he romanticized the origins of public education in Texas, called for general improvements in the school system, and advocated for a special tax to support the state's public universities.[37] The dean of the School of Education at the University of Texas at Austin, William S. Sutton, subsequently told Bralley about his high opinion of the speech, and overall, Bralley believed that it was a productive conference in which "the very finest spirit [was] obtained."[38] Clemente Idar probably read the *Houston Post*'s publication of Bralley's speech, as he published a Spanish translation of part of it, along with his own critique.

Idar never mentioned Bralley's views on levying a tax to support higher education or his suggestions for improving county schools; rather, he focused his sharp commentary on Bralley's analysis on the role of education in the Texas Revolution. Idar quoted Bralley as stating,

Texas has a unique history on account that its citizens, when still belonging to the Mexican government, revolted and gave as a principal reason the failure of their government to establish a system of public education. . . . Our ancestors, the only nation in the history of the world that revolted and went to war over the proposition that EDUCATION IS FOR EVERYONE and that the failure of government TO PROVIDE IT FOR EVERYONE is just cause for WAR.[39]

Unequivocally, Idar used Bralley's speech as an opportunity to highlight the hypocrisy of his own point: that the public school officials boasting that Texas seceded from Mexico on the principle of equal educational opportunities for all were themselves responsible for segregating ethnic Mexicans into separate schools.

He responded,

The "solid system of democratic education" of which the said Superintendent speaks in such beautiful words, does not have the slightest tinge of democracy, since democracy would not deprive Mexicans the pleasure of enjoying these "equal educational opportunities."[40]

Idar, then, directly addresses his own audience—unambiguously an audience very different from the one to which Bralley gave his speech—asking them to juxtapose the superintendent's idealism with the reality many Texas Mexican families faced, continuing,

Compare, our dear readers, the elevated concepts of the Superintendent of Texas with the facts, and you will find a difference that contradicts by being fully against educational democracy. . . . It is a true shame that the teachers and the citizens of Texas in the great majority do not participate in the same exalted notions of altruism that Mr. Bralley preaches. Nevertheless, we will . . . [call] to his attention the exclusion of the Mexican children of the DEMOCRATIC American public schools.[41]

When he says, "We will . . . [call] to his attention the exclusion of the Mexican children," Idar is not referring to La Crónica's ability to acquire Bralley's attention with its publications. It is highly unlikely that Bralley spoke or read Spanish, so he probably never read Idar's articles or knew of the consulate's inquiry about the state of public education for Mexican children. It is more probable that by "we," Idar was referring to the alliance between La Crónica and the Mexican Consulate, especially since he integrated the Bralley article into the larger campaign. Once the consulate completed its investigation, it would take its findings to the state department of education, and as the Idars and their readers hoped, Mexican children's educational experiences would improve.

Another indication that Idar was not speaking directly to Bralley is the ironic way in which he alluded to the "said Superintendent." Throughout his analysis, Idar continually referred to Bralley as "learned" and "illustrative," ironically speaking to the supposed wisdom his position as state superintendent implied by undermining that very wisdom in pointing out that Bralley never acknowledged that the public education system in Texas failed to provide equal opportunities to countless Mexican children. His comparison between Bralley's recounting of Texas exceptionalist history and Texas Mexican reality subverted Bralley's argument that the Texas public school system was the truest manifestation of democracy, and his emphasis of the word *democratic* in all capital letters highlights the ways in which the exclusionary public school system tainted that very word. Essentially, Idar contended that Mexican children and their daily experiences in Texas were living contradictions to the legacy of the idealized history that existed in contemporary Texan memory—of Texas igniting a revolution in the name of public education for all.

He also pointed out that in the 1830s, disgruntled Texans with educational grievances were able to revolt against Mexico in the name of public education with the support of the American government, as well as with the support of a large number of American citizens who moved to Texas to fight in the revolution. What viable solutions did Texas Mexicans of 1911 have to rectify their grievances? If Texas Mexicans followed the same example—taking up arms and going to war—to make the world understand that they, too, wanted education for their children, Idar argued, no one would come to their aid. They already lived their lives in open marginalization with little support from the Mexican and US governments. If they revolted, even for a cause as significant and egalitarian as education, neither government would support their insurrectionary activities. Texas Mexicans would have to undertake other methods for publicizing the lack of educational opportunities for their children.

LA CRÓNICA'S READERS SPEAK

The most important method for publicizing their grievances was to rewrite the narrative surrounding the relationship between ethnic Mexicans and the Texas public school system, an undertaking that involved enlisting the help of its readers and encouraging them to think about exclusion more broadly in terms of economic opportunity and social mobility. "The exclusion of Mexican children does not only consist of the decree from the Commissioner's Courts or of the School Trustees," Idar contended, but

> also there is exclusion, as can be proven when they are isolated to separate neighborhoods . . . when they attend the official schools and the American children insult them, fight them, slap them, until always making them forget the wish of feeding their tender minds with the sacrosanct bread of knowledge; also there is exclusion when entire colonies of Mexicans living 1 and 2 miles away from the American communities, in many places without schools . . . living and educating not "jointly" as Mr. Esteva [Ruiz] says.[42]

Idar wanted his readers to reflect on their own experiences and the experiences of their children to see clearly the ways in which dominant Anglo society excluded them, ways that included but were not limited to the public education system. He stated, "We know that the exclusion of the Mexican children in Texas is a fact, in some parts by express and direct prohibition, and in others indirectly, through bad treatment, through humiliation and antagonism."[43] The humiliating events that children experienced in Texas public schools were indications of larger societal problems that impacted every aspect of Texas Mexicans' lives and, as such, should be considered in any investigation into the exclusion of ethnic Mexicans. Many of his readers understood Idar's larger point, and they sought to help La Crónica prove that despite what the Mexican Consulate wanted to believe, Mexican children were being excluded from public schools in Texas. Readers from several counties sent in letters detailing their own and their children's experiences in the public school system, explicitly stating that they were telling their stories to help prove the reality of exclusionary practices.

Two weeks after Idar's initial article in mid-December, La Crónica published two letters from readers in Seguin and Pearsall, in Guadalupe and Frio Counties, respectively. Ramon Escobedo of Seguin stated that the claims Idar made about public schools excluding Mexican children were true,

> because in Seguin . . . the exclusion is applied to us equally, as our children are not admitted to the schools of the "whites," but they built us a schoolhouse that will have more or less 20 × 30 feet and without sufficient seats for the children . . . Children that come from outside the city are required to pay 25 cents monthly to rent the seat.[44]

In 1902, Seguin was the first town or city to formally segregate Mexican children, establishing the state's first "Mexican school," and other counties in Texas followed suit. As early as 1930, 90 percent of the schools in Texas were already segregated.[45]

Escobedo also stated that there were two or three escuelitas "outside the city that can say they are purely Mexican,"

> but to build them they had to impose a contribution between all the Mexican Colony, besides paying certain contributions that they demanded of us. In a word, Mr. Idar, we are in a lamentable condition with respect to the instruction of our children, and today I direct myself to you . . . so that if you like I can give you information that serves a little to refute Mr. Esteva Ruiz.[46]

Escobedo's letter manifests the ways in which childhood education was a form of cultural negotiation. He outlined his options in educating his children, the segregated public school with inferior facilities and a seat rental fee or the Mexican escuelitas that existed outside the city limits. Interestingly, he does not glorify the escuelitas or refer to them as a saving grace that enabled him to bypass the humiliation embedded in segregated schooling. Instead, Escobedo focused on the fact that those who organized the founding of the escuelitas "imposed" payments (referred to as "contributions") from everyone in the Mexican colony to cover the costs of constructing and maintaining a schoolhouse, as well as for other undisclosed expenses to pay for the communities' necessities. In many ways, Escobedo's rejection of the self-segregating characteristic of escuelitas foreshadowed the rise of the Mexican American Generation's full embrace of educational integration as central to their civil rights campaign. These activists, who would emerge twenty to thirty years after Escobedo penned his letter to *La Crónica*, wholeheartedly dismissed the escuelitas' self-segregation.

Either way, Escobedo unequivocally stated that he was filled with anguish about his options, saying, "Mr Idar, we are in a lamentable condition with respect to the instruction of our children." His struggle with accepting the dichotomy of secondary status the Texas public school system bestowed on his children and the "purely Mexican" curriculum of the escuelitas mirrors the dialogues and debates in which he undoubtedly engaged with the larger cultural worlds surrounding him. His dissatisfaction with either educational option for his children speaks to the larger negotiations Texas Mexicans carried out in their daily lives.

Another reader from Gonzales wrote,

We have a school where they give instruction to the Mexican children, but to it not one American child goes there. The teacher thinks she is superior and is little interested in the students. The result is that the Mexican parents observe the inefficiency of the school, they make the charge "that it does not matter to send them to school or to let them idle in the street." These circumstances have demoralized me so much and already I have made the resolution to move my residence, soon, from here to the county of Wilson, where the Mexican children have access to the school of the "whites" and to where I go with the goal that my daughter receive the due instruction. To change my home, I leave behind me my relatives, friends, and very expensive attachments of 17 years of permanence in this place, because I do not want to experience more humiliation.[47]

Despite having lived in Gonzales for seventeen years, this father was committed to making sure his daughter attended a quality public school rather than a quality escuelita. Gonzales is located fairly close to Seguin and New Braunfels, both of which had their own escuelitas, so it is likely that one existed in or around Gonzales. However, there are salient factors that we do not know: whether he moved to Gonzales when he was a child or an adult, which industry employed him, and the type of income he earned. Despite these factors, however, rather than move back to Mexico or send his child to an escuelita in or near Gonzales, he planned to uproot his family so that his daughter—a point worth noting, as many believed that ethnic Mexicans did not value education for girls—could attend an integrated school. Leaving extended family and a job behind meant he would have to find new employment and a new group of supportive friends, but integration meant better facilities and better teachers, even if the price for such benefits was Americanization policies and an Anglocentric curriculum. This man sacrificed his work, home, and family to give his daughter an opportunity to receive an education based on a traditional US model.

Elías Tavarez wrote about an argument his father had with the commissioner of schools in Smithville, Texas, in Bastrop County. His father inquired as to whether his children would be able to attend the new school, and the commissioner responded outright, "No, they do not admit people of color." Either highlighting the fact that ethnic Mexicans were legally considered White or pointing out the nonspecific use of the phrase "people of color," his initial retort was "White is not a color?" Following the antagonistic exchange, Tavarez's father responded that the county's public schools received four dollars a month for each child, and since their school received this money for his son as well, he should be able to enjoy the educational benefits for which this amount paid. The commissioner responded in anger.[48]

We do not know whether Tavarez's father considered sending his son to an escuelita or if it was a viable option, but what is clear is that he was well informed about developments within the local public school system, inquiring about when the new facility would be open. He was also aware of the amount the state paid for the education of each student, regardless of race. The school received the same amount of money to educate his son as it did to educate an Anglo child; therefore, he argued, each child should receive the same education.

Dámaso T. Alemán in Marathon, Texas, also responded to *La Crónica*'s call for personal testimony, but he wrote directly to the Mexican Secretary of Foreign Relations in Mexico City, which forwarded a copy of the letter to the ambassador in Washington, DC. Alemán stated,

> More than this segregation of our children from the children of the Americans it diminishes us to a degrading moral level and creates in the children the hatred of some to others; this will give in the future, all that happens in our days, that burn us barbarously in life with any pretext, but in the bottom you can see clearly the hatred the Americans have for our race.[49]

Alemán presented his own solution to segregation, stating,

> In the report rendered by your Lordship Mr. Esteva Ruiz . . . it says that the children of both nations are not together because they do

not possess the language of the country. We do not wish that they be in the same class but in the same building, then the contact with each other will give the result that they are fraternizing since they are small, creating mutual sympathies.[50]

Alemán's letter speaks to his concern for segregated schooling's corollaries for society as a whole: the perpetuation of racism. Segregation degraded ethnic Mexican children and taught Anglo American children that the former were inherently inferior. As evidenced in the widespread racism in Marathon, he argued, segregated schooling was the vehicle that continually facilitated and encouraged society's racial hatred. Having read *La Crónica*'s articles that published the Mexican Consulate's correspondence, he recognized the public school system's pedagogical reasons for segregating ethnic Mexican children, but argued that language should not be used separate children. He believed that if the children could be exposed to one another early in life, their contact and possible friendship would assuage the prevalent and pervasive racism.

Unquestionably, Alemán was looking to the future of ethnic Mexicans in the United States. In his letter to the Mexican Embassy, he pleaded with the minister of foreign affairs to help ethnic Mexicans not only have better educational opportunities while living in the United States, but also use their educational experience to develop economic opportunity, civic engagement, and political influence north of the Río Grande. Alemán was using childhood education to negotiate the long-term ethnic Mexican presence in the United States, and he asked the Mexican government to assist him in doing so.

Idar's articles responded directly to the letters. He stated that every time a Mexican paid the poll tax, property tax, business tax, or any other tax or contribution, a portion of that money funded the public schools. To any Mexican who had paid any of these fees, he stated, "We recommend that you inform us if between these contributions have been recorded for the construction of a schoolhouse . . . for American children and to which they [Mexican children] do not attend."[51] Their investigation was no longer simply trying to prove the Texas public schools were excluding and segregating ethnic Mexican children, but also was asserting the state was using ethnic Mexicans' money to sustain a humiliating and undemocratic institution.

La Crónica also attempted to obtain specific information from its readers systematically. In late January, the newspaper published a questionnaire with twenty-one items and asked its readers to fill them out and send them back to help its investigation. Among the questions were: "Are you a Mexican citizen or American citizen? . . . Do you speak English? Do you have children, brothers, or family members of the Mexican race, of school age who reside in this town? . . . Do they attend school? . . . If they attend say if it is an American public school or a Mexican private school [escuelita] that they attend."[52] The newspaper repeatedly stated that it was going to publish an article with the results of this questionnaire but never did, most likely because the investigation ended before they could compile all the information.

Despite the harsh tone of Idar's criticisms, the underlying theme of every article—the entire point in involving his readers and creating a questionnaire—was his confidence in the ability of the Mexican Consulate to rectify the segregationist policies of the Texas public school system. In one article, he unequivocally stated, "The Mexican government will do a splendid labor if they manage to give to the Mexican children the welcome that they worthily deserve in the public schools of Texas."[53]

THE CONSULATE'S RESPONSE TO *LA CRÓNICA'S* CAMPAIGN

Undoubtedly, *La Crónica's* coverage of the Mexican Consulate's investigation affected the way Creel and de la Barra subsequently interpreted Diébold's report, prompting them to expand the investigation to other Texas counties, but establishing a timeline for such influence is difficult. Five days after *La Crónica* published its initial article, Diébold sent a letter to Nicasio Idar asking for more information about which counties excluded Mexican children, making it a point to mention that "the cases that have arrived to your knowledge are in counties foreign to the jurisdiction of this consulate."[54] The copy of this letter is in the archival file in Mexico City only because Diébold sent it to de la Barra when he responded to his second inquiry about exclusion in Webb County (which the Eagle Pass consul prompted) in January 1911. Up to that point, it appears the conversations Diébold had with Nicasio and Clemente Idar about resuming the investigation remained off the record and did not involve the Mexican ambassador in Washington, DC. This fact might account for why the December 24, 1910, edition of *La Crónica*, titled "Consul Miguel Diébold Resumes His Investigations," is the only article missing from the archival file. It is possible Diébold never sent it to the ambassador.

In the January 12, 1911, edition of *La Crónica*, published almost a week before Diébold wrote his response to de la Barra's second inquiry, a short article states that if the Mexican Consulate was going to offer any kind of protection to Mexican nationals in Webb, Zapata, and Duval Counties, those residents needed to register themselves with the consulate. Likewise, they needed to inform the consulate when they married, had children, or had friends or loved ones who died. One also needed to present proof or testimony that one had not tried to become a US citizen.

In another letter to de la Barra, dated January 17, Diébold stated that he had interviewed Nicasio Idar, who informed him that all the evidence he had about the exclusion of Mexican children had already been published in *La Crónica*. Idar also told him that he was currently investigating the treatment of Mexican children in Frio and Guadalupe Counties, as well as others, and he would send all the evidence he acquired to Diébold. The Idars continued conducting their own research, and they published their readers' letters as early as December 31, 1910, and then again on February 9, 1911.

On January 19, 1911, *La Crónica* had stated that its own investigation prompted the Mexican Consulate to issue new orders and that its work was a central part of the thorough examination the Mexican Consulate promised to undertake. The consulate assured everyone that for their renewed inquiry: (1) the consul in San Antonio would be in charge of carrying out a thorough, statewide investigation; (2) the San Antonio consul was going to interview those who wrote letters to *La Crónica*, and the paper would publish each letter with the name and address of the author to facilitate contact between them and the consulate; (3) the consul in Laredo would get information from *La Crónica* as its investigation progressed and send it to the consul in San Antonio; and (4) all information pertaining to the investigation would be sent to the ambassador in Washington, DC.[55]

The investigation ended, and the Idars stopped publishing articles about it, in early 1911. At that point, the Mexican government had lost all control of the revolutionaries, and many of the consuls involved in the 1910 investigation found themselves consumed by the insurgency. By 1911, Creel, the minister of foreign affairs, had lost much of his landholdings in Chihuahua—which were vastly extensive. Fleeing Mexico and finding refuge in the United States, he was one of the elite against whom the revolutionaries fought.[56] Mexican Ambassador de la Barra became interim president of Mexico at the end of May 1911 when Díaz resigned.[57] By 1911, the Mexican Consulate had more pressing issues at hand than the treatment of ethnic Mexican children in Texas public schools.

The Idars attempted to rewrite the narrative surrounding the ethnic Mexican experience in the public school system—to construct a body of evidence that would counter the inaccuracies of the superintendents' and the consulate's official reports—but they did so for the sake of convincing the Mexican Consulate to campaign on their behalf to the US government. When the investigation ended so abruptly, the Idars and members of the Laredo ethnic Mexican middle class realized that Mexico could not help them negotiate their lives in the United States, and thus their children's imaginary citizenship no longer belonged wholly to Mexico, but rather encompassed cultural and political divides between the two countries.

Ten years later, in the 1920s, members of the Texas Mexican middle class, including a few of the Idar siblings, created civil rights organizations that prioritized US citizenship over Mexican citizenship and English over Spanish. Framing their argument for inclusion around their US citizenship and English literacy, these activists eventually competed with the Mexican Consulate and middle-class Mexican refugees for the loyalty of the large ethnic Mexican working class, and they considered their children's imaginary citizenship to be unequivocally American.[58]

In 1911, however, in the early throes of the Mexican Revolution, the immediate issue was the widespread poverty and lack of education of ethnic Mexican children, which implied that neither country claimed these imaginary citizens. Clemente's sister Jovita Idar, Leonor Villegas de Magnón, María Rentería, and María Villarreal founded their own escuelitas, whose purpose was to construct a complex variation of imaginary citizenship that pointed to a cohort of children who spoke proper Spanish, not "Tex Mex"; who understood the gendered nuances of Mexican history; and who could use this knowledge to help themselves build a future in the United States.

CHAPTER 3

REVOLUTIONARY AND REFINED

Feminism, Early Childhood Education, and the Mexican Consulate in Laredo, Texas, 1910–1920

Cada vez que se educa a una niña se funda una escuelita.
[Each time you educate a girl you found an escuelita.]
"Pensamientos y Aforismos," *La Prensa*, February 5, 1920

The Mexican Consulate conducted an investigation into the state of public education for ethnic Mexican children in south Texas in 1910. By early 1911, however, the Mexican government could no longer ignore the beginning of the revolution, and the organization abandoned the inquiry, much to the dismay of the Idar family. In September 1911, seven months after the Mexican Consulate hastily ended its investigation, the Idars hosted El Primer Congreso Mexicanista in Laredo, a conference that brought together members of the Texas Mexican middle class from all over the southern part of the state and northern Mexico to discuss the social, economic, and political discrimination against ethnic Mexicans in Texas. After witnessing the decline of the educational status of Mexican children in Texas and the growing violence against ethnic Mexicans in general, the Idars began taking a more aggressive course of action, and organizing the Congreso was a step in that direction.[1] Trying to establish a long-term impact, the Congreso founded La Gran Liga Mexicanista de Beneficencia y Protección (The Great Mexican League for Relief and Protection), which they envisioned having local chapters across the state. La Gran Liga's goal was to protect its members from any kind of discrimination and eliminate the segregation of ethnic Mexican children in the public school system.

During the conference, Texas Mexican women also organized themselves into their own charitable group, La Liga Femenil Mexicanista (The Mexican Women's League), whose main objective was the education of Texas Mexican children. Jovita Idar, María Rentería, Leonor Villegas de Magnón, and María Villarreal—most of whom were officers in La Liga Femenil Mexicanista—believed that the widespread poverty and illiteracy among their community's children were the most salient problems for ethnic Mexicans in

Laredo, and educated and modern ethnic Mexican women were a necessary resource in combatting these issues.[2]

Since these women understood that they would not receive any help from governmental institutions on either side of the Rio Grande—such as the Texas Department of Education, the US Justice Department, or the Mexican Consulate—they founded their own escuelitas and educated Laredo's children themselves to mitigate the hegemonic agenda of the English-only, Anglocentric curriculum of the public school system, the disenfranchising effects of borderland modernity, and the violent disruptions of the Mexican Revolution. Idar, Rentería, Villegas de Magnón, and Villarreal, who were revolutionary and refined, looked to ethnic Mexican children as a vehicle for stabilizing their community, and to childhood education as the most effective approach for ensuring Texas Mexican upward socioeconomic mobility.

Using childhood education as a tool for stabilizing the community, however, was not as straightforward as one might expect. First, there was the question of who was the community and with which nation did it identify? In the early part of the twentieth century, the education of ethnic Mexican children was a highly politicized endeavor, whether they attended a public school or an escuelita. As the southern progressive education movement gained traction in south Texas, the public school system implemented a curriculum designed to assimilate immigrant children using subtractive Americanization methods that sought to erase the children's native culture in favor of one more "American." Escuelitas, particularly those created with the intention of offering an alternative to the public school system, also had a political agenda. Teaching children Spanish literacy and Mexican history, these schools encouraged children to hold onto their native culture, and in many cases, they transformed their Tex Mex fluency into Spanish literacy. For the public school system and the escuelitas, the language of instruction, as well as the version of history, manifested the patriotic sentiments of parents and teachers of the United States and Mexico.

Each politicized curriculum became an instantiation for the nation-state it was supposed to represent, and the opposing views of the two agendas meant that ethnic Mexican children were subjected to two different versions of imaginary citizenship—each of which failed to provide them access to civil rights. Between 1910 and 1920, these were children whose citizenship American superintendents disdained and the Mexican Consulate neglected, so to which nation did they imagine themselves to belong? Idar, Rentería, Magnón, and Villarreal, who combined the revolutionary ideals of teachers in Mexico and the Victorian social mores of middle-class women in the United States, addressed this question with their unique pedagogical approach—one that prioritized Spanish literacy as a way to eliminate the use of Tex Mex, ratified narratives of Mexican women's history, and valued children's agency in labor and community engagement.

THE MEXICAN REVOLUTION AND EDUCATION IN MEXICO

When the Mexican Consulate ended its investigation of the condition of education for ethnic Mexican children in Texas, public education in Mexico was in a state of flux, and shortly thereafter it fell into rapid decline. The Mexican Revolution, which began in 1910, triggered the immigration of about a million refugees to the United States, altering the composition of the ethnic Mexican population in Texas. Porfirio Díaz, dictator from 1876 to 1911, encouraged foreign businesses to invest in Mexico, offering extensive tax breaks to railroad companies and ignoring the exploitation of natural resources. Looking to developments in the United States as his muse, Díaz attempted to modernize his country, but he carried out these goals through the use of violence and electoral fraud, engendering the displacement of workers and peasants.[3] The overwhelming amount of foreign investment that he encouraged, as well as the government's disregard for workers' rights, prompted William Randolph Hearst to write to his mother, "I really do not see what is to prevent us from owning all of Mexico and running it to suit ourselves."[4] By late 1910, peasants united with discontented political elites to bring down Porfirio Díaz.

Although Díaz's policies displaced workers and peasants, they expanded public education. The number of primary schools increased from about 5,000 in 1878 to close to 10,000 in 1907, and the number of students swelled to about 600,000.[5] Not only did the teaching profession grow to try to accommodate the increase in students and schools, but it also became professionalized and feminized. Aspiring teachers needed to attain an education that trained them in pedagogy, the humanities and the sciences, and multilingual literacy. In 1895, there were roughly 13,000 teachers, compared to the 21,000 in 1910; additionally, the percentage of male teachers fell from 58 percent in 1878 to 23 percent in 1907.[6]

These gains in public education did little to elevate literacy rates among adults. By 1910, at the beginning of the revolution, an estimated 68 percent of Mexican adults were illiterate, and the widespread chaos and violence devastated the growing but tenuous public school system.[7] Many schools closed, many teachers fled to safety, and many students lost their chance to pursue an education or find work. For example, Pedro Chausse, one of several Mexican immigrants in the United States that Mexican anthropologist

Dr. Manuel Gamio interviewed between 1926 and 1927, detailed how the decline of public education during the revolution affected the course of his life. He told Gamio, "Before leaving for the United States I attended school up to the third year of Preparatory School. Then I left there because the school was closed on account of the revolution. Having joined Carranza, I went to the capital first. When the campaign was over and I was not able to find employment, I went to join my brother who was already working in the United States."[8]

Though it appears Chausse immigrated to the United States after school age, numerous families headed north to give their children educational opportunities elsewhere. Immigration and Naturalization Service records from this time period are full of Mexican immigrants stating that they wanted to move to the United States so that their children or grandchildren could attend school. In every case, the school in Mexico had closed. For example, eleven-year-old Antonio Gómez told immigration officials that he stopped attending school in Mexico "because the teacher went away."[9]

In some cases, parents who remained in Mexico paid to send their children to an escuelita because that was their only opportunity for an education. Attending an escuelita during the revolution could be a dangerous act, however, making education a perilous pursuit for children and their families. For example, Louise Gates, who grew up in the mining town of Sierra Mojada, Coahuila, with an American father and Mexican mother, states,

> There [was] no school, because of course, there was no civilian government, no municipal government, and probably no pay, and probably the teachers would've been afraid anyway. So the schools were closed. So Papa sent for a teacher from Torreón for us, Jesusita Cuellar, very nice lady and very religious, and she promptly organized these catechism classes, because of course, there was no school for anybody. . . . We had to walk down the railroad track to the town, which was maybe three or four miles, for the classes. . . . And we'd watch for, always, for men on horseback, because by then if a man was on horseback, he was a revolucionario of one army or the other, because no one else had horses. And we would then get on the far side of the . . . railroad embankment, you know, and lie down and keep low until they passed. We just never felt too safe about them.[10]

Sotero H. Soria, who grew up on an hacienda during the revolution, states,

In those times there were no schools. Nevertheless, on the *hacienda* where I grew up, I had the great opportunity of learning to read and write my name. A fine person who was somewhat educated, helped those of us who wanted to learn. The payment that he received was about ten cents a week. Even now when I am sixty-seven years old I have no words to show my gratitude to that splendid man. Teaching me to sign my name was for me a great achievement.[11]

The lack of schools meant that education became a prized possession, something that could not be obtained without taking certain risks. Adults with little education taught children basic elements of literacy, and even during the Mexican Revolution—a time of absolute chaos—some children were fortunate enough to learn to write their names.

TEACHER AS A MODERN REVOLUTIONARY

In many ways, the female teacher epitomized the modern woman—a well-read feminist who allied herself with the working class and looked to education as the key to lifting up the ethnic Mexican community. As stated earlier, by 1910 the majority of teachers in Mexico were women, and Mexican historian María Teresa Fernández Aceves argues that teachers in Mexico during the revolutionary and postrevolutionary eras created ties with other feminists to "transform the social configurations of femininity, masculinity, politics, and citizenship in the Mexican twentieth century."[12] In fact, from the Porfiriato to the postrevolutionary period, these female teachers made up the bulk of feminists in Mexico.[13] Many scholars link Díaz's obsession with modernizing Mexico to the rise of the revolution, and historian Ana Macías argues that feminism in Mexico was another by-product of modernization.[14] In 1904, Dolores Correa Zapata, a schoolteacher whose textbook *La Mujer en el Hogar* [The Woman in the Home] was used in an escuelita in 1900 in the San Roman Church in south Texas,[15] founded Mexico's first feminist magazine, *La Mujer Mexicana*, along with Dr. Columba Rivera and María Sandoval de Zarco. This monthly, published until 1908 and edited solely by women, filled itself with voices and concerns of "female teachers, writers, doctors, lawyers, bookkeepers, telegraphists, and other white-collar workers whose ranks had swelled to the thousands from 1880 to 1904."[16] Additionally, Chicana and Mexican feminists did not limit their activism to within their own borders, or even just across the US-Mexico border. Sonia Hernández argues that "a global language of activism and survival was promoted and appropriated by women to make sense of their local conditions."[17]

Female teachers also had a more direct impact once the revolution began. Dolores Jiménez y Muro, a schoolteacher from Aguascalientes, was part of the editorial staff of *La Mujer Mexicana* in 1905. She was twice jailed in the Belén penitentiary for her revolutionary activities during both the Porfiriato and Victoriano Huerta's counterrevolutionary regime in 1913–1914.[18] Participating in a plot to bring Francisco Madero to power in March 1911, she penned the plan outlining the conspirators' goals and intentions.[19] Emiliano Zapata read Jiménez's plan and stated that the document articulated the principles for which he was fighting. When he was told a female schoolteacher wrote it, he requested she join him in Morelos. After Madero's assassination, Jiménez, then in her sixties, joined Zapata in the south and remained with him until his assassination in 1919.[20]

As the revolution carried on in Mexico, women teachers turned a profession considered "women's work" into a revolutionary role, and this revolutionary role did not subside after the civil war ended. Jocelyn Olcott explains that, after the revolution, the Secretaría de Educación Pública provided a gateway to social activism and community engagement for many female teachers.[21] Ana María Flores, a former postrevolutionary teacher in the Comarca Lagunera, remembers, "We were everything. We were the town's teachers, lawyers, counselors, midwives, organizers. . . . We did everything; we knew everyone."[22]

Ethnic Mexican women teachers in Texas took on a similar role; however, they needed to maintain a "gente decente" (decent people) approach to combat the rampant, and oftentimes violent, racism in Texas. Gente decente referred to one's social status, as opposed to one's socioeconomic class. As Leticia Garza-Falcón notes, "Very poor people can have class, while middle-class people can be common."[23] Even when sharing their revolutionary ideas with students, these women maintained a demeanor that was almost Victorian in how they dressed, spoke, and interacted with their peers.[24]

JOVITA IDAR, MODERN WOMEN, AND THE RECONCILIATION OF IMAGINARY DUAL CITIZENSHIP

One such Texas Mexican teacher who embraced gente decente methods throughout her life was Jovita Idar, who earned a teaching certificate from the Laredo Seminary in 1903 and was president of La Liga in 1911. From 1910 to 1914, her father, Nicasio Idar, published *La Crónica*, in which she, María Rentería, and Leonor Villegas de Magnón published articles on education, history, and culture. In her article "Debemos Trabajar" (We Must Work), published in November 1911, Idar articulated a philosophy guiding the labor of these teachers by equating the working woman—regardless of socioeconomic status—with the modern woman, stating,

> The modern woman, informed of and understanding the need for contributing her contingent to help the development of the learning of the people, bravely invades all fields of industry in all of their phases without fear and without laziness. Abandon comfort and inaction, for in the current age, so full of life opportunities, so replete with energies and hope, there is no room for social leeches.[25]

Idar's perceptions of the working class complicated her relationship to modernity, which was framed by the needs of her community and Anglo hegemony. First, when Idar referred to herself as a "modern woman," she attached a specific meaning to that phrase. Christine Stansell's *American Moderns* examines the impact feminism had on the modern woman in New York City at the turn of the twentieth century. Though these modern bohemians included men and women from various classes, races, and nations, they also embraced the idea of what Stansell calls "sexual modernism," placing free love next to free speech as part of their political agenda, as well as their own lived experiences.[26] Even the Mexican American flappers that Vicki Ruiz describes in *From Out of the Shadows* held different views on the modern woman than Idar and her cohort. Examining the ways Mexican American women experienced a traditional and patriarchal culture through their immigrant parents, in addition to an American popular culture, Ruiz notes that many of these young Mexican American women altered their appearance by bobbing their hair and wearing makeup while still retaining aspects of their native background.[27]

For Idar, Mexican Protestantism shaped what it meant to be a "modern woman." Historian Gabriela González contends that "the Social Gospel," specifically Methodism, framed Idar's cultural redemption approach to her social activism: "Jovita Idar, like the Progressive New Woman, exemplified a feminist ideal that was not completely divorced from Victorian concepts of womanhood but certainly challenged and stretched the boundaries of a male-dominated society."[28] Additionally, González argues that though Idar equated the modern woman with the working woman, it was a different concept than that of the working-class woman. The "subtext of [Idar's] message was that despite unequal economic relations, the working poor would be measured by bourgeois moral and cultural standards, which were believed to hold the key to better treatment for Mexicans in Texas."[29] Embedded in Idar's revolutionary ideas about feminism and education was a traditional view of the Mexican caste system. In one particular article, she wrote that one of the unfortunate effects of the decline of the Spanish language was the loss of the castes. In fact, the social, economic, and political changes that modernization engendered created a new hierarchy that collapsed all ethnic Mexicans into a single, low-wage category, regardless of educational background or citizenship status. Idar's more traditional views on the caste system, as well as her inclination to view the working class through a bourgeois lens, influenced her thoughts about Tex Mex and its relationship to education and citizenship.

Idar held equally complicated views on the education of Texas Mexican children, the complexity of which unfolded over the course of two articles published within a week of each other, "La Niñez Mexicana en Texas"(The Mexican Children in Texas) and "La Conservación del Nacionalismo" (The Conservation of Nationalism), published August 10 and 17, 1911, respectively. Idar began "La Niñez Mexicana" by admitting that "our country" is too occupied with the revolution to "attend to its children" living in the United States, so Texas Mexicans would need to deal with the problems of their community themselves. She argued that the most salient reason the "foreigners"—Anglo Americans—despised Mexicans was due "to the crass ignorance of an overwhelming majority of our compatriots."[30] She does not, however, attribute the "crass ignorance" to the lack of English literacy among the working-class children, stating, "With deep grief we have seen Mexican teachers teaching English to children of their race, without taking any account of the maternal language, which every day is being forgotten and every day suffers adulterations and changes that hurt the ear of any Mexican."[31]

Acknowledging that "it is not easy to instruct these great masses of workers," she proposed that "we, the parents of our Mexican children in Texas, should unite to cover the costs that a school requires."[32] Idar suggested that the community of Texas Mexican parents hire graduates from the normal schools of Mexico—Monterrey, Saltillo, or any other university town—to teach in their school. Speaking to the logistics of such an endeavor, she argued that these teachers, so young and full of hope and energy, had few expectations in terms of salary and would probably be willing to negotiate. She ended her article with one of the statements that scholars quote most often:

> Mexican children in Texas need education. Neither our government [in Mexico], nor the United States government can do

anything for them, and we have no other recourse than to do it by our own impulse in exchange for no longer being dismissed by the foreigners that surround us.[33]

In this first article, Idar argued that she and her community needed to create their own escuelitas to help prevent the loss and the erosion of the Spanish language—not to teach children English. She was not advocating for a community escuelita because of problems with public school attendance. In a way, the public schools were part of the problem because the English-literacy curriculum was not balanced out by a Spanish-literacy curriculum, and the lack of a proper education in Spanish literacy had given rise to what scholars and layman alike call Tex Mex.

Both Idar and Leonor Villegas de Magnón found Tex Mex painful to hear and interpreted it as an indication of the working class's ignorance that encouraged Anglo American racism. Many White Americans did attribute the code-switching between Spanish and English to a lack of intelligence and education. In 1930, less than twenty years after Idar penned her plea for more Spanish-language education, *American Mercury*—H. L. Mencken's highly respected monthly magazine that published work by W. E. B. Du Bois, Clarence Darrow, Langston Hughes, and Sinclair Lewis, among others—printed H. E. McKinstry's "The American Language in Mexico." "Although every other word your Nogales or Juárez peon uses may be English," McKinstry wrote, "he could not, to save his sombrero, put them together into a sentence intelligible to an American, that is beyond such simple household phrases as *all right* and *goddam*. . . . This mongrel jargon of the border is naturally shocking to the ears of the well-bred Mexican of the interior."[34]

It was also shocking to well-bred Mexicans who did not live in the interior of Mexico, but on the border, watching the proliferation of this code-switching unfold. Historical linguist John M. Lipski argues that a "transparent linguistic blend" is going to emerge any place where Spanish-speakers and English-speakers live in contact with each other, but the Mexican Revolution and the influx of Mexican immigrants to the United States it provoked were the impetus for new ways for purists and xenophobes to perceive Spanish north of the Río Grande.[35] "It was during this time period," he states, "that the Spanish of Mexican political émigrés was regarded positively, while the language of migrant laborers on either side of the border was implicitly racialized as belonging to a poor non-white population, was viewed with scorn, and was assumed to be a pastiche of non-standard Spanish variants combined with a hopeless jumble of English."[36] Magnón referred to it as the "chronic disease of the border," rhetorically asking, "Is our own language not rich enough to sustain a conversation satisfactorily?"[37] Sharing Magnón's view, Idar called for the community to create escuelitas not only to minimize racial tensions, but also to construct a Spanish-literacy education, arguing that the English-only schools in which many Texas Mexican children were enrolled were degrading their mother tongue. While taking note of Lipski's contention that "transparent linguistic blending" occurs wherever Spanish and English meet, the emergence of the habit on the US-Mexico border in this era of intense social, political, economic, and cultural change—and the reaction on the part of Idar, Magnón, and others—indicates the significance of language and education not only in negotiating Anglo hegemony, but also in how living in the United States was changing the composition, nature, and daily habits of these communities.

Idar must have received some criticism for "La Niñez Mexicana en Texas" because the following week she felt compelled to publish "La Conservación del Nacionalismo" to clarify her views on language and literacy. She stated that she never meant teachers should not teach Mexican children English,

> the language of the land that they inhabit, since it is the medium that has put them in direct communication with their neigh-bors, and that will enable them to assert their rights; what we wanted simply to mean, is that we should not neglect the national language.[38]

Another frequently quoted passage serves to explicate her point of view further:

> We are not saying that we should not teach English to the Texas Mexican children . . . we are saying that we should not forget to teach them Spanish, because as math and grammar are useful to them, English is useful to those who live among those who speak the language.[39]

At the root of Idar's initial proposed plan to start an escuelita with Mexican teachers—and her subsequent inclination to clarify that plan—was her concern about the role language, literacy, history, and culture played in encouraging children to think of themselves as belonging to a community and to a nation. Understanding the link between language and nationalism several decades before Benedict Anderson's groundbreaking *Imagined Communities*, she states, "Nations disappear . . . when the national language is forgotten."[40] She contended that teaching Texas Mexican children Spanish would preserve Mexico as a nation-state within the Mexican colony living within the political boundaries of the United States. A proper language curriculum was at the center of their effort to help ethnic Mexican children move beyond their community's poverty and illiteracy, and teaching Texas Mexican children English would empower them to attain social, economic, and political mobility.

Essentially, Idar spoke to the constructed nature of children's imaginary citizenship, and the role of children's agency in that construction. "We are the makings of the environment," she stated, and therefore, "if in the American school to which our children attend they teach them the biography of Washington and not the biography of Hidalgo," then Texas Mexican children will not know anything about their country—Mexico—nor will they feel any love or affection for it.[41] If adults do not give children opportunities to read in their country's language, to learn about their country's past, or to understand

Jovita Idar (second from right) worked for multiple newspapers, including La Crónica, El Progreso, *and* Evolución. *She is pictured here in* El Progreso's *print room in 1914.* NO. 084-0592, GENERAL PHOTOGRAPH COLLECTION, UNIVERSITY OF TEXAS AT SAN ANTONIO, SPECIAL COLLECTIONS—INSTITUTE OF TEXAN CULTURES. COURTESY OF A. IKE IDAR.

the expectations of their country's citizens—if children do not engage in those intellectual activities—they will become adults who "will look with indifference to the compatriots of [their] parents."[42] The problem, according to Idar, was that the imaginary dual citizenship of Texas Mexican children in Laredo was tipping over to the American side because of the influence of the English language in the Spanish vernacular.

MARÍA RENTERÍA, WOMEN'S HISTORY, AND RATIFYING NATIONAL NARRATIVES

Most of the women involved in the creation of La Liga were teachers, and members included intelligentsia from both sides of the border, in Laredo and Nuevo Laredo, Tamaulipas.[43] As education and poverty were the most important issues to the Liga Femenil Mexicanista, these women immediately began instituting their own course of action and opening escuelitas. An article in *La Crónica* written in December 1911 about La Liga Femenil states,

> The "League" . . . agreed to take charge of the education of poor children and to this effect, the honorable Professors María Rentería and Berta Cantú offered spontaneously and generously to give free education in their respective establishments.[44]

In 1911, at the age of eighteen, María Rentería moved to Laredo and, after being elected treasurer of La Liga, integrated herself into the active cohort of borderland feminists there.[45] A graduate of Mexico City's Normal School for Women, Rentería took out several advertisements for her escuelita in *La Crónica*, stating that she taught young girls how to read and write in Spanish, as well as arts and crafts.[46] Subsequent advertisements explained that she had merged her school with another escuelita, moving to a more central location. Rentería expanded her course offerings beyond kindergarten to include elementary levels, and she began working with another teacher, Amparo Vargas Orozco of Chihuahua, Mexico.[47] By 1917, it is unknown whether she still maintained her escuelita, but she was continuing to earn a living as an educator teaching at the Holding Institute.[48]

October 15, 1911, one month after Jovita Idar and her cohort founded la Liga Femenil Mexicanista, Rentería read an article she wrote to her fellow Liga members, "Leona Vicario y Rafaela Lopez," which was published in *La Crónica* the following week. Though we do not know which books Rentería used in her escuelita—or the extent of her budget to buy them—her article gives us insight into her approach to history and her belief that women were active agents who shaped national narratives. Rentería, as an early scholar of women's history, was far ahead of her time. María Teresa Fernández Aceves states that even today, Mexican historiography fails to include Mexican women's history. She claims that those who study women's history "still comprise a small academic ghetto."[49]

Rentería opened the article by stating that "both women and men have felt patriotic love," and they "have shown it a thousand different ways,"[50] including women taking on multiple roles to support their country.

> In studying history we find beautiful examples of mothers who sac-
> rificed themselves for their children, wives who braved thousands
> of dangers to save their husbands and enhance their homeland,
> and daughters who feared nothing and challenged everything to
> achieve the happiness of their parents and the honor and glory for
> their country.[51]

Rentería did not just give general idealizations of the ways in which women have helped their country. She focused on the lives of two women who were active historical agents in two different ways, one taking on a traditionally feminine role, and the other taking on a traditionally masculine one. She discussed the life of Rafaela López, a woman who epitomized the role of the sacrificing mother during Mexico's fight for independence. When a Spanish officer asked her about her son, whom he had taken prisoner, López stated, "The duty of a soldier and a patriot is to die in defense of their country, and all feelings to the contrary should be suffocated."[52] Days later, López, full of tears, saw the body of her son "shattered by enemy bullets," but she never lost her strength or courage. As a mother who sacrificed her child for the sake of her country, she is the ultimate heroine.

Rentería detailed other ways beyond the martyred mother that women helped Mexico win its independence by telling the story of Leona Vicario. Vicario did not bear sons that became Mexico's soldiers, but by the age of nineteen, she herself was a soldier and helped create a clandestine message system that carried information about the enemy's movements. After being captured and sent to prison, she escaped and married D. Andrés Quintana Roo, who was also an insurgent for Mexican independence.[53]

Rentería's article highlights the various ways women contributed to the founding of Mexico—from being the loving and patriotic mother to being the brave soldier. Her article not only combats the stereotypes of Mexican women, but also is an early form of women's history—interpreting women as active agents and valuing the labor that stems from their diverse roles as mothers, soldiers, and everything in between. We can assume that Rentería, as a teacher, as an early writer of women's history, taught her students a different curriculum than that taught in the public school system. She taught her students Spanish literacy and arts and crafts, but most likely, she also taught them that the dominant historical narratives in the United States and in Mexico were not the only narratives—women's labor was an integral part of national histories, even if it is often ignored. And in sharing this history with her students, who were all female, she worked to ratify her own historical narrative.

By inserting women's roles into Mexico's founding history during a time when the revolution had only recently begun, she was making a statement about the multidimensional roles women could play in Mexico's present and future. And by sharing her research with fellow teachers who espoused the same commitment, she not only ensured that their students would learn this different narrative as well, but also helped all of the women of La Liga understand that by taking on the role of educating Laredo's children in a time when no one else would, they were carrying out their own revolutionary act, following in the footsteps of Leona Vicario and Rafaela Lopez.

LEONOR VILLEGAS DE MAGNÓN AND THE REVOLUTIONARY NATURE OF CHILDREN'S AGENCY

Leonor Villegas de Magnón is not listed as an officer of La Liga, though she was a close friend and associate of the Idar family, and participated in El Primer Congreso Mexicanista.[54] By 1914, she had founded two organizations that would manifest her legacy, a nursing corps and a kindergarten class. She wrote about both in her autobiography titled *The Rebel*, which was never published in her lifetime, despite lifelong efforts on her part to see her story in print.[55] The nursing corps and medical relief program Magnón founded was La Cruz Blanca (The White Cross); she noted that the Mexican Red Cross helped only the wounded Federalist soldiers, and the revolutionary Constitutionalist cause needed its own medical relief program.[56] In 1914, La Cruz Blanca met Carranza and his Constitutionalist Army in Ciudad Juárez and followed them into Mexico City. They established a local nursing corps for each city they stopped in along the way, often turning abandoned or seized haciendas and mansions into hospitals. In May 1914, Carranza nationalized the White Cross, renaming it La Cruz Blanca Nacional.

Magnón also founded a kindergarten in a hall that her brother had used to organize his political campaigns. Magnón and her cohort's work in La Cruz Blanca was unequivocally revolutionary, as they were in direct contact with wounded soldiers and the future president of Mexico, and setting up hospitals and training new staff, but their work as teachers was even more so. Early childhood education, particularly in alternative institutions such as escuelitas, subverted the devastation the revolution left behind for Mexican children and the segregation and racism of the Texas public school system.

Two battles of the Mexican Revolution took place in Nuevo Laredo. The first was on March 17, 1913, when the opposing armies exchanged gunfire. Early that morning, Magnón left a note for her children that read, "When you get up, go to the house of your uncle. Wait for me there. I'll be back soon."[57] She and Jovita Idar organized a small group of women living in Laredo to cross the border and tend to the wounded. Magnón and Idar pulled the wounded from the battlefield, took them to the local hospital in Nuevo Laredo, and helped organize relief efforts in Laredo, bringing over food, clothes, and medicine. Five American doctors crossed the border to help Magnón and Idar aid the wounded.[58]

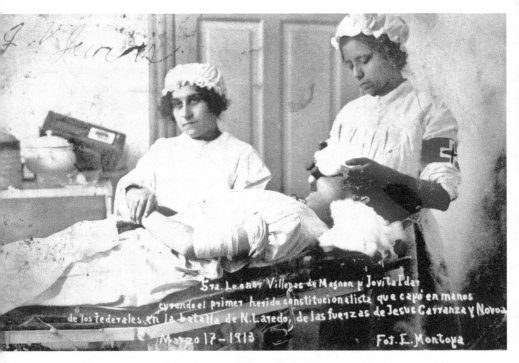

Leonor Villegas de Magnón (left) and Jovita Idar worked as nurses for La Cruz Blanca during the Mexican Revolution. PHOTOGRAPHER EUSTACIO MONTOYA DATED THE PHOTO MARCH 17, 1913. NO. 084-0597, GENERAL PHOTOGRAPH COLLECTION, UNIVERSITY OF TEXAS AT SAN ANTONIO, SPECIAL COLLECTIONS—INSTITUTE OF TEXAN CULTURES. COURTESY OF A. IKE IDAR.

The second, and much bloodier, battle took place on January 1, 1914. Carranza, leader of the Constitutionalist Army, decided that commanding all border cities was central to his strategy in overthrowing President Huerta, as it would enable him to prevent Huerta from receiving arms and weapons from the United States. By the afternoon of the second day, 75 percent of the 700 casualties were Constitutionalists, and hundreds of wounded men remained on the battlefield. President Huerta's Federalist soldiers hunted down the remaining wounded and killed them on site.[59] They burned the corpses from both sides of the conflict to prevent the spread of disease. The smell of burning flesh and the sight of Federalists bayonetting wounded men traumatized civilians on both sides of the border.[60]

Magnón's role as a teacher and her role as a revolutionary came together to have a direct impact on her young students in 1914. After the second battle of Nuevo Laredo, Magnón brought many of the wounded Constitutionalist soldiers across the border to Laredo, turning her home and school into makeshift hospitals. Referring to herself in the third person as "the Rebel," Magnón stated in her autobiography:

> Her young pupils soon became involved in the Revolution, too. One day, they were to find their school taken over by wounded soldiers. Their picture books and slates under their arms, the Rebel had walked them through the big room. Their work tables had been made into beds, their little chairs, into bed tables. Each child was introduced to the reality of the Revolution at the sight of the wounded soldiers who resembled the toy soldiers they used in counting games.[61]

Whereas María Rentería and Berta Cantú opened the doors of their escuelitas to impoverished children in Laredo for free, Magnón's students did not need such charity. Her students were both American and Mexican citizens, and many of them came from interracial families—making them biracial, bicultural, and bilingual. These interracial students were also part of Laredo's elite. In fact, many members of Laredo's wealthiest families sent their children to Magnón's escuelita, and rather than close her school to protect the middle- and upper-class children from the disturbing reality of the revolution, she integrated it into her curriculum. Giving children an opportunity to exercise agency and undertake important work was central to Magnón's parental and pedagogical approach.

In September 1911, as a participant in el Congreso Mexicanista, she published "Adelanto de los Mexicanos de Texas" (Advancement of Mexicans of Texas), in which she lamented the drawbacks of an upper-class mother's love. With the best intentions, she stated, these mothers enslaved themselves "to prepare their children for what seems like a bright future," but they actually limited their children's ability to appreciate the value of moral, intellectual, and physical work.[62] Women were the ones, with their intelligence, wealth, and knowledge, who shaped their children, or as she refers to them, their "little citizens," into being either productive members of society or slackers.

> Later we suffer bitter disappointments because our children turn out loafers, for having them avoid doing any work, because it was not necessary or because we consider it degrading, without understanding, poor mothers!, blinded by the love, that the physical work develops health and strength and that the moral and intellectual work is the most dignified and exalted of man.[63]

Unquestionably, Magnón was speaking to a middle- and upper-class readership, going as far as to state, "If in our youth we are taught all the classes of labor as a luxury, as an ornament, we would later avoid bitter suffering."[64] She identified the root of the problem in the lack of unity across class lines. One of the biggest obstacles to education for working-class children was the fact that many of them needed jobs to help their families survive. Upper-class mothers, knowing that child labor was a sign of an impoverished family, did not want anyone to mistake their children for those of the lower classes.

In 1912, very soon after *La Crónica* published her "Adelanto" article, Magnón opened her own escuelita.[65] It is likely the parents of her students had already read her views denouncing upper-class children's entitlement to lives of leisure, and it was well known that she had published pro-Madero and anti-Díaz articles as early as 1910.[66] Laredo's elite, however, chose to enroll them in her escuelita regardless, so they could not have been entirely surprised when she turned her school and home into makeshift hospitals and their children into makeshift nurses. Nor could they have been surprised when she founded La Cruz Blanca in 1914, two years after opening her school. Many of these families re-enrolled their children and enrolled their siblings when her school reopened after her return from her work with La Cruz Blanca. Magnón continued teaching until 1923.[67] These highly literate, wealthy families—the most prominent citizens of Laredo—were all part of the same social circles, and they all sent their children to a bilingual escuelita run by a revolutionary, modern woman.

"A group of pupils in Leonor Villegas de Magnón's first kindergarten." REPRINTED WITH PERMISSION FROM ARTE PÚBLICO PRESS—UNIVERSITY OF HOUSTON.

Magnón and her family themselves belonged to Laredo's elite. Her father, Don Villegas, left a very sizable inheritance to his children when he died, as well as a successful business, which her brother, Leopold, ran to much profit and growth. She and her brother, who was elected mayor of Laredo in 1920, both attended grade school and high school in San Antonio and college in New York. In 1912, Leopold, along with several other wealthy men, financed *El Progreso*, a Spanish-language paper that became Laredo's main source of news on the revolutionary battles in Mexico. Jovita Idar worked as a journalist for *El Progreso* as early as March 1913 to 1914, when she tried to prevent the Texas Rangers from demolishing the paper's facility.[68] During its tenure, the newspaper organized food drives and other fundraisers to benefit those who had experienced tragedy at the hands of the revolution.[69]

By sending their children to Magnón's school, Laredo's elite made a statement about the role of education in negotiating their own political views, as well as the imaginary citizenship status of their children. Politically, these parents sympathized with the Constitutionalists, offering aid in many forms throughout the decade, including the help of their children. They also valued bilingualism and the idea that socioeconomically and culturally, the United States offered many opportunities for upward mobility and enrichment. To secure the future of their families within this borderland model that relied on a symbiosis of the Mexican and American cultures and socioeconomic mobility, they sent their children to an escuelita that valued all of these things. As Idar argued, the school system in Texas had nothing to offer ethnic Mexican children, and the chaos in Mexico devastated the school system there. "Our children need education. . . . We have no other option but to do it by our own impulse," she argued, and though Idar was referring to impoverished children attending Spanish-language escuelitas, these wealthy individuals essentially agreed with her.

The Ligarde family is one such example. Having moved to south Texas from France, they assimilated themselves into the top tier of the Texas Mexican social hierarchy in Laredo, running in the same social circles as Magnón.[70] Honoré Ligarde was born in Bordeaux in 1855; his wife, Elizabeth Martin, was born in a French colony in Africa but raised in Bordeaux, where she met her future husband. In 1881 the couple moved to Laredo, where Raymond Martin, Elizabeth's uncle, had already established himself as a wealthy, successful businessman. In Laredo, the couple had four children: Fred H., Hermance, Amedee, and Antoinette.[71] Honoré began a brick-making factory in the 1880s and was elected to several county offices, including county commissioner, city alderman, county assessor, and tax collector.[72]

Honoré's son Fred published in the Spanish-language press under the name Frederico and was on Laredo's school board of trustees.[73] Two of Fred's daughters are in a photograph of Magnón's first kindergarten class in 1912: Louise, who went by Lulu, and Elizabeth, who went by Liche.[74] In a photograph of Magnón's last kindergarten class, taken in 1923, is Anita Ligarde, the daughter of Fred's brother, Amedee.[75] Amedee owned a brick factory, most likely the one his father began, and managed his father's ranch.[76] Anita's mother was Sara Sáenz Ligarde, who was a local organizer for the International Ladies' Garment Workers' Union in the 1930s.[77] By the time Anita enrolled in Magnón's last kindergarten class, the Ligarde and Villegas families had known each other for over a decade, at least. Before Magnón opened her kindergarten in 1912, Leopold Villegas, Magnón's brother, and Fred Ligarde served on a commission that organized a celebration for Mexican Independence Day in 1910.[78] The fact that two different members of the Ligarde family chose to send their children to Magnón's escuelita between 1912 and 1923 indicates their respect for Magnón as a pedagogical expert and intellectual in her own right. Ultimately, Magnón's decision to have her facility operate simultaneously as a school and a makeshift hospital allowed for her middle- and upper-class students to connect the ideals of their education with the radical ideals of the revolution, making a profound statement about the power of children's agency when exercised across class lines.

"Leonor Villegas de Magnón [far right] and María Villarreal [far left] visit the family of a fallen soldier." REPRINTED WITH PERMISSION FROM ARTE PÚBLICO PRESS—UNIVERSITY OF HOUSTON.

MARÍA VILLARREAL AND THE UNEXPECTED POWER OF TEACHERS

Magnón detailed in her autobiography, *The Rebel*, the role that the nurses in La Cruz Blanca played in aiding the Constitutionalists, and it is striking how many of the women who either worked as nurses or were women she encountered in Mexico along the way were teachers. One such example is María Villarreal, who worked in the hospital in Nuevo Laredo as a nurse for La Cruz Blanca after the Battle of Nuevo Laredo and was an officer in La Liga.[79] Born around 1893, Villarreal graduated from and subsequently taught at the Laredo Seminary, which was renamed the Holding Institute in 1914. Afterward, she opened up her own school in her home in Laredo when her mother became ill.[80] Her daytime students included children from both sides of the border, and she taught both Spanish and English literacy. At night she taught English and Spanish literacy to border patrol and immigration agents.[81] In 1927, she directed a new educational center for Laredo's Salvation Army that offered free education to impoverished children, as well as sewing classes to young ethnic Mexican women.[82]

Villarreal's work as a teacher gave a certain amount of power to the Constitutionalist cause. In *The Rebel*, Magnón detailed how she met a young teacher named María de Jesus who worked for the Constitutionalists. She was trying to take a secret message to General Carranza, but to do this, she needed a train ticket and different clothes, two things difficult to acquire during the revolution. However, de Jesus was surprised at how easily Villarreal was able to procure them.

After Villarreal dropped off the necessary items, de Jesus asked Magnón, "So easy as all that?"[83] Magnón responded, "Oh, nothing is impossible for María [Villarreal]. . . . She has taught many boys in Laredo, and her word is their command. I think she would make a good general."[84] As Villarreal left de Jesus at the train station, she stated, "You can dress here on the train. I have spoken to one of my pupils; he will take care of you. They are all my friends, these railroad people."[85] After Magnón and Villarreal helped de Jesus leave safely, Magnón stated, "María [Villarreal], tomorrow we return to our duties, just as if nothing had ever happened to us. You to your school, and I to my kindergarten."[86] Just as Magnón continued running her escuelita while opening a makeshift hospital, so, too, did Villarreal continue to operate her school while helping a revolutionary agent on her clandestine mission. These women's work as teachers gave them power on multiple levels. First, as Idar argues, education and work endowed women with integrity and respect. Second, the relationships they established with former students enabled them to receive help whenever they needed it, as those former students were current soldiers and railroad workers.

Both in Mexico and on the Texas-Mexico border, female teachers embodied the ideals of the modern woman, creating another form of the modern female revolutionary, adding to the martyred mother and the brave soldier about whom Rentería wrote. The very fact that they were relegated to do "women's work" such as teaching gave them a specific power that they would not have otherwise had, and put them in a position to cultivate children's agency for working-, middle-, and upper-class students. At the core of these women's work and rhetoric surrounding education was the idea that educating Laredo's children would (1) culturally redeem the Mexican race in the eyes of Anglo Americans because, as Idar stated, the majority of ethnic Mexicans in Texas lacked a formal education; (2) enable these educated children to attain some level of socioeconomic mobility; and (3) permit them to move independently between two worlds. All of these objectives put children in a position to realize the impact of their own agency for themselves and their communities.

An educated child became not only an abstract symbol of the future—when the border population would be able to move past the trauma of the Mexican Revolution, modernization in Texas, and progressivism in the public schools—but also part of a group of future citizens learning to be dutiful subjects of Mexico and informed subjects of the United States.

Women such as Leonor Villegas de Magnón, Jovita Idar, María Rentería, and María Villarreal merged ideas about feminism, childhood, education, and revolution in their writings and their labor, seeing childhood education as a meeting ground for their current social and political woes and the future prospects of Texas Mexicans.

CHAPTER 4

EDUCATION IN POST-MEXICAN REVOLUTION TEXAS, 1920–1950

The Mexican Consulate's investment in the future of Texas Mexican children intensified around 1920, when, for the most part, the revolution ended. Around the same time, however, progressives in south Texas sought to provide stability to the region's quickly changing industrial, bureaucratic, and political systems, and a key part of their efforts was the Americanization of immigrants.[1] In 1922, Annie Webb Blanton, the state superintendent of public instruction, denounced the existence of Spanish-language escuelitas as a hindrance to the project of assimilating future American citizens, arguing that the people of Texas had a right to tell "those of foreign descent, however long they may have dwelt within our borders," either to enroll their children in the public schools or to go back to their home country.[2]

While Blanton and her colleagues lamented the existence of any foreign language–based alternative to the public school system, the Mexican Consulate offered various forms of support to escuelitas throughout south Texas. Their direct involvement marked another turning point in escuelita history. On numerous occasions, they legitimized the escuelitas' work as essential factors in Mexico's postrevolutionary progress by attending the schools' "fiestas patrias" and giving speeches of encouragement, such as at the Mexican holiday celebrations and the students' end-of-the-year oral exams. They also gave support in the form of money and supplies. In 1927, the Mexican secretary of public education, via the Mexican Consulate's Department of Protection, sent Spanish-language reading and educational materials to an escuelita in Valentine, Texas.[3]

James W. Cameron's 1976 dissertation was the first work to examine the Mexican Consulate's role in creating schools for Mexicans living in the United States, focusing on those in southern California. Cameron states, "That these schools did not survive the years of Mexican repatriation and depression is not as significant as the fact that they were started at all. It showed that Mexicans in the 1920s were not as passive as many social scientists have led us to believe."[4] Taking on decades of scholarship that presented Mexicans and Mexican Americans as lazy, submissive, and indifferent to education, Cameron looked to these escuelitas as an example of Mexican American agency fighting against an unrelentingly Americanizing force. Much of the scholarship that refers to the consulate's involvement with escuelitas follows Cameron's lead in that it focuses solely on California and interprets them as an example of ethnic Mexican agency in the era of segregation, and as an example of "cultural maintenance."[5]

One consistency in escuelita history is that these little schools were always a mechanism that helped ethnic Mexicans overcome whatever obstacle was impeding their ability to negotiate their lives in the United States. The less static aspect of escuelita history is the nature of those obstacles, which tended to change over time, and thus the way ethnic Mexicans used escuelitas changed as well. The little schools that emerged after 1920 differed from those for which Jovita Idar advocated, as well as from those that arose in every rural corner of south Texas in the postbellum era. The Mexican Consulate attempted not just to counter the Americanization movement, but also to convince refugees of the revolution to return home so they could help reunite the nation after the civil war. These objectives demanded that these immigrants stave off Americanization and resist Tex Mex, that habit of code-switching that demeaned both Spanish and English, and in this regard, the escuelitas that they supported in the United States functioned as another form of hegemony. The consulate, however, could not escape ethnic Mexicans' growing desire for inclusion in the public school system, nor could it control how their escuelitas influenced the generation of students who attended them. Rather than encouraging children to look to Mexico for their identities, they ultimately used the skills they attained in the Mexican Consulate–sponsored schools to demand their civil rights as adult US citizens. Ironically, the activism for which the escuelitas prepared them facilitated the little schools' decline.

PROGRESSIVISM

American public figures and scholars of the era believed requiring cultural and linguistic assimilation from the immigrant masses would provide structure to an increasingly heterogeneous populace, and as sociologist Cybelle Fox notes, those speaking the loudest on the issue were "overwhelmingly native-born whites."[6] Theodore Roosevelt, who remained outspoken about foreigners, Americanization, and nationalism long after he left public office, contended that immigrants should be given a certain number of years to learn to read and write English, and if by then they had not attained English literacy, they should be deported. He also argued for "social loyalty," which called for "a citizenship which acknowledges no flag except the flag of the United States and which emphatically repudiates all duality of national loyalty."[7]

National loyalty framed the perspective of scholars who studied immigrants and assimilation. Emory S. Bogardus spent his time as a graduate student at the University of Chicago living and working in the Northwestern University Settlement House, where he taught, as he stated, "the English language and American principles to the foreign-born" from 1908 to 1912.[8] After earning his doctorate, he took a position as a sociology professor at the University of Southern California, teaching classes in "Americanization and Immigration" while founding the School of Social Work in 1921.[9] *Essentials of Americanization*, published in 1919, is based on his experiences as a settlement worker, researcher, and professor. Bogardus argued that Americanization was not a "big stick" or a "*laissez faire* policy," but "an educational process of unifying both the native-born and foreign-born in the United States in perfect support of American principles."[10] Both natives and foreigners could benefit from Americanization instruction, he contended, but the immigrants needed to "giv[e] up one set of well-known and, in part, precious loyalties for another set of loyalties," a process that involved "a deep-seated and delicate re-adjustment of mental and social attitudes."[11]

According to Bogardus, Mexican immigrants were the slowest to assimilate, partly because social workers in the United States had failed to understand how centuries of hardship had "broken the spirit and nearly destroyed the self-respect" of this mixed-blood, immigrant, and illiterate class.[12] By 1927, Bogardus had become a member of the Advisory Council for the American Eugenic Society, and his views on "the Mexican problem" hardened. He stated, "A situation is clearly abnormal when a race representing seven or eight percent of the population . . . furnished 28 to 30 percent of the charity cases."[13] Alfred White, a sociology graduate student at the University of California at Berkeley, made similar assertions in his master's thesis. He characterized Mexicans as lazy, arguing that they seek employment only "when hunger and shelter drive [them] to it." "Among the masses the standard of living is so low," he continued, "that the Mexican has to work but little to exist, hence the apparent laziness."[14] In the years before the Great Depression, the notion that Mexicans were prone to indolence and dependency became a dominant interpretation for sociologists and social workers, whose research drew from race-based arguments that these traits were embedded in Mexican biology and culture.[15]

As multiple key progressive figures put emphasis on using English literacy as a factor in promoting national loyalty, it is unsurprising that they also believed that American governmental or social organizations should bear the responsibility for carrying out any assimilation plan.[16] Roosevelt, for example, was wholly oblivious of what was going on in south Texas and of the role the Spanish language and the Mexican Consulate played in the lives of ethnic Mexicans living there. Large portions of this population had been US citizens for generations but remained unaware of their political citizenship and still did not speak English.

MEXICAN PROGRESSIVISM AND ESCUELITAS

The first school that the Mexican Consulate founded, La Escuela México, was in Belvedere, California, in 1926. Zeferino Ramírez, a Belvedere businessman and member of the Honorific Commission, built the school on his property and subsequently donated it to the Mexican Consulate. Another local businessman donated the desks, and Mexico's secretary of education donated the textbooks, maps, paintings, and other educational materials.[17]

The intersection between race and class in postrevolutionary Mexico functioned as the impetus for the Mexican government's decision to support escuelitas in the United States. Politicians, who were part of the Mexico City elite, looked disparagingly on the majority of Mexican citizens, who were rural peasants of diverse indigenous backgrounds.[18] Throughout the 1920s, the Mexican government attempted to use education to consolidate the numerous indigenous communities scattered throughout the country into a single Mexican identity as part of Mexico's postrevolutionary plan for uniting the nation. Drawing heavily from John Dewey—Moisés Sáenz, the secretaría de educación pública after 1924, studied with Dewey at Columbia University three years after *Democracy and Education* was published—the federal Mexican government relied on three tactics to carry out its mission: cultural missions that sent intellectuals into remote areas of the country to organize schools, rural normal schools that trained and certified young adults in the community to work as teachers, and the rural schools themselves that peasant children attended.[19] From 1920 to 1940, the Mexican government constructed more than 15,000 public schools.[20] In many ways, the work of the Mexican Consulate in supporting escuelitas mirrored the work of the secretary of public education in Mexico.

The consulate's work in Mexicanizing ethnic Mexican children as an oppositional struggle to American progressivism was a form of progressivism itself; its purpose was to instill a homogenous cultural and linguistic outlook to frame the daily lives of ethnic Mexicans. Just as American progressives had drawn the central tenets of their Americanization policies from the idea that an "American Mind" existed, the Mexican Consulate and its Honorific Commissions sought to erase the heterogeneity of the multiple indigenous cultures in Mexico and replace them with a homogenous Mexican way of seeing the world. And their experience in the United States was central to this objective.

Manuel Gamio, who studied under Franz Boas at Columbia University and earned his master's degree in anthropology in 1911, became one of the most dominant Mexican intellectuals during the 1920s.[21] One of the most influential advocates of indigenismo, Gamio argued that as two-thirds of the Mexican people were indigenous and from diverse populations, they needed to be incorporated into the modernizing nation or else their heterogeneity would undermine national unity. Essentially, he contended that Mexico should revere the indigenous populations, but at the same time, these populations needed to be properly civilized if Mexico would ever be as modern and advanced as the United States, the country that embodied his vision of the ideal nation.[22]

Interestingly, Gamio argued that these rural peasants, who were the majority of those that immigrated north of the border, became civilized and patriotic Mexicans after living in the United States.

> We have seen frequently that natives or mestizos in rural districts in Mexico have not much notion of their nationality or their country. They know their town and the region in which it is situated, and this is a "little country" for them. People of this type, as immigrants in the United States, learn immediately what their mother country means, and they think of it and speak with love of it.[23]

If a Mayan from the state of Quintana Roo, a Yaqui from the state of Sonora, or a former public official from Mexico City immigrated to the United States, the dominant Anglo society would label each one "Mexican" without any regard to their status within the racial and socioeconomic hierarchy in Mexico. Surviving in the United States meant that these indigenous peasants had to become modern citizens and learn valuable skills while living in a foreign country. And coupled with their newfound ability to identify as patriotic Mexicans, they became ideal elements for Gamio's concept of a homogenous Mexico. The Mexican Consulate's efforts to create escuelitas for immigrants and their children living in the United States were to nurture immigrants' relationship with their home country by encouraging the development of a Mexican national consciousness.

Further, opening escuelitas exposed ethnic Mexican children to a curriculum that served as an instantiation not for the heterogeneous Mexico that existed, but for the unified country that Mexican public officials wanted. Teaching ethnic Mexican children Mexican history through a lens of Mexican exceptionalism that diminished the role of indigenous populations was an attempt to initiate and subsequently perpetuate the notion of an integrated Mexico. Additionally, the books the Mexican secretary of education supplied to escuelitas encouraged ethnic Mexican children, whether they were born in Mexico or in the United States, to think of themselves as Mexican citizens.[24] Their age and geographical dislocation meant they could not yet exert any political rights, but their imaginary citizenship ratified the national narrative the government tried to create in postrevolutionary Mexico. The ethnic Mexican child, then, became an integral element in nation-building.

THE MEXICAN CONSULATE'S DEPARTMENT OF PROTECTION

South of the border in postrevolutionary Mexico, Venustiano Carranza and Alvaro Obregón understood that the hundreds of thousands of Mexican citizens leaving for the United States only added to the detrimental effects of the revolution in Mexico, and they approached the problem in two different ways. Carranza, president from 1917 to 1920, issued a propaganda campaign about the rampant discrimination ethnic Mexicans faced in the United States. When that did not slow the migration numbers, states stopped issuing passports to those wishing to leave for the United States to encourage their citizens to remain in Mexico. Those not given passports, however, either obtained them from a different state or crossed the border without the necessary papers.[25]

Seeing the futility of his (assassinated) predecessor's policies, Obregón, president from 1920 to 1924, decided to offer Mexican citizens living in the United States help, hoping that many of them would return and play a vital role in rebuilding the nation. When Mexican citizens chose to remain in the United States, however, even after the majority of the violence subsided, the government enacted policies that targeted its citizens' national loyalty.[26] Obregón encouraged the Mexican Consulate—which in 1920 only had fifty-one consulates in the United States—to develop programs designed to protect Mexico's citizens, keep them engaged with the home country, and nurture a patriotic love for Mexico.[27]

In 1921, the consulate founded the Department of Protection to offer aid to its citizens living in the United States.[28] Additionally, the consulate helped organize Comisiones Honoríficos, composed of Mexican expatriate men who wanted to help the consulate in its cultural and linguistic preservation work. Expatriate women could join Brigadas Cruzes Azules (Blue Cross Brigades). In 1920s Texas, there were thirty-five commissions and fifty-two brigades. Membership drew from the working and middle classes of both Mexico and the United States, though US citizens could not vote in elections or serve in any leadership capacity.[29] These expatriates did not receive any pay from the Mexican government, but they did receive the consulate's assurances that their labor was essential to rebuilding Mexico in a time of great need for unification and nationalism, and they became highly respected figures in their communities.[30]

Luis Montes de Oca, who took the position of consul general of El Paso's Mexican Consulate in 1920, and Eduardo Ruiz, the Mexican consul in Los Angeles, spearheaded the creation of Juntas Nacionales Mexicanas (Mexican National Board), an Honorific Commission that worked closely with the newly formed Department of Protection. Montes de Oca told the *El Paso Herald* in 1921 that his consulate alone received more than a hundred letters each week from Mexicans throughout the Southwest who detailed their unfair treatment at the hands of American employers and public officials. The Department of Protection conducted investigations into Mexican citizens' allegations of injustice and maltreatment. The job of the Junta was to conduct preliminary investigations of each Mexican citizen's complaint and write a report about its findings for the consulate, as well as register with the consulate as many Mexican citizens as it could. In some cases, the Junta could contact the employer or official against whom the charge had been made and mediate the issue itself rather than forward the report to the consulate. Montes de Oca oversaw the development of eight Juntas in his district: three in Texas, three in New Mexico, and two in Arizona.[31]

According to Montes de Oca, Mexican citizens living in the United States needed the consulate to help them negotiate the discriminatory practices that they encountered in their daily lives because these individuals were powerless to do so themselves. He told the *El Paso Herald*,

> Our government has always been highly paternalistic and naturally the lower class have always looked upon the higher for protection, if not means of livelihood. Ninety-five percent of the Mexicans in the southwest are of this class, and practically none of them know the English language or anything of the American laws, and for that reason are timid. This makes it easy for unscrupulous employers to exploit their labor and for petty officials to graft off of them in many ways.[32]

American employers and politicians found the Junta's work effective in mitigating problems between themselves and Mexican laborers. The manager of the Phelps Dodge corporation in New Mexico, E. B. Sawyer, said that the Junta's work had minimized many of the issues that had been arising "constantly" between the employer and Mexican workers, stating that "there is practically no friction between the employers after [the Junta's] organization." Texas governor Pat Neff also stated that he had seen improvement in employer-worker relations after the Junta's founding.[33]

Montes de Oca's perspective offers insight into the roles of class and nationalism among the Mexican expatriate community. First, the divisions between the members of the Mexican Consulate and the Mexican immigrant laborers justified the consulate's paternalistic approach to helping Mexican citizens living in the United States. Rather than help them adjust to life in a foreign country, they attempted to act as mediators between American employers and public officials and Mexican citizens, maintaining the paternalistic relationship that encouraged Mexican citizens to remain dependent on the Mexican government.

Second, the Mexican government sought to help them live in the United States while at the same time discouraging their acquisition of the English language or any knowledge about their rights as laborers—two facets of American society responsible for shaping individuals' lived experience in the United States. They feared that empowering their citizens would compromise their loyalty to Mexico. The consul members' elite socioeconomic status perpetuated the notion that while they could handle the ability to speak English and possess knowledge regarding the American legal system, those of the working class should not. If they did, they would be at risk of betraying their native country and settling in the United States permanently, a notion that persists today. As Martha Menchaca points out, even in 2011 the Mexican government believed "Mexican immigrants should remain Mexican citizens . . . that Mexicans should be able to work in the United States under some labor agreement but eventually return home."[34] Mexico's current resistance to encouraging its countrymen to become US citizens has deep roots in the revolutionary era, when about a million Mexicans, many of whom never returned, crossed the northern border.

In fact, most Mexican Americans living in the United States today descend from immigrants who crossed the border after 1880, the majority of whom came as a result of the revolution.[35] Nonetheless, the Mexican Consulate's paternalistic position did its best to ensure that many of these individuals would remain dependent on the Mexican government to survive in the United States. The consul members tried to promote Mexican patriotism at all costs, oblivious to the way their proselytism functioned as another form of hegemony, albeit one that opposed US Americanization policies. It served as a direct counter to Theodore Roosevelt's contention that American organizations—and only American organizations—should be responsible for helping immigrants adjust to life in the United States.

THE MEXICAN CONSULATE AND THE TEXAS PUBLIC SCHOOL SYSTEM, 1920-1927

After the consulate closed the investigation into the treatment of ethnic Mexican children in the Texas public school system in early 1911, it did not address the issue again until 1920, when Mexican nationals wrote letters detailing their children's exclusion. In July 1920, Desiderio Tagle, president of Agricola Mutualista, wrote a letter to the Mexican consul in San Antonio, Teódulo R. Beltrán, stating that the local public school in Fentress would not permit Mexican children to attend. Tagle and his mutual aid society founded their own school for the eighty-five ethnic Mexican children in their community after acquiring a building and hiring a professor.[36] In 1920, Fentress, a small town on the San Marcos River in Caldwell County, had a two-room schoolhouse, and as a result of an increase in the production of a local oilfield, the population grew throughout the decade, peaking at five hundred residents in 1929.[37] Beltrán wrote to the Fentress school board to request that they cease making any distinction based on nationality and allow Mexican children to attend school with American children. He also forwarded the letter to the secretary of foreign relations in Mexico City, M. Covarrubias, who asked Beltrán to let him know if the school board responded.[38] There is no indication as to whether or not it did respond, nor is there any information about the consulate's response to Tagle and his mutual aid organization's inauguration of an escuelita.

A similar situation occurred in November 1920 in Vanderbilt, a small town in southeastern Jackson County in east Texas. Ursino Amaya, F. Morales, Pedro Treviño, and Crispín Amaya wrote to the Mexican consul in San Antonio, Mauro Castro, stating that the school designated for Mexican children was half a mile outside of town, and it was the same school designated for Black children. These parents had informed their nearest consul representative in Galveston, but they had yet to hear anything back from him. They implored Consul Castro to use his influence to convince the school board to give them a "Professor that understands Spanish and can educate our children" because "we are truthfully interested in that our children receive an education."[39] Castro forwarded the letter to Dr. Cutberto

Hidalgo, the subsecretary of foreign relations in Mexico City. Hidalgo then sent the letter to the Mexican Embassy in Washington, DC. He informed Castro that he would contact him if the embassy responded, but aside from a record documenting the tribulations of the ethnic Mexican community in Vanderbilt, no other information regarding the outcome of the situation exists.

In 1922 in New Braunfels, the consulate took more aggressive steps in questioning public school segregation. L. Garza Leal, the Mexican consul in San Antonio, sent a letter to George Frederic Oheim, the president of the school board of the New Braunfels Independent School District, on May 24, and the *San Antonio Daily Express* published the letter on May 31. In his letter, Garza Leal stated that he had just found out that the New Braunfels "school authorities have segregated the Mexican children and the American children of Mexican descent" in the primary grades and also had denied them the privilege of attending the high school.

Oheim's June 2 response stated that the Mexican children in the elementary grades were segregated "not on account of their race, but for depagogical [*sic*] and administrative reasons; not knowing any English and learning this language slowly and with difficulty, these children can not keep up with others and require special instruction."[40] He also stated that Mexican students were allowed to enter the high school if they were qualified.[41] Oheim, like countless public school administrators and school board members across the Southwest, used the language barrier issue as an excuse to segregate ethnic Mexican children. No one ever interviewed these children to find out whether they spoke or understood English. The assumption that they spoke only Spanish was based on their race and surname, without any regard to citizenship.[42]

Garza Leal's next letter asked whether "Mexican children who speak English are required to attend the regular American school, since they would not come under the rule that requires for them the special school."[43] Oheim's response states that (1) all of the four schools in the New Braunfels Independent School District are "regular American schools"; (2) Mexican children are segregated because of the language barrier, not because of their race or place of birth; (3) Mexican children may enroll in the high school if they are qualified; and (4) any other questions about a particular case should be taken to the school board, which will make decisions on an individual basis. He never stated whether or not Mexican children who spoke English would be able to enroll in the elementary school for White children.

Garza Leal pointed out the equivocal nature of Oheim's letter, responding, "You have not answered my question in a clear way, but I think that I know what you mean."[44] He sent a letter to the president of the Honorific Commission of New Braunfels, letting him know the results of his investigation, which he conceded were "not completely satisfactory." He stated that Mexican children were segregated because of the language barrier, not because of their race, so he instructed them to communicate to the Mexican colony that the parents of children who do speak English correctly needed to ask the school board to admit their children to the elementary school for English-speakers. If the school board refused to help, then they needed to contact the state superintendent in Austin. And if the superintendent did not allow their English-speaking children to enroll in the elementary school for White children, then they should contact the Mexican consul's office again. He also stated that all Mexican children who are qualified had "the right to enter" the high school.[45]

For eleven months, Garza Leal was the Mexican consul in Houston, where he founded multiple Honorific Commissions and Mexican Blue Cross Brigades before being assigned to the San Antonio office, with a promotion, in April 1922. In June 1922, however, he was reassigned to the Los Angeles office. Two weeks after he sent his final letters to Oheim and the Honorific Commission in New Braunfels, he left Texas for California.[46] Garza Leal's multiple assignments throughout the Southwest were part of the larger instability of the Mexican Consulate. The constant shuffling of consuls throughout the region undoubtedly made it difficult for cases such as these to attain any kind of resolution. Between 1918 and 1920, for example, the Los Angeles office had fifteen different consuls.[47]

Garza Leal's brief inquiry did not change the New Braunfels Independent School District's segregationist policies, and it is unclear whether any of the ethnic Mexican parents whose children could speak English approached the school board about enrolling their children in the elementary school for White children. But what is surprising is Garza Leal's decision to ask Oheim if English-speaking Mexican children could attend the same elementary school as the White children. As noted earlier, the Mexican Consulate, especially toward the end of and following the revolution, was more interested in making sure Mexican citizens remained dependent on the Mexican government in hopes that they would return to Mexico. It is possible Garza Leal's letter to the president of the Honorific Commission intended to do just that, as he may have suspected that Spanish-speaking parents of bilingual children would be hesitant to approach the school board on their own.

Even if this was the case, however, there was still no reason to ask the president of the school board about the possibility of a Mexican child attending the elementary school for White children if the child spoke English. The fact that Garza Leal did pose the question hints at the consulate's—or, at the very least, individual consul members'—changing views on public education in Texas. In the 1910 investigation (discussed in chapter 2), the consulate was reluctant to believe that the segregation of ethnic Mexican children was exclusionary. Garza Leal's question points to the notion that there were ethnic Mexican children who could speak English but were still segregated in the Mexican schools. And the fact that Oheim could not provide a concrete answer illustrates how deeply embedded in race the district's language-based segregation actually was.

Oheim was born in Bavaria, Germany, in 1865 and came to the United States in 1880, becoming a schoolteacher, writer, historian, and editor in the German American community of New Braunfels. In 1899, he became a partner and editor of the German-language paper *New Braunfels Zeitung*, which published continuously from 1852 to 1957, when it merged with the *New Braunfels Herald*, an English-language newspaper. When Oheim fell ill in 1941, his son, Frederic, assumed the position of editor.[48] Outside of Oheim's work as editor, teacher, and school board member, he also wrote several manuscripts in German on New Braunfels history, including "Texanische Sänger-Geschichte in den Jahren 1852 bis 1856," and maintained a collection of German-language newspapers of Texas.[49]

Oheim, then, wrote local histories in German and collected German-language newspapers from Shanghai, Mexico City, New York, and small Texas towns such as Victoria, Seguin, and Hallettsville. His work promoting the German language and culture did not prohibit him from becoming a teacher and board member for the local school district, much less enrolling his five children there. Though Benjamin M. Baker, state superintendent for public instruction, complained in his 1886 annual report about the pervasiveness of the German and Spanish languages among the Texas population, by 1922, German no longer seemed a threat to the public school system, whereas Spanish still was.[50] Annie Webb Blanton singled out ethnic Mexicans as the state's biggest obstacle to overcoming illiteracy, stating, "In certain counties along our borders are many men and women, born and reared in the Lone Star State, who speak a foreign tongue and cherish the habits and ways of another country."[51] What is striking about Superintendent Blanton's statements, as well as Oheim's equivocal response to Garza Leal, is that no school district ever tested the level of English literacy of their Mexican students. And there must have been Mexican children in New Braunfels who spoke English; otherwise, the president of the Honorific Commission would not have asked Consul Garza Leal to inquire about their status.

The litigation history of Mexican American–initiated desegregation cases reveals how public school administrators used the cloak of lan-guage-based segregation as a cover for race-based segregation, a practice that occurred throughout Texas.[52] Eight years after Garza Leal and Oheim exchanged letters, the first Texas-based Mexican American–initiated de-segregation case occurred in Del Río, *Independent School District v. Sal-vatierra*. Throughout the trial, no one interviewed ethnic Mexican children to assess their English-language skills. The school superintendent testified that the district had been segregating Mexican children long before he took the position. It had become a common practice.[53] He also stated that his district never administered any tests to assess the ethnic Mexican children's language abilities, but still insisted that segregation "was in the best interests of Mexican children because of their language deficiencies." The testimony alleging that the Mexican children needed special instruction because of their inability to speak English, however, was strong enough for the school district to win the case on appeal.[54]

The following year, during the 1931 California case *Alvarez v. Lemon Grove School District*, ethnic Mexican parents sought help from the San Diego Mexican consul, Enrique Ferreira, who referred them to two lawyers who would represent them in the case: Fred C. Noon, who was fluent in Spanish, and A. C. Brinkley.[55] Part of the plaintiffs' strategy was proving that the district's assertion that Mexican children did not speak English was inaccurate, so Noon and Brinkley had ten Mexican students take the stand. All the children spoke English, and one of them could not speak Spanish, even though the child had been made to attend the Mexican school because of "language deficiencies."

The 1946 case *Méndez v. Westminster* also put ethnic Mexican children on the stand, and their answers not only exhibited their strong English skills, but also provided insight into the relations between them and American children. During the trial, the lawyers for the plaintiffs asked fourteen-year-old Carol Torres if she knew any children her own age who were not Mexican, and she responded, "Yes, there are plenty of white children, Americans as they say there." When the lawyer asked her to explain her statement further, she said, "Americans, as they say they are. They don't consider us—" before being interrupted by the court. The plaintiffs won the *Méndez v. Westminster* case, ending school segregation in California.[56]

Throughout 1922, Mexicans continued to send letters to the consulate about their children's exclusion, prompting Enrique D. Ruiz, the consul general in San Antonio, to write to the Mexican ambassador in October of that year stating that for a long time his office had been "receiving repeated complaints from Mexican parents" about public school segregation. Ruiz pointed out that previous steps the consulate had taken "have been entirely useless because nothing practical has been obtained."[57] The consulate's official response on the matter remained rather similar to its view in 1910, though it also seemed to admit that there were some documented cases of ethnic Mexican children being segregated based on their race. The ambassador responded that as there was a lack of "concrete" evidence regarding segregation, any allegation needed a thorough investigation before the consulate could act. He also reminded Ruiz that "in some cases the exclusion of Mexican children is due, not to reasons of race, but to their lack of knowledge of the language that hinders the labors of the schools in which the children who speak English receive instruction."[58] Language-based segregation, which officially came to the consulate's attention in 1910, enabled the organization to overlook the poor treatment of Mexican children in the Texas public school system. This stance conveniently served to discourage Mexicans from settling in the United States permanently.

Though no real change occurred as a result of Garza Leal's investigation, his act of putting the question "What about the Mexican children who speak English?" in writing as early as 1922 to the president of the New Braunfels school board was a step in questioning the traditional narrative of public school segregation in Texas, especially because Oheim was unable to answer the question with any clarity *and* because it silently challenged the official view of the consulate.

THE MEXICAN CONSULATE AND ESCUELITAS

With the founding of the Department of Protection in 1921, the consulate took a much more active role in engaging with the Mexican colony in the United States, and as the decade progressed, it intensified its efforts to aid ethnic Mexicans in opening escuelitas and Spanish-language libraries and gave moral support to escuelitas that were already in operation. In October 1921, Enrique D. Ruiz, the consul in Laredo (who in 1922 would become the consul general in San Antonio) attended an event in Hebbronville celebrating the founding of the Honorific Commission and the Mexican Blue Cross Brigade. While there, he gave a class at el Colegio Altamirano on Mexican civics, and reportedly, Consul Ruiz was pleased with the degree of progress and learning that the students had achieved.[59]

In its work in creating new escuelitas in the United States, the consulate was never able to provide a significant amount of funding due to the financial troubles and political instability that plagued the organization after the revolution. In the earlier part of the 1920s, the consulate organized Honorific

Commissions and Mexican Blue Cross Brigades in large cities and small towns throughout their consular districts and encouraged these groups to carry out charitable activities for their communities with consulate direction rather than consulate funds. Keeping the Mexican colony mentally and emotionally close to Mexico was at the center of the consulate's efforts, but there were other issues embedded in the larger agenda—namely, preventing the corruption of the Spanish language and countering the dominant society's racist stereotypes about ethnic Mexicans.

Key factors in the Mexican Consulate's role in founding escuelitas in Texas were its relationships with the Honorific Commissions and the Blue Cross Brigades, and the influx of Mexican teachers, many of them graduates from the state-sponsored normal schools who had immigrated to the United States as refugees of the revolution. In many cases, these teachers, after witnessing how the Spanish language had changed among ethnic Mexican children in Texas, approached the consulate about providing the children, most of them from poor or working-class families, with an opportunity to learn the language properly. The inclination of Mexican educators and consuls to preserve the integrity of the Spanish language was not only to counter Americanization but also to function as another form of hegemony. As the Americanization movement sought to assimilate immigrants, teaching them proper English and American customs and traditions, the escuelitas that emerged as a result of the consulate's postrevolutionary agenda and the large numbers of Mexican immigrants that flooded across the border took on a political mission. The creation of hybrid cultures and languages such as Tex Mex threatened the integrity of Mexican cultural traditions as much as American cultural traditions. Mexican chauvinism was the only way to counter American exceptionalism.[60]

In 1921, Mariano Avalos Santoyo, a former teacher in the Mexican state of Nuevo León, approached the Mexican consul in Hidalgo, Francisco Pérez (who also had the title of professor), about opening up a school for the Mexican children there. Santoyo stated that most of them were impoverished, and either they had not received an education at all or they had received a deficient one from the public schools. Santoyo argued that if the educational system in the United States "had reached the maximum level of perfection," the Mexican children were not benefiting from it, and as such, his project to open a school was "of urgent necessity."[61] Pérez promised that he would study Santoyo's proposal carefully and let him know what the consulate would be able to provide, but there is no indication whether the consul supported Santoyo's idea or if it ever came to fruition.

That same year, Francisco Morales, a member of the San Antonio mutual aid society Miguel Hidalgo, proposed building a school for the children of the city's Mexican colony, arguing that because all of them either were born in the United States or immigrated at an early age, they spoke a deficient form of Spanish since there was nowhere for them to learn how to read and write the language properly. The Mexican consul of San Antonio assured Morales that his mutual aid society had the consulate's "moral" support—although he did not offer any financial assistance—adding that "while it is true that [Mexican children] have not forgotten [Spanish], they possess a form so impure that it is painful to hear it."[62] The author of the *La Prensa* article that covered Morales's efforts expanded on the school's proposed curriculum:

> the history of their country; the geography of Mexico; their civic duties in that territory; their form of government, their institutions; its commercial and economic life, and above all, Spanish; but the pure Spanish; do not give them the slang, of the "troca" and of the "marketa" but that which our ancestors bequeathed us and that walks so badly dressed at this point.[63]

It is unclear whether Morales and the Miguel Hidalgo mutual aid society succeeded in establishing their escuelita, but what is clear is a striking abhorrence of Tex Mex. Morales, members of the Mexican Consulate, and the writers at *La Prensa* were witnessing the same development in San Antonio that Jovita Idar and Leonor Villegas de Magnón had witnessed in Laredo a decade earlier: the proliferation of children and adults code-switching between English and Spanish as a quotidian part of life.

Linguist John M. Lipski argues that the increasing numbers of Mexican immigrants during the revolution impacted not only the demographics of the ethnic Mexican population in the United States, but daily speech patterns as well. The ways that communities blended Spanish and English differed across time and space because a number of factors influenced local dialects—such as place, as in urban or rural setting; the ratio between Mexican immigrants and second-, third-, or fourth-generation Spanish-speakers; and the area of Mexico from where the immigrants originally came.[64] It was rather common for advocates of a "pure" Spanish and advocates of English-only education to agree that the popular way of blending the two languages produced a "degenerate Mexican Spanish" that was "the result of imperfect bilingualism."[65]

The 1921 consuls of Hidalgo and San Antonio promised to study the situation or stated that they gave their moral support, but there is no indication that they took steps to help create each school. However, as early as 1922, the conversations the consuls in south Texas were having with leaders of the Mexican colonies changed, in that they encouraged the leaders of the Honorific Commissions and Blue Cross Brigades to open escuelitas and libraries for their communities.

In June 1922, in one of many consular reorganizations, Samuel J. Treviño, who previously had been the consul in Laredo, was assigned to Port Arthur, Texas.[66] Born and educated in Monterrey, Treviño worked as sub-superintendent of Instituto Laurens, a private Methodist school there, before moving to Mexico City to work as the inspector of schools, a position he held for two years before entering the consular service in 1920.[67] Upon arriving in Port Arthur, he quickly began organizing Honorific Commissions and Blue Cross Brigades in the city and towns in the surrounding area, including Beaumont, Orange, and Taylor, as well as throughout the twelve counties southeast of Jefferson County that were also in his consular jurisdiction.[68] In October 1923, the Sub-Honorific Commission of Port Arthur opened a school named Escuela Juarez, and Consul Treviño attended the inauguration.[69] By February 1924, however, the Honorific Commission and the Mexican Blue Cross of Port Arthur had a dispute over their differing interpretations of the regulations for the Blue Cross. The two groups reached an impasse, and communication shut down. It is unclear whether or not the conflict between the two groups affected the stability of Escuela Juarez, or even how long Escuela Juarez remained open, but the disagreement became serious enough to warrant Consul Treviño's intervention.

In an attempt to act as a mediator, Consul Treviño held a conference in Orange, Texas, which every member of the Honorific Commission and the Blue Cross of Port Arthur attended. He spoke at length, outlining the official interpretation of the regulations of the Blue Cross, and argued that the benevolent nature of the institution meant that the organization should be focused on its charitable programs rather than being muddled in misunderstandings. He also spoke of the "harmony that should reign between the Mexican groups that live in this country, stressing that through patriotism they seek solidarity."[70] He believed their mutual love for their homeland should help them move beyond their differences, invoking Manuel Gamio's argument that living in the United States encouraged the racially and ethnically diverse Mexican immigrants to become more aware of their status as Mexican citizens, functioning as a unifying factor—something the Mexican government struggled to do after the revolution.

Additionally, he argued that an effective way to intensify "this harmony and this solidarity" would be to fill the community's urgent need for

a Mexican school and for a library. He noted that the building they constructed, which they were using as offices for the two organizations, would
be the ideal place for both the school and the library. He offered to donate
a large batch of books to the new cultural center. The people in attendance
agreed with his counsel; however, there is no record of a school or library
that may have come from their work, and it is unclear how the dispute and
resolution impacted Escuela Juarez.

Consul Treviño continued to use this tactic as a way to encourage ethnic
Mexicans' patriotic love for Mexico while at the same time manifesting to
non-ethnic Mexican populations the honor and beauty of Mexican social
and cultural life. By 1925, the consulate had reassigned Treviño to the Río
Grande Valley, and in May of that year he held a conference in Mercedes
attended by more than five hundred ethnic Mexicans. He implored them
to unite in creating what he called a "respectable front," arguing that their
proper "conduct" would illustrate Mexicans' virtuous nature in contrast to
the prejudice and racism that surrounded their daily lives in the United
States; their "respectable front" would "make [Anglos] see the great qualities
that the Mexicans treasure."[71] Three months later, he met again with ethnic
Mexican leaders in Mercedes and urged them to unite by building a Mexican
school for their children and a library for their community.[72]

It is unclear whether or not a school and library materialized as a
result of Treviño's efforts, but what is clear is that he believed that founding
centers for cultural preservation would not only fulfill the ultimate goal
of helping ethnic Mexicans maintain allegiance to Mexico, but also help
them look to their mother country as a symbol of unity. Their unity and
"respectable front" had the potential to counter both Americanization and
racial prejudice. Rather than promote Americanization as the solution to
racism, by encouraging ethnic Mexicans to assimilate, Treviño promoted
Mexican cultural preservation—or rather, he promoted the idea of a Mexican consciousness in the minds of immigrants who, most likely, had little
notion of a unified country while living in Mexico during the Porfiriato and
then the revolution.

As the decade progressed, the Mexican Consulate played a more active
role in establishing schools, especially after 1925, as seen in the work of the
Vásquez brothers, Ismael and Alfredo.[73] Ismael was born in Encinillas in
Chihuahua, Mexico, in 1885 and moved to Texas with his family as a young
child. Alfredo was born in Fort Davis, Texas, in 1888.[74] By 1910, both men
were married and living in Del Río along with their father, who was a tailor.
Ismael was a clerk in a general store, and Alfredo was a barber with his own
shop. Up to this point, it appears the family had been reporting that although

their father was born in Mexico, both sons were born in Texas.[75] By the early 1920s, the brothers were working for the Mexican Consulate.

It is difficult to assess whether or not Alfredo's birth in the United States complicated his ability to work for the consulate. On the one hand, tensions between the United States and Mexico during the second half of the Mexican Revolution were such that American citizens were no longer able to work as consuls for the Mexican government. Wealthy American businessman Jack Danciger, a committed Carranza supporter, bought the Kansas City Spanish-language newspaper *El Cosmopolita* and used it to publish articles denigrating Carranza's opponents. He also used his political connections to meet with President Woodrow Wilson and urge him to recognize Carranza's Constitutionalist government. As a result of Danciger's work on behalf of the Constitutionalists, Carranza appointed him to be the Mexican consul in Kansas City in September 1915, but in June 1916, as tensions between the United States and Mexico escalated, Danciger was forced to resign.[76] On the other hand, during the 1920s, one of the ways the Mexican government sought to maintain its ties with Mexican immigrants living in the United States was to reassure them that their children who were born in the United States were still Mexican citizens according to their country's constitution.[77]

It is likely that Danciger was forced to resign as consul because he was Anglo American, and Alfredo Vásquez was able to obtain his position because he was technically a Mexican citizen since his parents were born in Mexico. However, even if this technicality allowed Alfredo to work for the Mexican government, it does not account for his response to the 1930 census. He stated in the 1900 and 1910 censuses that he was born in Texas and was a US citizen, but in 1930, as a consul in Kansas City, he stated that he was an "Alien" who was a Mexican government official born in Mexico, who immigrated to the United States in 1911, and though he spoke English, his principal language was Spanish.[78] Ismael also claimed to be born in Texas in the 1900 and 1910 censuses, but in the 1930 census, while a Mexican consul in Denver, he stated that he was born in Mexico, immigrated to the United States in 1908, and was a naturalized citizen.[79] Ismael did not apply to be a naturalized citizen until 1950, when he was working as a salesman in San Antonio, long after his career as a consul ended.[80]

During their tenure as Mexican consuls, both brothers lied about their citizenship status. Alfredo emphasized his Mexican-ness by lying about where he was born, and Ismael emphasized his American-ness by lying about his status as a naturalized citizen. Scholars have written extensively about the ways Anglo Americans in south Texas collapsed all ethnic Mexicans into a single "alien" group—regardless of citizenship or socioeconomic status—and how they used this assumption to justify many common discriminatory practices. The Vásquez brothers were able to invert these assumptions to their advantage, moving between American and Mexican citizenship to advance their careers. Although their cultural identities—tied to their use of Spanish and English, and the fact they spent most of their lives in Texas among the rest of the Mexican colony—remained the same, their national identity had fluidity.

Additionally, the Vázquez brothers were about fifteen years older than most of the men who founded the League of United Latin American Citizens. For the members of LULAC, their status as American citizens was central to how they defined themselves and their nascent organization, and they only allowed US citizens to become members. The Vásquez brothers went in the other direction, particularly Alfredo, an American citizen by birth, who emphasized his right to Mexican citizenship by declaring himself one in the 1930 census. In seeking out paths of perseverance, both groups looked to education as a survival tactic. Other founders of LULAC—Alonso S. Perales, M. C. González, and Eduardo Idar—advocated for public school inclusion for ethnic Mexican children, but the Vásquez brothers, on behalf of the Mexican government, encouraged members of the Mexican colony to create cultural centers—libraries and schools—to preserve the Spanish language and Mexican cultural traditions in Texas. As the 1920s progressed, the degree to which they were willing to involve the Mexican Consulate intensified.

In July 1925, Ismael, then consul in Laredo, announced that he was part of an "integrated commission" composed of local trade and businessmen and the Methodist Church, which had raised $1,500 to build a school for Mexican children on the corner of San Darío and Washington Streets. Additionally, the Eagle Pass Lumber Company had donated 25,000 bricks for construction.[81] By early September, the school had been finished, and Vásquez oversaw the school's inauguration, which included Bible readings from Reverend Zenón Moraida and Reverend Félix Segovia of the Mexican Methodist Churches in Laredo and Nuevo Laredo, respectively, and Reverend E. García from the Mexican Baptist Church in Laredo. It also featured piano and violin performances by local musicians and a history lecture by Gustavo Garza López, the first chancellor of the Mexican Consulate in Laredo.[82] Although the Mexican Consulate did not cover the cost of building the school, it helped organize the accumulation of resources and directed the school's opening and curriculum.

The following year, Alfredo Vásquez, as the consul in Brownsville, took more aggressive steps to help ethnic Mexican communities create their own cultural centers. In October, he wrote to the secretary of foreign relations in Mexico City that the Honorific Commission and the Mexican Blue Cross

Brigade of Río Hondo, about twenty-six miles from Brownsville, had raised $600 to purchase two plots of land: $150 to buy the property and the rest to construct a building that would be a school for Mexican children as well as the offices for the two organizations.[83]

Vásquez asked if it would be possible for the Mexican government or the consulate general in San Antonio to purchase the property in their name so that regardless of "the future or past difficulties that arise between the Colony," the property would always be "exclusively for the Mexican Colony, whether they be those that live there now, or new families that arrive to live in this place."[84]

Vásquez's proposition for the property to be purchased in the Mexican government's or consulate's name would have political implications if successful. First, it would allow the Mexican government to claim the labor of the Mexican colony. Ethnic Mexicans living in the Río Hondo community worked together and pooled their resources to raise $600. To use that money to buy two plots of land in the name of the Mexican government would have meant that all the work involved in raising the money and all the intentions of community-building at the center of raising the money were done in the name of Mexico. Second, and concomitantly, it would have meant that long after these ethnic Mexicans left Mexico's borders, they would continue to look to Mexico as their provider and protector.

The Mexican minister of foreign relations requested that the consul general in San Antonio, Alejandro P. Carrillo, ask the consular lawyer if such a move was even legal. Birkhead, Lang, and Beckmann, the San Antonio law firm that represented the consul general, stated that it would be best for the charitable societies to purchase the property in their own names, and advised that at least two of the people involved in the transaction be American citizens, not just residents of Texas.[85] While the consulate was trying to figure out the best solution to Vásquez's proposal, Felix Alvarado, president of the Honorific Commission in Karnes City—the county seat of Karnes County, where Gregorio Cortez and Sheriff W. T. Morris had their now infamous misunderstanding twenty-five years earlier—wrote to the consulate informing them that the Mexican Blue Cross Brigade of that city had recently purchased a plot of land in its name. Although both groups were benevolent in nature, the Mexican Blue Cross was officially registered as a charitable organization in Austin so was exempt from paying taxes, but the Honorific Commission was not.[86] Perhaps influenced by Alvarado's letter, the consulate decided that the property should be purchased under the name of Carrillo, who, in addition to being the consulate general in San Antonio, was the executive president of the First Division of the Mexican Blue Cross.[87]

Interestingly, while the Spanish-language press widely reported on the consulate's efforts to build escuelitas, the English-language press did not. Many of the consuls were highly respected by members of the Mexican colony and members of the American press. They seem to have done their job of encouraging ethnic Mexicans to open escuelitas and Spanish-language libraries—a direct contrast to the English-only instruction of the public school system—without angering the press or public school officials. For example, Consul Ruiz of Laredo, who gave a class on Mexican civics to the students of el Colegio Altamirano in 1921, received a glowing review of his work from the *Laredo Weekly Times*, which stated that he had "proved to be a most indefatigable worker, promoting a feeling of fellowship and friendship among Mexicans and Americans and doing everything in his power to advance the interests of both peoples."[88] And while Annie Webb Blanton, the state superintendent of public instruction, expressed her indignation at the fact that many Mexicans and Mexican Americans—she did not distinguish between the two—on the Texas-Mexico border could not speak English, she never mentioned the consulate as being part of the problem.[89]

The consulate also framed the purpose of escuelitas carefully when speaking to those outside of the Mexican colony. Daniel Garza, the consul in Houston, told UC Berkeley economist Paul S. Taylor, who was conducting research for his work *Mexican Labor in the United States*, that the purpose of the Mexican private schools was "to aid the American schools because the children will know the Mexican language." Noting that the parents paid tuition for their children to attend, he stated that the schools taught Spanish and English, and took place in the afternoons after the public school day ended.[90]

THE ESCUELITA CURRICULUM

Despite the Mexican Consulate's interest in fostering loyalty to Mexico in the two decades after the Mexican Revolution, south Texas escuelitas helped their students negotiate their existence in the United States, particularly since the public school system often failed ethnic Mexican children. Much of what we know about the curriculum comes from the memories of those who attended escuelitas during childhood. All of those with firsthand experience in an escuelita, including those I interviewed, say the curriculum was more academically challenging than the public school's. Whereas the escuelitas' curriculum offered students the opportunity to learn grammar, arithmetic, geometry, history, literature, and current events, the public school curriculum for ethnic Mexican children was strictly focused on teaching them English. Additionally, many schools implemented policies that required ethnic Mexican children to remain in first grade for multiple years.

In 1929, Taylor interviewed members of the education community in Big Wells, including an escuelita teacher, a committee member of the Honorific Commission, and the Mexican public school teacher, providing multiple perspectives on the role of escuelitas in ethnic Mexican education. Juan Llanos taught in an escuelita that was open five days a week from 4 to 8 p.m. for students age six to eighteen, and both Mexican immigrant and Texas Mexican children attended.[91] He held his classes in the Mexican public school building.[92] Parents paid five cents a day for each of the first two children, but other siblings could attend free. His curriculum included "hygiene, diet, clothing, the cause [of] infant mortality," as well as "gymnastics, manual training, drawing, Spanish, grammar, arithmetic, geometry."[93] Juan Cortez, a member of the Big Wells Honorific Commission, argued that Llanos's escuelita provided their children with an education, and the public school did not. "The teachers don't teach my children," he said. "They have been to school several years and don't learn anything. The Americans say we don't want education. But we pay our own teachers because we want to learn."[94]

Llanos said, "We teach the children their own language as the French, Italians, and Americans do in Mexico," and noted that "The better educated they are, the better they will live here."[95] Like Jovita Idar, he credited a Spanish-literacy education for helping his students get further ahead in the United States, though he admitted the value of knowing English. He himself took English classes from Faye Parr, the teacher at the Mexican public school, stating, "A man who speaks both Spanish and English is worth two."[96]

Undoubtedly, Llanos's escuelita was providing a service to the ethnic Mexican children of Big Wells. Parr, who also offered private English-language classes to adults, including Llanos, stated that the teacher who taught in the Mexican public school before her "used to go to sleep sometimes in school and [go] home early."[97] She stated that the children did not learn anything. The public school system was set up in such a way that the Mexican schools only went through the elementary grades. If ethnic Mexican students went beyond fifth grade, they would have to attend the American (White) school. Parr stated that in Big Wells, Mexican children were not permitted to enter the American middle or high schools, so they had no access to education beyond fifth grade. She also said the citizens of Big Wells often chided her for teaching Mexican children, arguing that education would only make them demand higher wages for picking onions, a staple crop in the region. She admitted her own ambivalence toward her students, saying, "I don't believe in equalizing myself with them, but I would let them come to the American school."[98]

Miss Dunham, the public school teacher in Valley Wells, about twenty miles southeast of Big Wells, shared Parr's ambivalence. "People here treat the Mexicans just about as we do the Negroes in Arkansas," she said. "I sometimes wish I had been raised in the north so I would not have the feeling I do. I can hardly touch them (Negroes and Mexicans)."[99] Dunham recognized her own inability to see beyond the ways in which racialization framed her notion of social hierarchy, and how that impacted the power dynamic between her and her students. Nonetheless, it is likely that her views affected her teaching methods, despite her own self-awareness. Certainly not every public school teacher in Texas felt that ethnic Mexicans and African Americans were inherently inferior, but evidence abounds that many of them did. Undoubtedly, escuelitas provided a more challenging curriculum and a space where students were not made to feel subordinate and unintelligent.

Taylor's interviews are so significant because they document aspects of the escuelita curriculum and how it compared to that of the public school system in rural Texas in the era after the Mexican Revolution ended and before the Great Depression began. And while his interviewees mentioned the subjects taught, they did not mention which books they used, or whether they used books at all. The people I interviewed noted that their escuelitas did not have books, not even El Colegio Altamirano, because no one in their communities could afford them.[100] Rather, many of the students in these little schools read Spanish-language newspapers such as *La Prensa* and wrote their notes in tablets that their teachers made.[101]

There is one book, however, to which multiple interviewees referred. It underwent numerous printings in the United States and Latin America for almost a century and earned its author honorary memberships to the Society of Geography and Statistics of Mexico and the Scientific Literary Academy of Guatemala in April 1869: *Libro de Lectura No. 1*, by Luis F. Mantilla. But this text—which made its way into the hands of Texas Mexican children, as well as children throughout Latin America—was not written by a Mexican, or even by a Spaniard. Mantilla was Cuban, born in Havana in 1833. He earned a degree from the University of Sevilla before becoming a professor at Colegio El Salvador, a university in his hometown. Little is known about his work there, but in July 1862 his belief in Cuba's independence from Spain impelled him to leave the island for New York City.[102]

Mantilla was one of hundreds of individuals who left Cuba for the United States because of the events leading up to the Ten Years' War (1868–1878), the first of three Cuban struggles for independence.[103] The vast majority of the exiles settled in New York or Key West, Florida, and where they settled largely depended on their class. Members of the Cuban elite settled in New York, working as writers, publishers, and teachers, while members of the working class settled in Key West, typically finding work in one of the many cigar factories there.[104] Mantilla worked as a professor of Spanish language and literature at the University of the City of New York (later named New York University) from 1869 until his death in 1878.[105]

While living in New York, he befriended other Cuban political exile intellectuals. Nestor Ponce de León, a close friend of José Martí, was born in Havana and immigrated to New York in 1869. De León owned a publishing house and printed diverse works on Cuban history and culture, such as Francisco Calcagno's *Biográfico Cubano* and several of Mantilla's works—though Ivison, Phinney, Blakeman and Company, a large publishing house in the United States, published *Libro de Lectura No. 1*.[106] Though living abroad, these exiles, including Mantilla, involved themselves in the struggle for independence from afar, organizing and raising money for the rebels and calling themselves the "central republican junta of Cuba and Puerto Rico." Their political activities did not pass without notice. In November 1870, though they still lived in New York, a Spanish military court in Havana found Mantilla and his fellow Cuban political exile Nestor Ponce De Leon guilty of treason for their work in aiding the rebel cause, sentencing them to death and ordering that their property be confiscated.[107] They could never return to Cuba.

Though Mantilla's political activities in New York were notable enough to warrant a death sentence from the Spanish military, he is not remembered as a Cuban revolutionary. When he is remembered at all, it is as the professor who wrote Spanish-language textbooks for children. In fact, *Libro de Lectura No. 1* was one of the two most widely used textbooks in Mexico from the earliest days of the Porfiriato (1876–1910), and it was known simply as "el Mantilla." During Díaz's dictatorship, respected pedagogues sought to professionalize the teaching profession, and the Mexican government opened more public schools and colleges to train teachers.[108] Mantilla's *Libro* was published just as this emphasis on education was becoming more widespread. More reading and writing primers for children were published between 1890 and 1900 than in the three previous centuries combined, and more than 80,000 copies of *Libro* were exported to Central America annually.[109]

Most of the book's passages discuss animals, children, and the family, but a few passages mention Cuba, and one seems to allude to the island's struggle for independence and Mantilla's support for the rebels. "We go to Havana. / It is a very light boat. / Navigate this boat well. / And bring your flag."[110] Cuba did not win its independence from Spain until the Spanish–American War in 1898, so this passage from the fourth edition—published in 1876, two years before Mantilla's death—implies that the group of people traveling to Havana on a boat with their own flag intended to free the island from its previous colony status, bringing with them a new future of peace and independence. These subtle nods to the Cuban independence movement were not lost on Mexican publishers. At the Louisiana Purchase Exposition in 1904 in St. Louis, Missouri, the Herrero Brothers Publishing House displayed all of their publications, including Mantilla's *Libro de Lectura No. 1* and *No. 2*.[111] In the Mexican editions, *Havana* was replaced with *Veracruz*.

Mantilla's *Libro* impacted not only the children in Latin America and Spain, but also ethnic Mexican children in Texas. Josefina Andrade, who grew up in San Antonio during the 1920s and 1930s, stated that in her westside neighborhood, the book was known simply as "la Mantilla." Her mother bought a copy at the Mexican bookstore in downtown San Antonio and used it to teach her and her sister Spanish literacy.[112] Jovita Idar, the teacher and feminist journalist from Laredo, used Mantilla's *Libro* in the escuelita she founded after moving to San Antonio.[113] Transnationalism is a central part of escuelita history, but it is not necessarily restricted to the United States and Mexico.

THE LONG GOODBYE: THE DECLINE OF ESCUELITAS AND THE RISE OF MEXICAN AMERICAN CIVIL RIGHTS ACTIVISM

The Mexican Consulate carried out its work in Mexicanizing the colonia mexicana throughout the 1920s, offering support to escuelitas by providing books and materials, as well as opening Spanish-language libraries and attending the little schools' fundraisers and events. But the rise of the Mexican American Generation in that same decade and their pursuit of educational equality challenged the consulate's approach to dealing with Mexican citizens living north of the Río Grande. The historical record of the late 1920s and early 1930s documents the destabilization of escuelitas as a way of life in south Texas, marking the beginning of their decline. As late as 1930, the superintendent of public instruction noted the continued presence of escuelitas in south Texas, stating, "As late as the current year we have signs of the determination of some to have Spanish schools." He detailed how a superintendent in the Río Grande Valley reported that a group of families in his district sent their children "to a school organized over-night in which Spanish was to be used exclusively."[114]

As early as November 1928, *La Prensa* lamented the closing of multiple escuelitas in San Benito, a small town in the central part of Cameron County. The article stated that the superintendent of the local school district had visited an escuelita sponsored by the Benito Juarez Mutual Aid Society and posted a notice stating that (1) the escuelitas were not compliant with state building regulations and (2) schools should not "teach another language that is not the official one of the country."[115] The fact that the Spanish-language press lamented the decline of escuelitas while the Anglo American superintendents noted their resilience speaks to the late 1920s and early 1930s as a time of transition in escuelita history. One side viewed their existence as threatened, the other as threatening.

Scholars argue that in the first three decades of the twentieth century, two emerging ethnic Mexican middle classes in Texas—the Mexican immigrant middle class (closely associated with the Mexican Consulate) and the Mexican American middle class (young men and women in their twenties and early thirties)—competed for the loyalty of the ethnic Mexican working class.[116] The Mexican American middle class founded civil rights organizations that differed from the prevalent mutual aid societies in ethnic Mexican communities. Whereas the mutual aid societies offered insurance, funeral benefits, and other services to fellow ethnic Mexicans in need, these new organizations focused on political activism in pursuit of Mexican American civil rights.[117]

The notion of a hegemonic struggle implies that there were two distinct sides, but there was significant overlap throughout the 1920s. In 1921, eight ethnic Mexican men—seven were Texas Mexicans and US citizens, one may have been a Mexican citizen—all between the ages of twenty and thirty, founded the Order of the Sons of America (OSA), which required its members to be US citizens.[118] This organization established councils in areas of urban and rural Texas, bringing ethnic Mexicans living in remote places together under the umbrella of civil rights activism and debating which language their children should know, English or Spanish. For example, in 1927, the second vice president of the Alice council, Manuel Sáenz Escobar, suggested they organize summer escuelitas to teach their children English to prepare them to enter public school. Frank Perez, the council's president who was also a Mexican citizen, reflected on his experience in an escuelita in San Diego, Texas, remembering how his community hired a teacher trained in Mexico. He noted that the curriculum was more rigorous than that of the public school system. The council decided that their summer escuelita would teach children both Spanish and English.[119]

The Alice council's partial commitment to the English language and US citizenship standards for members, despite the organization's official stance on the issue, manifested how the OSA served as a transition between the Mexican nationalistic fervor of the consulate and the unequivocal embrace of the English language and American patriotism by the Mexican American middle class by 1929. [120] Subsequent organizations adhered to the decision to exclude non-US citizens, which most likely was a response to Texas's new voting law. In 1921, Texas enacted legislation that prohibited noncitizens from voting in any elections. [121]

A few months after the OSA Alice council debated the benefits of bilingualism, Alonso S. Perales, J. Luz Sáenz, and J. T. Canales, among others, founded the Comité Provisional Organizador Pro-Raza (Provisional Pro-Raza Committee), which organized the Harlingen Convention of 1927. The organizers wanted to unite all the various civil rights groups in south Texas in the hope that their activism would be more effective, but one of the most significant issues that needed to be resolved was the status of Mexican immigrants in the new association. Z. Vela Ramírez, an escuelita teacher in Kingsville, attended the convention and published an editorial in Harlingen's *El Comercio* the day the convention began. Ramírez called "the unification of the Raza community" one of "the real problems in this country," noting the "responsibility of solidarity" that existed between immigrants and citizens despite the two groups' different "social actions and politics." [122] The various speakers called for making American citizenship a requirement, which caused 75 percent of the crowd to leave. Unification did not happen at the convention, but nonetheless, the heated discussions provoked questions about community and identity. [123] Mexican American activists spent the next two years trying to unify four different organizations, and in 1929 they founded the League of United Latin American Citizens (LULAC), arguably the most significant Mexican American civil rights organization of the twentieth century. [124]

Ultimately, the Mexican American Generation won the hegemonic struggle, not only convincing ethnic Mexican working-class families to enroll their children in the Texas public school system and to look to the United States as the foundation for their political and civil rights, but also convincing the Mexican Consulate to abandon its support of escuelitas in favor of endorsing their own push for educational equality. By 1930, the consulate's attention turned to the issue of the educational segregation of ethnic Mexican children in the US public school system, maintaining files on exclusion in Del Río and Mission, Texas, as well as various localities in California. Unlike the files on educational segregation in the 1910 investigation, these documents do not excuse the practice. [125] The last files pertaining to escuelitas in Texas are from 1927. [126]

While many scholars have pointed to World War II as the main catalyst for Mexican American activism, its origins date to before World War I. [127] At the turn of twentieth century, Texas Mexican intellectuals were lambasting segregation and unequal treatment before the law. Their civil rights work continued throughout the 1910s and 1920s, culminating in the formal organizing of LULAC in 1929. Despite the exigencies of life during the Great Depression, LULAC initiated the first Mexican American–initiated desegregation case in Texas, *Independent School District v. Salvatierra* in 1930, as well as investigating the dismal lack of educational equality in San Antonio throughout the 1930s.[128] The momentum that Mexican Americans sustained during the 1930s may have stalled during the war, but it picked up again with a certain fierceness afterward, particularly with regard to educational equality and integration. In 1948, Hector P. García, a World War II veteran and doctor in Corpus Christi, organized about seven hundred Mexican Americans to establish the American GI Forum, which fought for equal rights and educational equality. The organization helped Mexican Americans gain access to their veterans' benefits, advocated for equality in burial rights, and, along with LULAC, initiated the 1948 *Bastrop v. Delgado* (1948) and *Hernandez v. Driscoll* (1957) cases, which challenged the pedagogical justification of segregated schools.[129]

La Prensa reported on the rise of these Mexican American civil rights activists, just as it reported on the decline of escuelitas. Though the newspaper never made the link between the two explicit, the timing of these two developments was not coincidental, as their dynamics were greatly impacted by the Great Depression and both world wars. The Great Depression had a catastrophic impact on many ethnic Mexican communities. By the early 1930s, a third of the entire US labor force was out of work, and people of color were the first groups to be laid off. As if high unemployment rates were not enough, by 1930, many large cities throughout the country, not just the Southwest—such as Chicago, Denver, Detroit, Los Angeles, and San Antonio—launched a series of repatriation campaigns that sent thousands of Mexican immigrants and their American-born children to Mexico. Initially, the Mexican Consulate supported these repatriation efforts, believing that the experience these immigrants had gained working in the United States would make them a vital factor in strengthening Mexico's workforce. Some scholars estimate that the Mexican Consulate paid the train fares for about 1,500 people to go to Mexico in the spring of 1931.

Many repatriates for whom the Mexican Consulate paid fares struggled to survive in Mexico, being unable to find work and adjust to an economy that was in many ways worse than that of the United States. By 1932, the Mexican Consulate went from paying train fares to warning those headed south that it would be unlikely that they would be able to find work. Despite the Mexican government's public withdrawal of its support for these repatriation campaigns, the various cities across the country, often in collaboration with the Department of Labor, continued to repatriate ethnic Mexicans until the late 1930s. While it is difficult to calculate an accurate number, some scholars estimate that between 1929 and 1937, an average of 80,000 people were repatriated each year.[130] The proliferation of escuelitas began tapering off at the moment when Mexican American activists emerged in earnest, and thousands of ethnic Mexicans were repatriated to Mexico.

Escuelitas may have sharply declined throughout the 1930s, but they never fully disappeared. Those who attended escuelitas run by Mexican refugees in the 1930s, 1940s, and 1950s have fond memories of their experience, rather than feeling as though they were caught in the middle of a linguistic hegemonic struggle. Additionally, the escuelitas' curriculum—arithmetic and grammar studies—gave them a solid foundation for when they enrolled in the public school. In 1930, at age four, Belisario Flores attended an escuelita in Eagle Pass founded by a group of nuns who were refugees of the Mexican Revolution, where he learned arithmetic and basic Spanish literacy. He enrolled in the public school system in the early 1930s, after his family moved to San Antonio, where his teachers were surprised that by the time he began the first grade, he could already write his numbers and add and subtract. Adelina Flores, Belisario's wife, also attended the nuns' escuelita, and she recalls that the women were extremely strict, though effective teachers.[131]

Adelina Flores attended two little schools as a young child, the one the nuns began and one that was held in the home of Mrs. Johnson, a stern Anglo woman who offered English lessons to Mexican girls so that they would have some skills before entering first grade. She recalls, "[Mrs. Johnson] understood our parents worked for measly wages, so she would tell us, 'They are paying for you, making a sacrifice, so you better learn English.' And we learned with her."[132]

Belisario Flores attended another escuelita during the summer of 1936, at the age of ten, after moving to San Antonio. It took place at Navarro Elementary School and was taught by Professor Felix García, "a strict and dignified man." He said his parents "still had that closeness to the mother tongue, so they wanted my brother and I not to forget our language." In addition to teaching Spanish literacy, García taught his students "urbanidad de la humanidad"—or politeness, civility, and courtesy. Flores became the first Mexican American to be promoted to the rank of general in the US Air Force, and he credits his "beautiful 'escuelita' days" with instilling in him an early appreciation for learning and courtesy.[133]

Rolando Hinojosa-Smith, professor emeritus of English at the

University of Texas at Austin, recalls that he and his four siblings attended three different escuelitas all within a few blocks of his family's house on North Texas Avenue in Mercedes, and all of them were taught by refugees of the Mexican Revolution. He went to one during the summers of 1934 and 1935 and was taught by Professor Cuéllar.

> [He] would buy *La Prensa* . . . and then would put his chair on top of the desk, and then he would read current events for us. . . . Our vocabulary increased tremendously because of the newspaper that he would read, and you could always ask what a word meant after the reading of the particular article.[134]

Professor Cuéllar would read to the class for thirty to forty-five minutes, and afterward the students would go to the blackboard and copy what he said, which was one of the methods he used for teaching the children how to write. There were between fifty and sixty children between the ages of five and eleven in Professor Cuéllar's escuelita, located in a building next to the barbershop. Hinojosa-Smith's sister attended Señorita Amelia's escuelita, and his brother attended Doña Albinita's escuelita, which she conducted in her house.[135] He argues that the proliferation of escuelitas in his neighborhood, along with the large public library, speaks to the importance of education within the ethnic Mexican community of Mercedes during the Great Depression, and cites several of his neighbors who, despite financial constraints, graduated from college, particularly from the University of Texas at Austin. Hinojosa-Smith remembers that one such neighbor, Ray Hernández, "who was a very good student,"

> had to quit in the tenth grade, and my father thought it was a crime . . . well, he gets drafted in World War II, and serves in Italy, comes back and on the GI Bill, he finishes high school—this guy is twenty-something years old going to high school with us, but he graduates—and then he comes to [UT] and earns a master's in math.[136]

After completing his degree, Hernández returned to Mercedes and became a teacher. Upon his death, his former students came together to pay for a plaque placed on his tombstone, a testament to the impact his work had on his community.

Hinojosa-Smith states, "I come from a family of readers. . . . We would read Spanish and English. . . . Education was always stressed, not only in my family . . . but many other families [as well]."[137] Recalling that there was no distinction between literature for children and literature for adults in his household, he states that his father often crossed the border to purchase Spanish-language books in Río Rico, Reynosa, and Matamoros. Though the family placed importance on literacy in both languages, the children were never penalized for mixing them. Hinojosa-Smith remembers, "If I began a sentence in one language and finished it in the other, Mom or Dad would not say anything. . . . We would just mix them back and forth, make jokes back and forth, mixing both languages and having plays on words."[138] He credits the importance placed on literacy and education during childhood, of which the escuelitas were a significant part, for his own success, as well as the success of his siblings and childhood friends and neighbors.

Doña Albinita García de León was the aunt of Clotilde and Hector García, the latter the founder of the American GI Forum. The siblings also were her escuelita students, and when she became older, Clotilde helped her aunt run the escuelita.[139] José G. García, Albinita's brother and Clotilde and Hector's father, was a graduate of the state-sponsored normal school in Victoria, Tamaulipas, where he worked as a teacher before immigrating to Texas. He published his own Spanish alphabet primer that Albinita used in her escuelita. As friends and neighbors of the Garcías, Hinojosa-Smith's family had a copy of this primer in their family's collection.[140]

Doña Albinita, whose escuelita Hinojosa-Smith's brother attended, continued to run her school at least until the late 1940s, when Ruben Manuel Vásquez was enrolled. Vásquez, who was García de León's great-nephew, remembers that all the students, including himself, came from poor families, and that he was one of the few who had shoes to wear. Doña Albinita taught her students the Spanish alphabet, arithmetic, and Spanish poetry for children.[141] She also placed an emphasis on taking care of one's environment in a manner similar to Montessori classrooms, prioritizing daily activities such as washing dishes and having an afternoon snack, called "merienda" in Spanish.[142] Vásquez recalls,

> My brother and I would go to my uncle's grocery store and pick up some day-old bread and overripe fruit, which we would take to my aunt and she would separate the good bread and cut away the moldy parts, the same for the fruit; she would cut away the bad parts and serve the better parts to the class.[143]

At the age of seven, Vásquez and his family moved to San Antonio, where he enrolled in the local public school and learned to identify as a Mexican American.[144]

The García family in Mercedes, Texas, 1926. Hector García is standing at the far left. Clotilde García is standing at the far right. José G. García, standing in the back, was a teacher in Victoria, Tamaulipas. He wrote a Spanish-alphabet primer that his sister Albinita García de León used in her escuelita. The García children attended this escuelita, as did the brother of Rolando Hinojosa-Smith. HECTOR P. GARCÍA PAPERS, MARY AND JEFF BELL LIBRARY, TEXAS A&M UNIVERSITY-CORPUS CHRISTI.

Around 1950, José A. Nieto attended a summer escuelita in Presidio, Texas, taught by two sisters, Socorro and Consuelo Hata, of Mexican and Japanese ancestry. He recalls that the school was in a large storage building on their father's farm. "There were sacks of grain and hay bales all neatly stacked and all was very clean," he states. "I can smell the hay and grain still."[145] The students studied arithmetic and geometry, and he states, "The geometrics were a 'discovery' for me. I sometimes think they might have set me on my life's course since I became a mechanical engineer many years later."[146] Though the sisters gave all their instruction in Spanish, all the class readings were in English, particularly old copies of *Life* magazine, which provided these children on the Texas-Mexico border with pictures from around the world.[147]

José E. Limón, the Julian Samora Endowed Professor in Latino Studies at Notre Dame, attended an escuelita in Corpus Christi between 1953 and 1956 during the summers and on Saturdays. Señorita Tafolla, who charged twenty-five cents a lesson, taught between five and seven children in her living room. Limón remembers, "We all spoke a fairly fluent Spanish, but Ms. Tafolla taught me the basics of writing the language, especially accents." She also instructed the children in declamaciones, Mexican patriotic speeches, in preparation for September 16, Mexican Independence Day.[148] As a single older woman with some education, Señorita Tafolla "taught children to make ends meet but also no doubt with some ideals in mind such as the maintenance of the Spanish language, especially in a racially hostile Corpus [Christi]."[149] Upon turning eleven and entering junior high, Limón no longer attended Ms. Tafolla's school.

The Mexican government's plan to Mexicanize the Mexican colony in the United States in the hope that they would return never produced the expected results. By the 1930s, the consulate no longer supported the notion of founding cultural centers that housed escuelitas and Spanish-language libraries throughout the Southwest. Most of the refugees who came north during the revolution remained in the United States, with long-term effects for the ethnic Mexican population north of the Río Grande. Their decision to remain not only altered the composition of the ethnic Mexican population in the United States, but also provoked further questions about what it meant to be a Mexican American. And certainly by the 1950s, La Prensa no longer reported on the goings-on of escuelitas throughout south Texas. But despite the lack of attention from the Mexican government and the Spanish-language press, escuelitas endured, albeit on a much smaller scale. Whereas Hinojosa-Smith recalls fifty to sixty children enrolled in his escuelita in Mercedes—a number consistent with other schools of that era—Limón's escuelita, twenty years later, had between five and seven children.

Many Mexican American activists, especially those who were part of the Mexican American Generation, were former escuelita students, and in carrying out their campaign for educational equality, they drew from their experiences in the little schools in two different ways. One group sought to incorporate the escuelita curriculum into the public school system, demanding a more inclusive narrative of Texas and US history. Another group used the escuelita model to teach children English, just as the OSA Alice council proposed in 1927. Though escuelitas declined rather steadily beginning in the 1930s, they have always maintained a lasting influence not only in Mexican American educational history, but also in the institutional history of Mexican American studies.

ESCUELITAS AND THE MEXICAN AMERICAN GENERATION'S CAMPAIGN FOR EDUCATIONAL INTEGRATION

"I don't think all my sisters went there, but I know for sure Laura did. And then Head Start came in, and Crucita closed her escuelita," Norma Cantú, the oldest of eleven siblings, tells me. She and the three siblings born immediately after her attended these little schools while growing up in Laredo, where they learned Spanish literacy and math skills before they entered first grade. Her five youngest siblings all attended Head Start, so they never had the same escuelita experience, though Cantú did try. When she was twelve, Cantú, now the Norine R. and T. Frank Murchison Professor of the Humanities at Trinity University, opened her own summer escuelita. For twenty-five cents a week, she taught Spanish songs and games and the English alphabet to her younger siblings and other neighborhood children, many of them enrolled in Head Start.[1] The Cantú siblings' relationship to early childhood education spans the transition from escuelitas to state-funded preschools, a shift that occurred with the rise of the Mexican American Generation, a "political generation" whose activism began as early as the 1910s and continued into the post–World War II era.[2] These individuals fought for educational equality, initiating desegregation court cases in the decades before and after the war, but the forgotten roots of their campaign extend back to when many of them were escuelita students.

Escuelitas provided many Mexican American activists with the tools they needed to advocate effectively on behalf of La Raza, and ironically, their very activism hastened the little schools' demise. With their Mexican-centric curriculum flourishing in an alternative space, escuelitas implied divisions between them and the dominant US society at the moment they were seeking inclusion. By the 1940s these little Spanish-language schools no longer worked as a cultural negotiation tactic for Mexican Americans, who labored tirelessly to emphasize their status as US citizens. While they disregarded the escuelita model with which they were familiar, Mexican American activists from across the political spectrum integrated aspects of them into their campaign for educational integration throughout the 1940s and 1950s. Both progressives and conservatives wholly believed a Mexican American child's imaginary citizenship belonged to the United States, but oftentimes, the similarities ended there. Many of them disagreed on how that imaginary citizenship should be negotiated, and the ways in which they drew from the escuelitas as they pursued educational equality reflect this difference. Progressive activists attempted to alter the system to make it more inclusive of Mexican American children, while conservative activists attempted to alter Mexican American children to make them more acceptable to the system.

Progressive activists never challenged English-only pedagogy as an exclusionary practice; some, like George I. Sánchez, endorsed it. Instead, they looked to the curriculum as one of the most important mechanisms for change. Mexican Americans such as Sánchez, J. T. Canales, Carlos Castañeda, and various writers for *LULAC News* attempted to incorporate the ethnic Mexican experience into the Texas historical narrative.[3] As former escuelita students, these Mexican American activists learned early on that the narrative in the public schools was not the only one.[4] The alternative narratives of the escuelitas may have evolved outside the realm of the state schools, but they could be integrated into the dominant curriculum not only to provide a more complete understanding of Texas's past, but also to demonstrate the loyalty and inclusion of Mexican Americans in the present. These activists understood that the way the Alamo was remembered and taught was perhaps more important than the event itself. Female teachers, including María Elena Zamora O'Shea and Jovita González, were integral if overlooked members of this group of progressive activists.

Conservative activists such as Felix Tijerina drew from another aspect of the escuelitas—the model itself. The Texas constitution of 1876 outlined a segregated public school system that separated White and Black students. Since the turn of the twentieth century, public school systems throughout the Southwest segregated ethnic Mexican children, arguing that they did not speak English well enough to attend school with Anglo Americans. School officials claimed the segregation was pedagogically based, not race based —an important distinction since Mexican Americans were legally White. Multiple initiatives created small schools that operated outside the nine-month school year to teach children basic English-language skills before entering the first grade. These activists left the escuelita curriculum behind, but appropriated the escuelita's structure to aid in their push for educational equality.

ESCUELITAS AND THE MEXICAN AMERICAN GENERATION

In the 1980s, Mario T. García first articulated his conceptual framework for what he called "the Mexican American Generation" in an attempt to understand these men and women activists who were full of contradictions—contradictions that seem especially egregious in a post–Chicano Movement world. For example, looking to the United States as their country, these Mexican American civil rights activists made US citizenship a requirement for membership in their organizations and claimed that all their meetings needed to be conducted in English. As if these views on citizenship and language were not contrary enough to the Chicano Movement's revolutionary mentality of the 1960s and 1970s, they argued for inclusion based on their legal whiteness and for legislation restricting Mexican immigration—tactics that, on the surface, appeared to undermine the subsequent generation's "Brown is beautiful" ideology. Scholars continue to wrestle with the legacy of these activists, trying to make sense of how their accommodationist tactics seemed to internalize Anglos' disparaging views of ethnic Mexicans. In doing so, their discourse largely focuses itself on immigration and Whiteness.[5]

Less developed is the historiography on this generation's activism for educational equality, which attributes their advocacy to their views on citizenship and Whiteness—that is, Mexican American children are legally White and US citizens and therefore entitled to full integration. A key element missing from these historiographical discussions is the way the Mexican American Generation's educational history informed their activism. While World War I, the Great Depression, and World War II facilitated this generation's transformation from Texas Mexican to Mexican American, the process of transformation began before these individuals were old enough to serve in the military. Childhood education—in the escuelitas as well as the public schools—and the two nations those institutions represented played a central role in it.

Though these Mexican American activists were products of the Texas public school system, many of them attended escuelitas as young children. J. T. Canales attended an escuelita on his family's ranch, and the first English-language school he attended was a public school in Nueces County when he was ten years old.[6] Hector P. García, founder of the American GI Forum, and his sister, Clotilde P. García, attended an escuelita that their aunt, Doña Albinita, ran in Mercedes. As a young adult, Clotilde helped her aunt run the escuelita and care for the children. Doña Albinita maintained her little school into the 1960s and probably used a Spanish-language primer that her brother (the García siblings' father) José G. García—a professor at the Instituto Científico y Literario del Estado in C. Victoria, Tamaulipas, from 1905 to 1910—wrote and had published in Mexico.[7] José de la Luz Sáenz attended two different escuelitas in Alice run by Pablo Pérez and Eulalio Velázquez. Alonso S. Perales most likely attended Velázquez's escuelita as well. A publisher and printer of his own Spanish-language newspaper, *El Cosmopolita*, Velázquez also opened his personal library to the group of young men to whom he taught Mexican history. Both Perales and Sáenz corresponded with Velázquez for decades after they left Alice.[8]

When Alonso S. Perales published *En Defensa de Mi Raza* in 1937, he sent a copy to Eulalio Velázquez, who had moved back to Mexico and was living in Querétaro. In a letter thanking Perales for thinking of his "old friend," Velázquez wrote, "I admire your strength, persistence and intelligence in your laudable defense of the Mexican people that live on the other side of the Río Bravo."[9] If the former escuelita teacher, now in his seventies, was bothered by Perales's decision to exclude non-US citizens from membership to LULAC, he did not mention it. Rather, he praised Perales's "valuable collaboration" with a "big group of intelligent and educated young people— méxico-texanos," a collaboration he "celebrated." He also noted Perales's perseverance in continuing the fight for equality despite the "resentment and hostility of strangers."[10] For Sáenz and Perales, the civil rights campaign they launched in the 1920s and continued into the 1930s was not antithetical to the ideology of the intellectual and social world of their youth. It was a sign of progress in the fight for equality, and their accommodationist approach received the imprimatur of a prominent figure in their escuelita days. Their strong cultural ties enabled them to limit membership to US citizens, to require English to be the official language of their organizations, and to vocalize an explicitly unambiguous patriotism for the United States. These tactics were made all the more sincere because of their own security in ethnic Mexican cultural forms.

Unequivocally, escuelitas played a role in the early stages of these men's and women's lives—in fact, they were one of the last generations to live in a society where escuelitas were ubiquitous. Recovering these individuals' experiences in these little schools provides another facet of their process of identity formation—where it began, what it included, and how these moving parts culminated in their accommodation politics. They took aspects of the escuelitas with them as they walked out of a Mexican-centered social world and into an American-centered political one where they could claim their civil rights as US citizens. Escuelitas provided them with a strong foundation of Spanish-language literacy, which not only influenced how they engaged

with the multiple social spheres around them, but also helped them reconcile the demands of Americanization with their own demands for social,
economic, and educational inclusion.

WOMEN OF THE MEXICAN AMERICAN GENERATION

The role and experiences of women—including their education in the escuelitas and their tenure as leaders—is another overlooked factor in the
way we remember the Mexican American Generation. Not exclusively, but
often, women were the teachers, the leaders of escuelitas and public schools
in their communities, and in this capacity they were often at the forefront
of everyday activism. When conceptualizing his generational framework,
García focused his study on leadership, and as he noted, "The vast majority
of leadership positions were held by men. Although the Mexican-American
Generation consisted of both men and women, it was mostly dominated
by men."[11] García's assessment of the founders of LULAC, of the School
Improvement League, of muckraking journalists, and of intellectual and
political leaders is accurate—they were all men.

Other academics, however, have questioned the "narrow construction
of analytical categories" that lead scholars to interpret civil rights activism
historically as men's work.[12] Cynthia Orozco states, "The study of men's organizations will not fully capture women's participation," and she also notes
that the "work women performed in their homes . . . privileged men with
leisure time to participate in politics."[13] Examining these men and women as
members of a larger civil rights campaign that began as early as 1900, Gabriela González has looked beyond García's generational model to call attention to the gendered, class-conscious, transnational, and intergenerational
dimensions of activists who "sought to redeem the Mexican masses . . . by
encouraging them to become identified with the United States."[14] Women's
activism spanned both sides of the border and drew from the politics of benevolence and respectability, as well as the politics of radicalism. It operated
inside and outside of the construction of LULAC and other organizations.[15]

If we want to continue to use the phrase *Mexican American Generation*,
we need to clarify and refine our definition of it. First, we need to move
beyond the narrow focus on the men who founded formal organizations.
A number of scholars have demonstrated that as significant as these more
formal organizations were, others also contributed to the civil rights movement, including women who campaigned for equality in significant, if often
unglamorous and unnoticed, ways. Second, we need to rethink how we
define leaders. Expanding our definition of civil rights activism will allow

us to locate the obvious and subtle ways women were leaders in their communities and, perhaps more importantly, in their own homes. As education
and childhood are vehicles for normalizing social constructions, the home,
as well as the school, is the site where the perpetuation and rejection of
those constructions are negotiated. Finally, we need to pay attention to how
activists' political ideologies shifted within their own lifetimes, how they
differed from those of other members of their cohort, and how these shifting
ideologies reflected their interactions with members of older and younger
generations. We talk about a "Mexican American Generation," which is a
useful and pithy framework for historicizing the different approaches for
civil rights activism throughout the twentieth century, but as scholars
continue to expand subjects and sources and construct more nuanced and
complex analyses of the past, we are really talking about an intergenerational
Mexican American civil rights movement that endured for several decades.[16]

THE TEACHER AS AN INTERGENERATIONAL MEXICAN AMERICAN REVOLUTIONARY

Mexican American female teachers, whether they taught in an escuelita
or the public school system, have always been leaders in ethnic Mexican
communities—intellectuals committed to education as a vehicle for socioeconomic mobility and racial uplift. The very nature of a teaching career—imparting knowledge and training a younger generation within the
confines of a progressive-education institution—gave their work a grassroots
dimension few other professions had. As historian Laura Muñoz states, few
Mexican American women in the first half of the twentieth century were
able to obtain jobs as public school teachers, and it is difficult to recover
information about those who did. The experiences of these teachers "point
to an active dialogue that occurred among Mexican American educators,"
one that played a "critical role in shaping a Mexican American cultural
consciousness."[17] Recovering the experiences and impact of these teachers
provides another entry into uncovering women's political activism in the first
half of the twentieth century.

María Elena Zamora O'Shea and Jovita González are two such teachers
whose intellectual biographies and educational histories reveal the contributions female educators made to public discourse and the school curriculum.
And, concomitantly, they also reveal one dimension of escuelitas' influence
on progressive activists of the Mexican American civil rights movement.
Both women attended escuelitas as children and learned Spanish literacy
and a different trajectory of Texas and Mexican history. Their work as

teachers provided them with firsthand knowledge of the consequences that the Anglocentric historical narrative had for race relations in Texas. Though both women most likely felt confined in their role as public school teachers— those Mexican Americans who made progress in obtaining doctoral degrees and professorships in the first half of the twentieth century were all men— they nonetheless used their pedagogical platform to question the dominant historical narrative and offer an alternative one that had its origins in the escuelitas of south Texas. Just as the work of Jovita Idar, María Rentería, Leonor Villegas de Magnón, and María Villarreal demonstrates the ways in which escuelitas provided a space that supported women's power within a patriarchal ethnic Mexican population, the work of Zamora O'Shea and González demonstrates how the push to integrate the escuelita curriculum into the public schools and popular discourse provided a space that supported women's agency within a patriarchal Mexican American movement.

NEGOTIATING THE TRANSITIONS FROM ESCUELITAS TO THE PUBLIC SCHOOL SYSTEM: EDUCATOR AND WRITER MARÍA ELENA ZAMORA O'SHEA

María Elena Zamora O'Shea was born in south Texas on July 21, 1878, to Porfirio Zamora and Gavina Moreno.[18] Both of her parents descended from Spanish land grant families that settled in the northern part of Nuevo Santander, the area between the Nueces River and the Río Grande.[19] Though she was born on her father's ranch, Rancho La Noria Cardeneña, in Hidalgo County, the family moved to her mother's family's ranch, La Posta del Palo Alto, in Nueces County.[20] Throughout the latter half of the nineteenth century, a growing number of ethnic Mexicans, including members of Zamora O'Shea's family, lost their Spanish land grant properties through bureaucratic and violent tactics designed to displace them. Despite the institutionalization of racist practices, life in rural south Texas provided a rich upbringing for the daughter of a wealthy and powerful ranch owner. Her father, a high-ranking officer in the Mexican military, won commendations for his role in the Battle of Puebla on May 5, 1862, and attained much power in Mexican politics, even though he lived in south Texas.[21] In one letter to the editor of the *Dallas Morning News* that she wrote near the end of her life, Zamora O'Shea bluntly stated, "I was raised with a silver spoon in my mouth."[22]

    In 1935, just before the Texas Centennial, Zamora O'Shea published *El Mesquite*. Set in south Texas between the Nueces River and the Río Grande, the stories in the novel are told from the perspective of Palo Alto, an old mesquite tree that recounts the social, cultural, and political history of several generations of the García family. In an autobiographical account of the ranches of southwest Texas that preface the novel, Zamora O'Shea notes that there was no public school on or near the ranch where she and her family lived in Nueces County, arguing that it was impossible to establish a school system in a ranching society where all the settlements were so far apart.[23]

As discussed in chapter 1, the progressive education movement arrived in Texas in 1884 with the passage of a school reform bill that ended the community system in favor of the district system and required an English-only pedagogy.[24] This new approach to public schooling facilitated the expansion of the state's education system, which ultimately had a major impact on Zamora O'Shea's life. In 1882, when she was four years old, Hidalgo County had seven public schools; by 1890, there were nineteen. All of them were ungraded, and not one of them was a high school.[25] Founded in 1852, Hidalgo County is 1,596 square miles, so in 1882, there was one school for every 228 square miles, and in 1890, there was one for every 84 square miles.[26] The great distances between schools, and the severe shortage of them, explains why ranches typically had their own escuelitas.

In many ways, Nueces County's history of public education closely resembles that of Hidalgo County. In 1882, the county maintained eight schools, seven for White children (including ethnic Mexican children) and one for Black children. In 1890, there were thirteen schools, eleven for White students and two for Black students. Families also paid an average of $2.10 per month for tuition.[27] As Nueces County was 847 square miles, in 1882 there was one school for every 121 square miles, and in 1890, there was one for every 77 square miles.[28] The county schools, one superintendent stated, were "not accessible by railway," making it difficult for students who lived great distances to attend and for teachers to arrange teaching institutes, professional development days that schools tried to organize once a year.[29] While the progressive education movement oversaw the dramatic expansion of the school system beginning in the 1880s, it would be decades before rural communities in south Texas had access to public education.

The children of Zamora O'Shea's family's ranch did not have a public school until 1887, when, she writes, "Judge Fitzsimmons of Corpus Christi inspected our part of the county and established the first public school in our section."[30] Throughout his tenure as county superintendent, Joseph Fitzsimmons maintained an optimistic outlook for the ethnic Mexican students under his charge. In 1882, he stated that the county's Mexican residents were "only recently made to understand the value of the Public Schools, and their children are rapidly acquiring a knowledge of the English language." In 1886, he noted that they were "gradually becoming accustomed to the use of the English language and methods of instruction." And in 1890, he hypothesized that since the county schools had begun to employ "competent teachers" who understood and spoke Spanish, "the population of these frontier counties will soon become good American citizens fully understanding their duties and rights as such."[31]

A native of Dublin, Fitzsimmons left Ireland for the United States during the Great Famine (1845–1849) and enlisted in the US Army in 1848.[32] By 1850, he was a sergeant stationed at Fort Duncan in Eagle Pass, fighting in the Indian Wars. In 1853, when he moved to Nueces County, he applied for citizenship and helped found a Catholic church in Corpus Christi.[33] A Texas Ranger during the Cortina War of 1859, he enlisted in the Confederate Army, serving from March to June 1863.[34] Like Sam Houston, however, he was a Unionist, and from 1864 to 1865, he volunteered for the US Civil Service in New Orleans and then Fort Gaines, Alabama.[35] Like other superintendents, Fitzsimmons interpreted Americanization and acquisition of the English language as signs of progress, but unlike other superintendents, his annual reports did not equate ethnic Mexican poverty with indifference to education. Nor did he perceive ethnic Mexican culture as being antithetical to the modern era. His own background as a devout Catholic who left Ireland during a time when scholars estimate a million people starved to death and another million left the island might have helped him understand the ethnic Mexican plight. His military record indicates that he valued the notion of American citizenship but most likely believed that the racial inferiority of Indians and Blacks made them unworthy of it.[36] His superintendent reports, however, indicate that he did not consider ethnic Mexicans to be ineligible for citizenship. In Nueces County, during Zamora O'Shea's childhood, the public school system unfolded under the auspices of a non-Anglo Catholic immigrant, but in her early adulthood, it came to be one of the most virulently racist public school systems in Texas.[37]

Navigating the racism and sexism of south Texas public education proved to be quite a feat, and Zamora O'Shea acknowledged the role of those who supported her in overcoming these obstacles. It was their "encouraging words," she states, "that kept me up."[38] One of the people she mentions is R. Marsh, Hidalgo County's superintendent from 1902 to 1914—the same period that Zamora O'Shea worked as a teacher at the King Ranch and then as a principal in Alice. As discussed in further detail in chapter 1, Richard Alvis Marsh was not only the county superintendent, but also the editor of the *Hidalgo Advance*, a publication that promoted the county as a site of technological and economic progress. A native of Kentucky, Marsh, a former watchmaker, enlisted in the military in 1869 under the alias Robert Belt, but he deserted in March 1870 after nine months of service.[39]

Four years later, he arrived in San Antonio at the age of thirty and quickly became familiar with the social traditions and multiple educational institutions of south Texas. Eventually he moved to Starr County to take a teaching position at Fort Ringgold in Rio Grande City.[40] In 1887, he married Virginia Johnson, a fourteen-year-old Hidalgo County native with a seventh-grade education whose parents were born in Mexico.[41] By 1900, Marsh had established himself in Hidalgo County as a public school teacher, a husband, a father of four children, and the master of two live-in Mexican servants, neither of whom could speak English. By 1903, he was convinced that the escuelitas were "fast disappearing" under his direction of the public school system.[42]

It is possible that some of Marsh's views on escuelitas were influenced by his wife's background. Her father, George Johnson, was a farmer in Hidalgo County, and one of the family's neighbors was J. Sergio Hinojosa, a teacher. Hinojosa may have been employed in a public school, but considering that Hidalgo County had fewer than seven schools in 1880 and Hinojosa was a Mexican immigrant, it is far more likely that he taught in an escuelita on one of the local ranches. Virginia Johnson may have been one of Hinojosa's students, and as she attended school only through the seventh grade, the foundational literacy skills she attained during early childhood may have come from Hinojosa's ranch school.[43]

It is also possible, however, that Marsh was influenced by Zamora O'Shea as much as she was influenced by him. She looked to Marsh as a mentor—referring to him as one of a select group of people that offered her support and encouragement as she pursued a teaching career, despite her father's desire to see her become a lady of the house. It is highly likely that she shared her experiences in these little Spanish-language ranch schools with Marsh, someone whose influence was so substantial that she made note of it in print almost twenty years after he died.[44] Further evidence of their relationship may lie in their similar views on ethnic Mexicans and education. Zamora O'Shea's initial exposure to education was in Spanish. Her father prized learning and knowledge, so despite the lack of public education, he maintained a school on the family's property where, she states, "every child living in the ranch learned to read and write in Spanish."[45] She herself was educated in this escuelita that her father maintained. In 1880, the teacher at the escuelita at Rancho La Noria Cardeneña, Zamora O'Shea's father's property, was José María Casada, a native of Mexico whose fifteen-year-old son, Manuel, attended school. In fact, many of the children who lived on Rancho La Noria Cardeneña attended school, even young adults as old as fifteen and sixteen.[46] Despite this pride in her family's commitment to the Spanish-language education of the children who lived on the ranch, she did not see the escuelita model—a method that served the rural population of south Texas well for many decades—as a relevant institution for the modern era.

Andrés Tijerina notes that the pride that she felt in her family's ancestry—descending from Spanish land grant families on both her mother's and her father's sides—gave Zamora O'Shea a "sense of superiority."[47] That sense of superiority was embedded not only in her family's noble past, but in their present socioeconomic status. She states, "Those of us who learned English at the time were sent away to boarding schools. As the poor working people could not afford that luxury, they remained ignorant."[48] The first English-language school she attended was the Ursuline Convent, where she enrolled as a boarding student, and she then attended the Holding Institute in Laredo. Subsequently, she became the first Mexican American to enroll at Southwest Texas State Normal School in San Marcos.[49] Her family's financial ability to send her to more urban places with opportunities for higher education—much more than what the rural areas of south Texas could offer—separated her from those whose poverty kept them "ignorant."

Her reflection on twenty-three years of teaching is another indication of the complexity of her views on education in south Texas. She states, "My determination to see my people awaken from the lethargy in which they had fallen, helped me for many years I worked for them and among them. Today in my old age I hope that they will forget all prejudices and begin to teach their children as my father taught me *that this is our grand Lone Star State.*"[50] Though she deeply admired and respected the people of south Texas and their traditional culture, she understood that modernity on the Texas-Mexico border had ushered in permanent changes with a devastating impact for Texas Mexicans. New technologies and social institutions, particularly public school expansion, made English-language literacy imperative for those who wanted inclusion—a truly uphill battle, as many rural areas of south Texas neglected to enforce compulsory attendance laws in favor of using ethnic Mexican children as cheap labor for the agricultural industry. And many ethnic Mexicans families could not survive financially without their children's wages, hence the disregard for compulsory attendance laws in the first place.[51]

Second, despite the number of obstacles that stood between ethnic Mexicans and education, Zamora O'Shea advocated for an inclusive version of Texas history that she hoped would combat ethnic Mexicans' present-day exclusion. She believed that if Mexican Americans were going to be part of an inclusive historical narrative, they needed to move past the "lethargy" into "which they had fallen"—that is, their own prejudices and reluctance to embrace American educational and linguistic conventions—no matter how hegemonic those conventions might have been. Only then would they be able to incorporate themselves into American social and political institutions. Zamora O'Shea articulated this perspective in *El Mesquite*, when Santos Moreno, one of the patriarchs of the maternal family line, reflects on the reasons for his own loss of land. He says, "Now [my cattle and lands] are gone. I perhaps did not know how to hold them. . . . This new government of ours has many strange laws. I do not know the new language, and therefore do not know the laws." Pleading with his son-in-law, he continues, "I want you to do your utmost to educate my grandchildren so that they will know the laws of the country to which they have been born. Spare no expense, send them away to other parts if necessary, but see that they acquire the knowledge of the language and laws of their country."[52] Rather than pointing out the structural racism of Texas land laws, the lack of public education, and the rampant discrimination against Texas Mexicans in the years following annexation, Moreno blames himself for his loss of land: he did not try hard enough to assimilate or to use his new country's justice system. He wants his children to learn from his mistakes and send their own children to the faraway public schools, not the escuelita on the ranch.

Zamora O'Shea and Marsh's views on escuelitas may have overlapped, but in more significant ways, their views diverged. Both believed that the escuelitas served their purpose in the days when there was no public education, and in that capacity, they were an unequivocal indication that the ethnic Mexican populations of south Texas cared very deeply about educating their children. But in the modern era, with its promise of progress and inclusion, they were no longer useful. While these little schools were a sign of an enlightened population before the expansion of the public school system, escuelitas in the modern era helped keep the south Texas ethnic Mexican population in a state of "lethargy" that hindered its political and economic advancement. But whereas Marsh's superintendent reports and articles in the *Hidalgo Advance* point to his belief that Americanization policies served the region by turning ethnic Mexican students into a dependable and easy-to-manage labor force, Zamora O'Shea's personal correspondence and published works point to her belief that though the escuelitas had outlived their usefulness, their curriculum had not.

The body of Zamora O'Shea's work points to the notion that the historical narratives of the public schools and of the escuelitas were not mutually exclusive. John M. González argues, "Public school education remained [Zamora O'Shea's] great hope for improving conditions for the Texas-Mexican community,"[53] and while this is certainly the case, oral history, family archives, and the land itself remained her great hope for improving conditions not just in the public school system, but also in the larger political world in which it existed. She wanted to integrate ethnic Mexican methods of history-remembering into the larger historical narrative that mistakenly depended wholly on archives that failed to represent all voices of the state.

Zamora O'Shea understood that traditional archives lacked the necessary materials for historians to be able to construct historical narratives that depicted the Mexican contribution to Texas accurately.[54] Her solution to the problem was for family archives and oral histories to provide the foundation for a narrative counter to the one that dominated the public school curriculum.[55] Historians of the early twentieth century looked at history writing as a scientific venture—one that was free from subjectivity and based on fact. Zamora O'Shea does not point out that objective history is an impossible endeavor because historians' interpretations will always be influenced by the time in which they live. Instead, she argues that historians need to be more cognizant of collecting *all* the "facts" before they write their narratives. Referring to the war for Texas independence, she states, "Sometimes I have wondered why it is that our forefathers who helped with their money, their supplies, and their own energies have been entirely forgotten. History should be told as a fact, pleasant or unpleasant."[56] The ways in which ideas about race superiority and inferiority impacted history-writing allowed Anglo American historians not only to fail to draw from Mexican American sources, but also to be completely oblivious to the fact that they existed at all.

One such example of Zamora O'Shea's intervention in this problem of archival representation occurred in February 1936, when Marjorie Rogers, a lawyer from Marlin, Texas, published an article about the Angel of Goliad in the *Dallas Morning News*.[57] The Angel of Goliad was a "beautiful, kind hearted woman" who came to Texas with Colonel Telesforo Alavez in 1836, Rogers wrote.[58] When Santa Anna ordered that Colonel Fannin and his men be killed in Goliad in March 1836, she intervened throughout the crisis, saving the lives of many Anglo Texans and providing medical attention and food to several others before the infamous massacre. Rogers's article quotes extensively from the written accounts of three men who witnessed the mercy of the Angel of Goliad: Dr. J. H. Barnard, Benjamin Franklin Hughes, and Reuben R. Brown.[59]

These written accounts established the common narrative about the Angel of Goliad and were already well known to researchers and historians in 1936. Based on how these men referred to her—as "Madam Alvarez, Alavez, Alvesco, and Panchita"—everyone assumed that she was the wife of Captain Alavez. Rogers's article included information from the Archivo de Secretaría de Guerra y Marina (Ministry of War and Navy Archive) in Mexico City, which stated that "the legitimate wife of Capt. Telesforo Alavez was Maria Augustina De Pozo, a resident of Toluca," and that it was possible that he "picked Panchita up on the road as he traveled with General Urrea [to Texas]."[60] Rogers knew that the marital status of Panchita was an important aspect of her identity, especially to many of the male historians, both amateur and professional, whose work focused on the war for Texas independence.

Harbert Davenport earned his law degree from the University of Texas at Austin School of Law in 1908. Over time, he became a judge and local historian, publishing several articles in the *Southwestern Historical Quarterly* and, from 1939 to 1942, serving as president of the Texas Historical Association. In the 1930s, he wrote an unpublished essay that surveyed the primary and secondary sources on the Angel of Goliad, including Rogers's article.[61] After its publication in the *Dallas Morning News*, Davenport asked Rogers for more information about her research. She stated that she hired "a young man who speaks and reads Spanish well" to search the archives in Mexico City.[62]

Perhaps Davenport could not believe that the woman who saved the lives of several Texas heroes was a mistress rather than a lady of distinction. While he acknowledged the documents Rogers brought forth, he was still inclined to believe that the Angel was not "a pseudo-wife."[63] Both Rogers and Davenport, however, agreed that the Angel of Goliad's "true identity has been lost to posterity."[64]

A month after Rogers's article was published, Zamora O'Shea published the "Sequel to the Angel of Goliad" as a letter to the editor of the *Dallas Morning News*, and she raised a number of issues with the way Rogers (and Davenport) had approached the topic. First, she points out that the reason the Angel's "true identity" and fate have been lost to "posterity" is because Anglo Texans' preoccupation with Santa Anna meant that every other Mexican involved in the secession had been forgotten, with devastating consequences for Anglo-Mexican relations in Texas.[65]

"Sequel to the Angel of Goliad" opens in 1902, when Zamora O'Shea was teaching at the Santa Gertrudis Ranch (King Ranch). She recalls that on Friday afternoons, two older men—one of whom was Matias Alvarez, the son of the Angel of Goliad—would go to the schoolhouse and listen to her read "from Spanish newspapers, or translated stories from the books studied by the children." One particular Friday, Zamora O'Shea read passages about the

Battle of Goliad from Pennybacker's *History of Texas*.[66] Don Matias asked, "Is that all they say about Goliad? . . . They do not say that any one helped those who were hurt, or that any of them were saved?" When Zamora O'Shea responded, "No," Don Matias answered by telling her his family history. His father, Telesforo Alvarez, had an arranged marriage and did not love his wife. He could not divorce or remarry, but the Catholic Church did "accept separation or annulment." Zamora O'Shea recounts, "He and Dono [*sic*] Francisca (Panchita) decided to take life into their own hands and be as happy together as the world would permit them."[67] Living in Matamoros after the war for Texas independence, Alvarez and Panchita had two children, Matias and Dolores. Shortly thereafter, Alvarez abandoned his family.

In the decades that followed, mother and children moved to various ranches in south Texas, eventually settling in Brownsville "so that [Matias] could send his children to school." In 1884, Matias met Richard King, a former friend of Captain Alvarez. He offered Matias work at the Santa Gertrudis Ranch, and when Matias moved his family there, he took his mother, the Angel of Goliad, with him. As a teacher on the King Ranch, Zamora O'Shea taught some of his grandchildren and met the Angel herself. She notes that she felt compelled to write the "Sequel to the Angel of Goliad" after reading Rogers's article "so that the citizens of Texas might know that at the home of the Kings, the Alvarez family had found shelter."[68] After the article was published, Father Joseph G. O'Donohoe, the lead organizer for the Centennial's Catholic exhibit in Dallas, interviewed Zamora O'Shea about her experience and sent a report to Davenport. This report contains many more details that were not in her initial letter to the editor. O'Donohoe's notes state that Panchita, Matias, and his family "were very white, had no Indian blood in them at all," and that the Kings respected her past. She was buried in an unmarked grave on the ranch."[69]

Davenport and Rogers were preoccupied with whether Panchita was an honest married woman or a young mistress, but for Zamora O'Shea, this was irrelevant. Her main point was that the Kings—"the pioneer family of the Southwest"—took her in. They provided her son with work, her grandchildren with an education, and at the end of her life, her body with a final resting place. Undoubtedly, the Kings were central to many historical narratives of the era, especially during the Texas Centennial, and tying them to the fate of the Angel of Goliad emphasized how ethnic Mexican and Anglo Texan histories were intertwined. Additionally, her narrative highlights the role of the bilingual teacher—not the monolingual male historian—whose relationship with the people granted her access to sources not part of the official archive. She was the one who translated the public school curriculum for workers, enabling them to critically engage with the material, and it was their critical engagement that developed a more inclusive narrative. She was the one who could implement the transition from escuelitas to the public schools, creating a space in which the curriculum could be debated, and a more inclusive narrative could be constructed.

For Zamora O'Shea, all of these conclusions were as true at the time she wrote "Sequel to the Angel of Goliad" as they were when she taught on the King Ranch. Just as she was a go-between in 1902, she remained so in 1936, except rather than facilitating cultural exchange and discussion between ethnic Mexican family history and the public school curriculum, she attempted to fill in a gap that neither the archives in Mexico nor the United States could fill. Zamora O'Shea stopped teaching in 1918, when she left south Texas for Dallas with her husband and five-year-old son. Subsequently, her research served as an extension of her professional role as an educator, and she intervened in the construction of historical narratives in myriad ways: by writing letters to the editors of newspapers, publishing her own longer works, giving public talks, and maintaining personal correspondence with professional and amateur historians around the state—a process Leticia Garza-Falcón calls "writing as teaching."[70] When she died in 1951, her son was the informant. He listed her occupation as "school teacher," though he was a young child when she left that profession.[71] That was the narrative surrounding her identity that had been passed down.

EDUCATOR AND HISTORIAN JOVITA GONZÁLEZ: A CASE STUDY IN BECOMING

Another Mexican American female educator and progressive activist who worked to reconcile the escuelita curriculum with that of the public school was Jovita González.[72] Unlike Zamora O'Shea, González spent her entire career as a teacher, intervening in the construction of historical narratives from within the public school system—"writing as teaching" while still teaching. She was born on her family's ranch in Roma, in Starr County, on January 18, 1897, and was baptized in March of that year. She was not born in 1904, as most scholars have believed.[73] The inconsistencies surrounding González's birthdate were of her own making.[74] In the 1930 census, she reported that she was twenty-eight years old, born in 1902, and she used that same birth year in her application for a Rockefeller grant-in-aid in 1934.[75] Shortly after her marriage to E. E. Mireles in 1935, she began using 1904 as her birth year, and she stuck to that date for the rest of her life.[76] Two years after they were married, Mireles submitted a petition to become a naturalized citizen, in which he stated that his wife, Jovita González, had been born January 18, 1904.[77]

While her birth certificate also states that she was born in 1904, she did not file that document until 1951. Since it was filed several decades after her birth, she needed two witnesses to swear under oath that they were there when she was born, and that to the best of their knowledge, the month, day, and year were accurate. Her witnesses were Roque Guerra and Patricia Guerra de Salinas, her cousin and aunt, respectively, on her mother's side.[78] Guerra and Salinas might have been present when González was born, or they might have heard the news very shortly afterward, as these relatives were also neighbors. In 1951, Roque Guerra was about sixty-eight and Patricia Guerra de Salinas was about seventy-eight.[79] It is entirely possible, even likely, that so much time had passed since that January day in 1897 that seven years made no difference at all to Guerra and Salinas. They might even have believed that their cousin and niece Jovita González was born in 1904.

In terms of examining González's trajectory of identity formation, however, seven years makes a dramatic difference. For example, by 1927, González had earned her BA in Spanish from Our Lady of the Lake College in San Antonio, and by 1930, she had completed her thesis and graduated from the University of Texas at Austin with an MA in history. Many scholars have established González as a foundational figure in the field of Mexican American history, largely (but not entirely) due to her thesis.[80] "Social Life in Cameron, Starr, and Zapata Counties" traces the history of south Texas from Spain's earliest colonizers to the Texas Mexican rural classes of the 1920s. Drawing from county courthouse records, archives, and newspapers in Texas and Mexico, and oral histories with border residents, "Social Life" not only examines the profound impact that economic and political transformations had on Anglo-Mexican relations and Texas Mexican identity, but also makes an early feminist contribution to the burgeoning discipline. Paul S. Taylor and González met in 1928 in south Texas while he was conducting research for his book *Mexican Labor in the United States* and she was conducting research for her master's thesis. Of González, who was supposed to be twenty-four at the time, he wrote, "She understands, analyzes, and presents better than any American of Mexican descent whom I know, the significant aspects of the contact of the two peoples [Anglo and Mexican] in the area."[81] Dozens of subsequent scholars were similarly struck by how a twenty-six-year-old—her alleged age when she finished her thesis—could possess such a complex, erudite understanding of ethnic Mexicans' relationship to the social, cultural, and educational shifts taking place on the Texas-Mexico border. González articulated the impact these transformations had on ethnic Mexicans, particularly Mexican American women, with clarity and perspicacity.

Not that González was not a gifted historian and cultural critic—because she certainly was—and not that scholars in their twenties are incapable of conducting meticulous research and writing discerning prose—because they can—but she wrote her thesis in an era when there were not any secondary sources on Mexican American history to consult. In the late 1920s, Castañeda had only begun to build the García Collection, and in this capacity, he connected her with relevant source material, but on the whole, archival repositories could offer little help. It was an era when many ethnic Mexicans were still trying to make sense of the larger changes that had such a direct impact on their daily lives. "Social Life in Cameron, Starr, and Zapata Counties" was written not by a twenty-six-year-old, but by a thirty-three-year-old who had already accumulated a wealth of experience in the ethnic Mexican social and cultural world before deciding to pursue her professional ambitions in the United States as a Mexican American.

In 1910, González and her family left their ranch, called Las Víboras, for San Antonio because, as she states in her short autobiography, "as a poor man, my father felt that the only heritage he could leave his children was an education."[82] Specifically, her parents wanted González and her younger sister, Gertrudis (Tula), to receive an English education; all the González children, including Jovita, had received Spanish instruction in an escuelita at the ranch. In 1900, for example, González's older sister Hortencia was six. Though Hortencia attended school and could read and write, she could not speak English, and neither could her mother and siblings. González's father, Jacobo, a teacher, was the only family member who spoke English, and as a bilingual patriarch, he oversaw the creation of an escuelita on the family's property. González notes that as more ranchers moved to the area where her family lived, the growing community looked for a teacher to provide a "Mexican education for their boys." "That man was my father," she states. Girls were not permitted to attend this school.[83] After the family moved to San Antonio, Jacobo became a member of Hijos de México (Sons of Mexico), a patriotic organization that collaborated with the Mexican Consulate to aid in the well-being of Mexican citizens living in the United States.[84] He briefly worked as a clerk before finding work as a Spanish teacher, an occupation he maintained at various places in San Antonio until his death in 1930.[85]

González attended San Antonio High School, and in the fall semester of 1914, she became a founding member and officer of the Spanish club.[86] She graduated in May 1915 at the age of eighteen, one of 144 graduates that spring.[87] By the end of that summer, she had earned her teaching certificate and accepted a position at a public school in Seguin.[88] The following year, she moved to Moore, in Frio County, where she spent two years teaching in a public school.[89] A couple of months into the fall semester of 1916, she founded La Asociación Guillermo Prieto, an organization that sought to ensure the "instruction and advancement of the Mexican children of Moore," as *La Prensa* reported.[90] It is unclear whether the association was supposed to help students succeed in the public school or provide them with Spanish-language instruction, but as *La Prensa* congratulated González "for her commitment to propagate education among the Mexican children," it seems more likely the organization promoted Spanish-language literacy.[91]

Of the twenty-four members of La Asociación Guillermo Prieto, she was the only teacher, so her knowledge and experience must have played a central role in an organization dedicated to education.[92] And in the public elementary school at Moore, she was the only Mexican American teacher. *La Prensa* reported that she had the titles of Spanish teacher and director of the Mexican Department, and in this capacity she helped organize an end-of-the-year "fiesta escolar" (school party) in the public school.[93] Students performed public recitations of poetry, dialogues, and plays, much as they would in El Colegio Altamirano in Hebbronville or any other escuelita in south Texas.

González's experience in an escuelita, as well as her teaching experience in Moore, provides more depth to certain passages of her thesis. In "Social Life in Cameron, Starr, and Zapata County," González wrote about several escuelitas, noting that they "followed a course of study superior to that offered by the public schools."[94] She states:

> An oral, annual public examination was held at the close of the scholastic year. A Board of Examiners known as the *réplicas* composed of the leading Mexican citizens decided whether the children passed or failed the year's work. During the examination, which lasted from two to five days, the children were examined in all the subjects studied. . . . The hall was decorated with Mexican flags, laurel wreaths, and pictures of Mexico's heroes hung from the wall. . . . Mothers whispered to their little ones the meaning of it, and told them of a country that had once been theirs, but had been snatched away by American greed.[95]

The escuelitas exposed children to a counternarrative about the US-Mexico War, one that never would have been taught in a public school— that Texas had once been part of Mexico, and it was taken as a result of

"American greed." Despite the difficult history of losing their land, the escuelitas enabled ethnic Mexicans to revel in the educational achievements of
their children and be surrounded by symbols of Mexican sovereignty in the
face of racial, cultural, and linguistic hostility. González provides a great deal
of detail about the structure of escuelitas and the way parents and children
engaged with the curriculum—but without citing any sources.[96] These passages in her thesis were drawn from her extensive firsthand knowledge and
experience in these little schools, and from her experience of being a young
teacher in rural Texas who, early in her public school teaching career, drew
from escuelita pedagogical practices.

As González gained more teaching experience, her pedagogical approach shifted, particularly after she took a position in 1926 as a Spanish
teacher at Saint Mary's Hall, an all-girls private school in San Antonio.[97] No
longer was she so heavy-handedly drawing from escuelita traditions. Rather,
she began creating her own bicultural approach to teaching, and her thesis
provides insight into the impetus for this bicultural transformation. In her
final chapter, "What the Coming of Americans Has Meant to the Border
People," she quotes an extended statement from a "young married man" from
Edinburg in Hidalgo County:

> The fact that we received an entirely Mexican education, I am
> a product of the Colegio Altamirano in Hebbronville, made it
> difficult for us to understand American ideals. And it is our place
> and our duty now to learn American ways, to send our children to
> American schools, to learn the English language, not that we are
> ashamed of our Mexican descent, but because these things will
> enable us to demand our rights and to improve ourselves. . . . My
> children are to receive a public education here, and when they
> graduate, I shall send them to Mexico for at least two years in
> order that they may perfect themselves in the Spanish language
> and that they may know Mexico as Mexico is.[98]

While he implies that escuelitas helped invoke pride in students' Mexican ancestral past, he also articulates that they inhibited the ability to pursue
not only socioeconomic mobility, but also rights as American citizens. Education was at the center of uncovering the political and cultural identities
of Texas Mexicans. But since there was not a curriculum that reconciled the
two languages and histories, the young man advocated sending his children
to two different schools in two different countries. Equally important, these
bicultural identities developed with consequences. He continued:

We are going now through a very painful period of transition and
like the white black bird do not know yet just what we are. Mexicans from across the river look down upon us and call us by what
to them is the vilest epithet, *Texanos* and the Americans do not
consider us as such, although some of our Texas-Mexican families
have lived here for generations. For years we have been part of a
big political machine, our vote has not been individual, but now
that we are becoming conscious of the meaning of citizenship we
want to exert our privileges as individuals. Our labor is arduous,
the future welfare of the Texas-Mexican depends on what will be
accomplished during this generation.[99]

Texas Mexicans were going through a period of self-realization that
had significant implications for their relationship to Mexicans and Mexico,
as well as to the US political system and the Texas political machine. Ethnic
Mexican children, with their exposure to both educational traditions, were
better prepared to understand and confront the dramatic changes that
their parents were enduring by 1930. González reinforces the salient role
bicultural identities and education would have in mitigating the social and
political struggles brought about by economic transformations:

Young Texas-Mexicans are being educated. Behind them lies a
store of traditions of another race, customs of past ages, an innate
and inherited love and reverence for another country. Ahead of
them lies a struggle of which they are to be the champions. It
is a struggle for equality and justice before the law, for the just
demands of full-fledged American citizens. They bring with them
a broader view, a clearer understanding of the good and bad
qualities of both races. They are the converging elements of two
antagonistic civilizations; they have the blood of one and have
acquired the ideals of the other. They, let it be hoped, will bring to
an end the racial feuds that have existed in the border for nearly
a century.[100]

While Texas Mexicans demanded their rights as citizens and as individuals, their bicultural, bilingual, and bi-educational experiences would
also be working toward a solution for the racial animosity prevalent on the
Texas-Mexico border. González's objective was not only to document how
economic changes impacted the ethnic Mexican social and cultural world,
but also to understand how ethnic Mexicans could use those changes to

attain socioeconomic mobility while claiming their civil rights. "The old type caballero is now an American business man and the girl who lived in conventual seclusion has become the modern college girl," she wrote in her 1934 application for a grant-in-aid from the Rockefeller Foundation.[101] She must have seen the escuelitas vanishing too, as she, the college girl from Roma, sought to establish herself as a historian and cultural critic while earning a living as a teacher.

The political and economic shifts that she examined in her work in many ways framed the transformations in her teaching methods. While there was no longer a direct connection between the escuelitas' end-of-the-year celebrations and that of her classes, as there was in her early days as an educator in Moore, ideas about Texas history and folklore from a Mexican American perspective remained ingrained in her approach to pedagogy, and she directly involved her students in her own research. In 1929, while enrolled as a master's student at the University of Texas and still a teacher at Saint Mary's Hall, she was the faculty sponsor for the school's new Spanish club. The student organization called itself Margil, named after "Padre Margil, who came from Spain and started the first missionary work in the Southwest."[102] Apparent in her work with the Saint Mary's Hall Spanish Club is González's view that Texas history began with Spain, and that studying the Spanish language required studying the history of Spanish colonization, Spanish arts and culture, and current events in Spanish-speaking countries.[103] Additionally, González collected folk songs from Las Víboras, her family's ranch in Roma, as well as from other areas of south Texas, and taught them to her Spanish students. In April 1934, John A. Lomax visited Saint Mary's Hall to record González and five of her students singing the songs that she collected. This scene, photographed by Lomax's son Alan, manifests a transitional moment in González's pedagogy.[104] She no longer focused on Mexican-centric organizations that advocated for a Spanish-language education. Rather, she created a course of study heavily based on her research that reconciled the escuelita and American educational traditions. With this new bicultural and bilingual curriculum, Mexican Americans would not have to send their children to two different schools.

As González constructed the revolutionary curriculum that enabled her students to perform for the Lomaxes, she was in the midst of seeking grant money to pursue her research. From March to May 1934, she submitted her application materials for a grant-in-aid from the Rockefeller Foundation. "My people are being transformed," she wrote in her grant proposal. "The rapid disappearance of what for nearly two hundred years formed a border culture has made me want to recapture for posterity, the value, the beauty,

Jovita González (far right) with a group of her Saint Mary's Hall students singing Mexican folk songs for John Lomax. PHOTOGRAPH BY ALAN LOMAX, APRIL 1934. LOMAX COLLECTION, AMERICAN FOLKLIFE CENTER, LIBRARY OF CONGRESS.

and the poetry of what used to be."[105] González received a $2,000 grant, which was part of a larger proposal on "folklore of the border people" that J. Frank Dobie, an English professor at the University of Texas at Austin, submitted to David H. Stevens, the director of the Rockefeller Foundation Humanities Division. Dobie's project proposal stated, according to Stevens's office diary, that he, González, and J. Evetts Haley—all experienced field researchers—would collect material on the topic for their own "individual programs," while capturing the vaquero's "rich tradition fast vanishing under Americanization drives."[106] Referring to González's separate letter of application, Stevens noted her "intent to write a literary-social record combining the folklore and cultural history of her own Spanish-American group."[107]

Dobie integrated his recommendations for González and Haley into his own proposal. He briefly recounted his first meeting with her when she presented her paper "Folklore of the Texas Mexican Vaquero" at the 1927 Texas Folklore Society conference. Dobie wrote, "The freshness and charm of this paper captivated us all." After listing her academic credentials and goals for her project, he noted that she had been "held down by a financially dependent family" and wrote, "She is a woman of charm as well as of bright intelligence. I doubt if she will go as far as Haley will go, but it seems a pity that she can not have here [a] chance to achieve at least a part of the work that she wants to do and that is worth doing."[108] Despite Dobie's ambivalence about González's potential success, Stevens decided the Rockefeller Foundation would allocate $8,000–$10,000 to the University of Texas for the collaborative project. Haley and González would work "under Dobie's direction."[109] González's $2,000 went to Saint Mary's Hall in quarterly payments, which released her from a year of teaching. In May 1935, just as her Rockefeller grant was about to end, she wrote Stevens asking for another six months to revise her already 300-page manuscript, which she was calling *Dew on the Thorn*. The extensive editing that remained was where "the real artistic creation begins," she stated in her letter. John Marshall of the Rockefeller Foundation denied her request.[110]

About six weeks after she received Marshall's denial letter, *La Prensa* announced her engagement to E. E. Mireles. Following their wedding at the end of July, they moved to Del Río, where Mireles worked as an educator and night school administrator. González left Saint Mary's Hall behind and joined Mireles as a public school teacher in the San Felipe Independent School District.[111] She and Mireles lost their jobs three years later, in 1938, and González spent a year seeking other opportunities to further her education. She must have been aware that only a small cadre of Mexican Americans had attained PhDs by the late 1930s, all of them men: among them Aurelio M. Espinosa (Stanford), Arthur Campa (University of New Mexico), Carlos Castañeda (University of Texas), and George I. Sánchez (University of Texas). Though her status as a Mexican American woman with a master's degree also made her part of a select group, she struggled to move into an even more elite category—that of Mexican American women with PhDs. In fact, had she achieved her goal, she would have been the only one.[112]

It is likely that in 1938 González believed she had already started work toward a doctorate in folklore. Her academic credentials listed in the Saint Mary's Hall yearbook, *La Reata*, changed in 1934 after she received the Rockefeller Foundation's grant-in-aid. Whereas previous bios listed her BA and MA degrees, in 1934 and 1935 they included "PhD work University of Texas, Universidad Na[c]ional de Mexico."[113] As there is no record of González as a doctoral student at the University of Texas, she must have been referring to her Rockefeller Foundation–funded research.[114]

From fall 1938 to spring 1939, she tried to continue with her doctoral work, applying to PhD programs at Stanford, the University of California at Berkeley, and the University of New Mexico, and writing letters to those she knew who had connections with noted professors of folklore.[115] When nothing came of her efforts, she tried to establish herself as a public intellectual in San Antonio, writing to Carlos Castañeda to see if he would recommend her to San Antonio Mayor Maury Maverick for an appointment to the La Villita Restoration Committee, a WPA-funded project of which Maverick was the head. Castañeda did, indeed, write to Maverick, calling González "eminently qualified" as "a nation wide authority on Texas Folklore." He also offered his own services as an advisor on the project.[116] Maverick stated that he might be able to hire González, but more importantly, in a handwritten note at the bottom of the page, he asked that Castañeda and Charles W. Hackett, a University of Texas professor of Latin American history, serve as advisers—at the Rockefeller Foundation's request.[117] González never did work for the La Villita Restoration Committee, but Castañeda and Hackett did.[118]

After González's efforts to enter a doctoral program and work as a public historian failed, González and Mireles moved to Corpus Christi, where they accepted positions as educators in the local public school system. González continued to work on her manuscripts, *Dew on the Thorn* and *Caballero*, a historical romance set in the nineteenth century that she cowrote with Eve Raleigh, but never made any progress in getting them published.[119] Teaching had always been a site of negotiation for women's inclusion in the larger Mexican American civil rights movement—particularly in the campaign to integrate the curriculum—and the significance of this profession intensified after her relocation to Corpus Christi. Her pedagogy and revisionist scholarship had been intersecting for over a decade before she settled in Nueces County, but the culmination of these intersections occurred when she turned to writing instructional material for children, *Mi Libro Español: Libros 1–3* and *El Español Elemental: Libros 1–6*. Children's literature offered González an outlet for sharing her research on Texas history, the Spanish and English languages, and ethnic Mexican culture when no other opportunities were available.

Mi Libro Español and *El Español Elemental* were her only new publications after 1940, an era when Good Neighbor policies at the national and state levels were influencing public sentiment about the teaching of Spanish in Texas public schools.[120] When Mireles and González began their Spanish program in Corpus Christi in 1940, it was still illegal to teach Spanish in public schools in Texas, the only exception being schools located on the Texas-Mexico border. The Corpus Christi Independent School District received special approval from the state before the 1940 school year began. The program was so successful, however, that in March 1941, the Texas legislature approved a bill that gave any public school in Texas the right to institute one.[121] Other schools throughout the state, as well as some in Louisiana and New Mexico, also adopted Corpus Christi's Spanish curriculum and textbooks.[122]

González coauthored the first two books of the *Mi Libro Español* series with Mireles and R. B. Fisher, the superintendent of the Corpus Christi public school system from 1938 to 1940. Books 1 and 2 were published in 1941, and book 3, coauthored by González and Mireles after Fisher died, was published in 1943; the couple also coauthored all six books for the 1949 *El Español Elemental* series. Though each of them played some role in the production of each text, archival evidence indicates that González completed much of the historical and cultural writing for both series.[123]

These Spanish-language textbooks focused on Anglo-Mexican historical collaboration, drawing inspiration from the Pan American movement. Pan Americanism argued, as one historian notes, that America and Latin America's "shared common origins in Western Christian culture and civilization" meant that any social, cultural, and political differences were not manifestations of inferiority or superiority. The corollary of a shared past was a shared future.[124] While Pan Americanism played a salient role in González's work of the 1940s, its origins in Texas went back to the Progressive Era, when Florence Terry Griswold founded the Pan American Round Table in San Antonio in 1916. The organization believed that women—unlike men, who were weighed down by the impersonal interactions of business and politics—were in a unique position to foster friendly relationships based on cooperation and understanding. The main objectives for the Pan American Round Table were to improve relations between Mexico and the United States and to help women and children who were refugees of the Mexican Revolution. By 1921, there was the Pan American Round Tables of Texas, and by 1944, shortly after González and Mireles published the third book of the *Mi Libro Español* series, the existing Round Table chapters throughout Texas and Latin America formed the Alliance of Pan American Round Tables.[125]

Pan Americanism directly impacted how Mireles and González structured the Spanish program's curriculum, which encouraged all children, regardless of race, to learn about Latin American language, culture, and history, and helped them understand that it was their language, culture, and history too. Pan Americanism, as these texts construct it, was rooted in the notion of a universal childhood, which became a vehicle for both normalizing and perpetuating Pan Americanism. It established childhood as a time when harsh realities such as racism do not exist because children do not see the constructed divisions that cut across adult experiences, such as race, ethnicity, class, and nationality; rather, children see age only as a uniting factor. Since childhood was the only defining characteristic for children's lived experiences, young students needed to be bilingual so they could participate in the unifying factor that their age brought, allowing them to interact with other children across racial, ethnic, class, and national lines.

González and Mireles constructed a curriculum with positive implications for contemporary race relations because, as the texts note, the historical links between Mexicans and Anglos go much further back, to the days of the Spanish explorers. Texas Mexicans descend from the Spanish, a population that played a dominating role in Texas history for a very long time. In fact, Anglos did not begin moving to Texas until three centuries after the first Spaniard—the first White man—explored Texas. As the texts explain, since Anglo Americans and Texas Mexicans are both descended from Europeans, these cultures should view each other as equals and friends rather than as adversaries.

Every passage about a Tejano emphasizes the salient role he played in Texas history, and every passage about an Anglo highlights the ways in which that particular Anglo engaged with and appreciated Latin American culture—an appreciation ingrained in the earliest days of North America's two great countries, the Republic of Texas and the United States of America. Lorenzo de Zavala, a revolutionary and hero of Texas, designed the Texas flag and his wife sewed it, emphasizing the defining role that they played in creating an iconic symbol of Texas's past and present.[126] Stephen F. Austin spoke and wrote in Spanish fluently, writing all correspondence to the Mexican government in Spanish and signing his name "Esteban."[127] Jorge Wáshington was a great admirer of Latin American countries, inviting Francisco de Miranda, a Venezuelan revolutionary, to New York.[128] And James Bowie, after saving the life of the governor of Coahuila y Tejas, married his daughter Úrsula Veramendi.[129] Through these readings, González sought to introduce Corpus Christi students to an entirely new interpretation of Texas history, one that would improve relations between Anglos and Mexicans rather than exacerbating them.

In the first half of the 1940s, Texas schools bought thousands of copies of *Mi Libro Español*, yielding a royalty check for $1,237.71 in 1943. But by 1949, W. S. Benson, the publisher, found it difficult to maintain this level of sales, writing to Mireles, "There seems to be greater resistance than formerly to teaching elementary Spanish, the superintendents claiming there is no time for it, or they don't have qualified teachers."[130] Despite the waning popularity of the Spanish readers, González continued teaching Spanish and Texas history in Corpus Christi until her retirement in the early 1960s. In her almost fifty years as an educator, González's pedagogical approach went through multiple transformations. In her early days teaching in Moore, she drew from the escuelitas in obvious ways, founding a coalition to support ethnic Mexican children's education and ending the semester in escuelita fashion. She walked away from these explicitly escuelita-inspired tactics when she began teaching at Saint Mary's Hall. By 1940, her approach to teaching was firmly rooted in the structure of the public school system. What was consistent throughout her almost fifty-year career was her commitment to building on the escuelita curriculum, developing it for a Mexican American and Anglo-Texan student body.

The escuelita movement had declined sharply by 1940, and while these little schools certainly still existed throughout south Texas for decades afterward, their diminished numbers manifested the changing needs of ethnic Mexicans in Texas. Examining Zamora O'Shea's and González's educational and professional trajectories through the lens of escuelita history illustrates just how closely tied those changing needs were to the rise and fall of those little schools. Whereas escuelitas implied divisions in the first three decades of the twentieth century, their Spanish-language course of study, when integrated in the public school curriculum, indicated an advancement in the campaign for educational equality and reconciled two disparate educational traditions in Texas. Zamora O'Shea and González, while hindered by patriarchal attitudes of male Mexican American leaders, used their roles as teachers to negotiate their own participation in the civil rights movement as intellectuals and activists, and normalize an integrated curriculum that promoted harmony and unity in past and present Anglo-Mexican relationships.

ESCUELITAS AND THE TEACHING OF ENGLISH

Zamora O'Shea and González, as teachers, activists, and intellectuals, were part of a much larger Mexican American campaign for educational equality that borrowed heavily from the escuelita tradition in two ways. First, as discussed at length above, they incorporated new historical sources and interpretations into the Anglocentric narrative of the public school system and public discourse—sources that escuelitas had been drawing from to construct their revisionist interpretations for decades. This progressive approach, which González and Zamora O'Shea both used, tended to provoke questions about the politicization of history, making the curriculum and public discourse contested spaces that sparked ire in those who used Anglocentric interpretations of the Alamo and Santa Anna to justify tense race relations in the present. The second approach emerged in the 1950s, and rather than drawing from the curriculum and content of the escuelitas, it borrowed from the structure itself, creating informal little schools that functioned outside the nine-month school year to teach Mexican American children English. This approach, much more conservative in nature, tended to appease many White public officials, who endorsed the idea that teaching Mexican American children English before they entered first grade would solve their troubled relationship with education.

Hector P. García, a World War II veteran and founder of the American GI Forum, was a practicing doctor in Corpus Christi. He grew up in Mercedes, and as a child he attended an escuelita that his aunt maintained for decades, and experienced firsthand the effectiveness of the escuelita model in early childhood education.[131] In 1954, he had an idea to create, as George I. Sánchez wrote, "summer kindergartens for children who do not speak English."[132] García and Sánchez were both passionate advocates of educational equality for Mexican American children, and García often turned to Sánchez for help and advice. Sánchez, a professor of education at the University of Texas from the early 1940s to the early 1970s, spent his career researching the how and why of public school segregation, as well as the detrimental effects of the discriminatory practice on children. He adamantly opposed segregation in any form.

In 1942, over a decade before he heard about García's idea to create an English-language summer school, he summarized some of his research findings to the Mexican Consul General in San Antonio, who inquired about the language justification for separation: Was segregation justified if Mexican children could not speak English? Sánchez outlined three significant points regarding the segregation of Mexican American children. First, while a lack of English literacy was often the reason given for segregation, no schools ever conducted assessments to find out how much English the children knew. Second, the real basis for segregation was "their Spanish name, their appearance, their parentage, and economic status, etc."[133] Finally, he argued that children's lack of English literacy was no basis for segregation in the first place. He contended, "'English' is not synonymous with education and deficiency in English is not necessarily indicative of deficiency in the other vital elements in the school's program. In other words, segregation as now practiced in some school systems is not only pedagogically unsound but also prejudiced and contrary to the principles of education in a democracy."[134] Sánchez was an "integration purist," to use Carlos K. Blanton's phrase.[135] He even advocated abolishing the Spanish Parent-Teacher Association, telling M. C. González, the newly elected state chairman of the Spanish-Speaking PTA, "The fact that [these families] speak Spanish is not sufficient reason to isolate them from the many benefits which accrue from joint action and from relationships and goals which have nothing to do with language."[136] It would be more beneficial, Sánchez argued, to do away with the PTA altogether than to have a segregated one.

As an integration purist, then, Sánchez interpreted García's idea to open a summer kindergarten for Mexican American children as a plan of action that validated the decades-long rhetoric that segregation was a necessary element of pedagogy, rather than racial discrimination. Sánchez counseled García:

> It would be a bad strategy for us to concede that our children are so incapable of doing normal work when they enter the first grade that they need a pre-First kind of training. If we did this we would be endorsing the very principle upon which some schools set up a separate (segregated) first grade . . . our children can do the work of the first grade substantially as well as Anglo children, even when our children start off without knowing English.[137]

Pedagogical segregation was a cloak for race-based discrimination, an argument Sánchez's research proved unequivocally.[138] Creating a program that separated Mexican American children to teach them English legitimized the notion that pedagogical segregation was not only a valid approach to education, but also a necessity—when it was never the real reason for segregation in the first place. Sánchez actively endorsed revising the public school curriculum to include Latino history and cultural studies in the larger narrative, editing a four-volume Inter-American series for students in grades three through six, published by Macmillan.[139] But he despised using the escuelita model to teach children English.

Not all Mexican American activists thought the two approaches were incompatible ideologically. E. E. Mireles, Jovita González's husband and co-author of *Mi Libro Español* and *El Español Elemental*, founded the Corpus Christi Independent School District's Spanish program in 1940 and oversaw it for multiple decades. In 1956, two years after Sánchez strongly advised García to abandon any attempt to begin an English-language summer school, Mireles founded one that taught Mexican American children 500 English words and 120 common expressions before beginning the first grade. That summer, 150 students from three different elementary schools enrolled in Mireles's preschool program, and by the summer of 1959, the school board had nearly doubled the funding for the program, which admitted 593 students from eleven different schools.[140] Mireles did not find his work running the Spanish program and the English program philosophically contradictory because of his abhorrence of Tex Mex and the widespread use of this code-switching in south Texas. Whereas Sánchez believed that a separate English-language kindergarten for Mexican American children validated the deceitful rhetoric surrounding pedagogical segregation and ignored racism and discrimination, Mireles believed that the prevalence of Tex Mex was evidence that Mexican American children in south Texas could not speak either language properly, and that the absence of these language skills reflected poorly on them not only in the United States, but also in Mexico.

In 1952, Mireles received a master's degree in Spanish at the Instituto Tecnológico y de Estudios Superiores de Monterrey. His thesis focused on the Spanish program in the Corpus Christi district, and the second chapter identified the "Tex Mex dialect" and "Discrimination" as the two most significant obstacles he and other administrators faced. According to Mireles, eliminating Tex Mex was one of the Spanish program's priorities, as it was a chronic problem children learned from their parents that hindered a "good sound way of life." Mireles explained what he believed were the origins of the "bad practice," stating:

> Since the Spanish-Speaking people in Texas were more or less isolated from Mexico after Texas independence, they began to drift away from normal development under the Latin culture and their language became stagnant. As a result of this stagnation and slow development, archaic expressions in Spanish were kept in Texas whereas they were discarded in Mexico. . . . Many of these words are not understood by educated Spanish-Speaking people and if understood, do not create the right impression.[141]

According to Mireles, Spanish spoken in Mexico evolved into a modern language, but Spanish spoken in Texas remained undeveloped, becoming a signifier of the uneducated Texas Mexican masses. Linguist John M. Lipski contends that the "varieties of Spanish included in the Mexican American category have never been cut off from Mexico" and therefore "the Spanish of Mexican Americans is not monolithic, but covers a broad range of social and regional variants, reflective of the immense linguistic diversity of Mexico itself."[142] While there are rustic variants in "Mexican American Spanish" (a phrase Lipski uses instead of Tex Mex or Spanglish), they are not a defining characteristic. Lipski notes that these pessimistic views manifest purists' and xenophobes' discriminatory perceptions of the "underclasses," and argues that "the true nature of the Spanish-English interface must be sought from an additive rather than a subtractive viewpoint."[143] "[C]ode switching is neither 'confusion' nor a hopeless tangle of two languages," he continues, "but rather a deliberately chosen strategy . . . a natural result of fluent bilingualism."[144] The emergence and proliferation of Mexican American Spanish was one of many strategies ethnic Mexicans used to negotiate their lives in the United States. And Mireles's own views, and the work he did in support of those views, were his own strategy.

Mireles's discussion of discrimination was far less severe, stating, "Everywhere in the school system one hears nothing but praise for the Latin children and how marvelous progress has been made in their education and how they are moving towards their proper place of equal opportunities in their community."[145] By the early 1950s, racial discrimination, Mireles contended, no longer impeded the potential for Mexican American educational advancement, but Tex Mex continued to stifle intellectual development.

Felix Tijerina, the most prominent figure to appropriate the escuelita model, also believed that it was not discrimination that led to high dropout rates for Mexican Americans, but a lack of English-language skills.[146] Whereas Mireles highlighted Tex Mex as the main culprit, Tijerina focused on a lack of English proficiency generally, a stance that helped him gain allies in the Texas legislature and among high-ranking businessmen. Unlike progressive activists such as Jovita González, Zamora O'Shea, Sánchez, or Castañeda, Tijerina was far less concerned with revising the curriculum than he was with helping Mexican American children linguistically prepare to enter the first grade.

Elected to four terms as LULAC president, from 1956 to 1960, Tijerina embodied the rags-to-riches trajectory at the center of the American Dream. Though he fought allegations of his foreign birth for years, all evidence indicates that he was born in Nuevo León, Mexico, and his family moved to Houston in 1915 to get away from the violence of the Mexican Revolution.[147] At the age of nine, when the family still lived in Mexico, his father died, and he, his mother, and his siblings lived in "deplorable conditions and near starvation," as his uncle described it.[148] After immigrating to south Texas, he found a job picking cotton to help support his family, and within a few years, the Tijerina clan moved to Houston, where he worked as a busboy in a Mexican restaurant. Eventually, Tijerina learned English and opened his own restaurant, becoming a wealthy business owner.

Tijerina identified his inability to speak English as his biggest obstacle–not poverty, discrimination, or the revolution that dislocated his family.[149] Though he focused much of his first term as LULAC president on expanding the organization outside the Southwest region, he spent much of his three subsequent terms focused on education—most notably the 1957 founding of the Little Schools of the 400, a preschool program focused on teaching Mexican American children 400 English words before they entered first grade. Initially envisioning his English-instructional project as a radio program called *Escuelita del Aire* (Little School of the Airwaves), Tijerina changed his mind when he met Isabel Verver, a seventeen-year-old sophomore in high school who hoped to become a teacher. Verver convinced him to change the format of the lessons from a radio show to a classroom setting, and to let her teach the classes, recruit the first group of students, and find a location to begin that summer. Elizabeth Burrus, a teacher in Baytown who had extensive experience teaching Spanish-language children, put together a curriculum that identified between 400 and 500 words that every first-grader should know. She also outlined an approach that emphasized conversation over reading, and active learning over rote memorization.[150]

Verver began her little school with four pupils, and just as escuelita students had to undergo their examinations, recitations, and musical performances publicly, so too did Verver's students at the end of their first week. She had her students give a public demonstration of the English-language skills they already had attained. By the end of the second week of that first summer session, she had forty-five students.[151] The Little Schools of the 400 expanded from Houston but never grew beyond nine schools throughout Texas. Tijerina, while receiving moral support from LULAC, as well as from the state legislature, never received any funding. He paid for most of the program out of his own pocket, paying Verver twenty-five dollars a week that first summer in 1957.

Early on, when he first began the program, Tijerina met with a number of political figures and informed them of his pilot project, including state senator Henry B. González, state representative Oscar Laurel, the Texas Good Neighbor Commission, Texas Department of Public Safety, the Railroad Commission, the Texas Health Commission, the Texas Commission of Education, and Governor Price Daniel.[152] Daniel, impressed with

Tijerina's ideas about how to fix the Mexican American "problem"—broadly defined—appointed him to the Hale-Aiken Committee, which was working on a proposal to reform Texas education laws. The following year, Tijerina organized a one-year-anniversary celebration of the Little Schools of the 400 and made Governor Daniel the guest of honor.[153] Multiple newspapers and radio stations in Houston covered the event, making note of the governor's speech, in which he took charge of LULAC's institutional history while still drawing from revisionist history to emphasize consensus. He began with the contention that the purpose of LULAC was "to promote better relations between Spanish-speaking and English-speaking people in the United States. LULAC was organized," he continued, "to uphold and defend the rights of all Americans."[154] He never mentioned LULAC's commitment to combating racism and discrimination for Latin American citizens or its history of initiating desegregation cases before and after *Brown v. Board of Education*.

For Daniel, providing an inaccurate history of LULAC—aggrandizing its origin story as one that prioritized harmony with Anglos above all else—was not enough to justify the state's support for the Little Schools of the 400. He turned to Texas history to validate Tijerina's project, stating,

> Texas has an important investment in its citizens of Mexican descent. This state owes much to them. It is an often forgotten fact in history that Mexicans fought side by side with Anglos in the Texas War for Independence 122 years ago. They died together at the Alamo. They shared the victory at San Jacinto. Twenty-four men of Mexican descent were among Sam Houston's heroes at San Jacinto.[155]

Though not Daniel's intention, his speech manifests the level of success the Mexican American civil rights activists who rewrote the historical narrative during the Texas centennial twenty years earlier experienced. Though Daniel acknowledged that the Mexican contribution to Texas independence remained "forgotten," he also maintained that because of that contribution, they were deserving of Texas' "investment." While activists concerned with integrating the narrative still had much work ahead of them—Chicano students of the late 1960s would cite the Anglocentric narrative as one of their grievances—by the late 1950s, their revisionist narrative influenced the perspective of the governor of Texas, who used it to justify his support for Tijerina's initiative.

The revisionist narrative, however, was not part of the way LULAC promoted the pilot project. In 1957, Tijerina and some of his closest LULAC supporters founded the LULAC Educational Fund, a nonprofit corporation to oversee and raise money to support the Little Schools of the 400.[156] Its board of directors included Tijerina; J. W. Edgar, the commissioner of education; J. O. Webb, the assistant superintendent for Houston public schools; and two attorneys and one district judge. It also included prominent businessmen, including an executive from the Humble Oil Company and the president of a radio station. A pamphlet circa 1958, mailed to LULAC members to solicit donations, outlined the progress and future goals of the preschool program. It included multiple photographs of children at their desks with their hands enthusiastically raised straight in the air. The caption under one of the photos reads, "These are but a few of the thousands of children who, with your help, can become worthwhile citizens of our great State."[157] The final text of the pamphlet argues, "Latin-American children can, with better education, become important factors in the economic and cultural growth of our State . . . become better citizens, better neighbors, or become an economic burden to the community."[158] These promotional materials, as well as Tijerina's correspondence with supporters, imply that previous generations of Latin American children evolved into adults who strained the economy, lacked understanding of civic responsibility, and with no education and no other options, turned to a life of crime. The state of Mexican American communities of south Texas, Tijerina suggested, reflected this trajectory, with the central factor in this kid-to-criminal pipeline being their inability to speak English when they began first grade.

In 1958, Tijerina presented the success and cost-saving benefits of the program to the Hale-Aiken Committee and the LULAC Educational Fund board of directors, stating that school authorities "noticed the great difference between a child that received the 400 Basic Word Vocabulary and one that did not."[159] The committee unanimously supported the project and committed itself to presenting the program to the state legislature the following year. HB 51, the corollary of the Hale-Aiken Committee's proposal to the state legislature, created a state-funded preschool program for non-English-speaking children ready to begin the first grade.[160] The state legislature fully supported Tijerina's pilot project, and the Preschool Instructional Act stipulated that any district with at least fifteen eligible students could open their English-instructional summer preschool, with the expenses covered by the state and district. The first state-sponsored schools opened in the summer of 1960. Though LULAC was no longer responsible for raising funds to support the program, it continued to solicit donations to fund a public relations campaign to raise awareness of the state-sponsored preschools.[161]

The Preschool Instructional Program garnered much attention in the

Josephine Falcón and students, Fort Stockton, Texas. Preschool Instructional Program, no date. FELIX TIJERINA COLLECTION, MSS 108-178, HOUSTON METROPOLITAN RESEARCH CENTER, HOUSTON PUBLIC LIBRARY.

national press. In July 1961, *Coronet Magazine* published the article "Now Juanito Can Read," which extolled the benefits of teaching 400 English words to Spanish-speaking youngsters. Tijerina sent copies of the article to his contacts in public service across the state and the nation. Egon R. Tausch, the executive director of the Texas Council on Migrant Labor, wrote that he hoped "more parents among our migrant farm workers could be brought to realize the desirability of leaving their children at home to attend the preschool English classes."[162] He noted that the work Tijerina and his LULAC supporters had completed thus far had reduced immeasurably "the apathy among the parents toward their children's education."[163] Reminiscent of the Texas superintendents of the late nineteenth century who equated ethnic Mexican poverty with indifference to education, Tausch and other supporters of the program attributed migrant families' need for their children's labor as a lack of concern for their future.

The month after the publication of the *Coronet* article, the *Saturday Evening Post* covered the story with "Texas Helps Her Little Latins," which noted that despite teachers' dedication, "at least 70 per cent of the children will not be promoted at the end of the term. Many of them eventually will have to repeat second and third and fourth grade too. Their schooling will be a limping experience, with failure their usual reward."[164] Additionally, the article gave its national readership a brief history of LULAC: an organization with 12,000 members, founded for the purpose of "promoting good relations between the Latins and Anglos." At the top of LULAC's priorities, the article stated, was to "help migrant farm families locate homes, find jobs for Latins, interpret for them when they get in trouble and, if necessary, provide bail money."[165] The narrative that Tijerina and the LULAC Educational Fund outlined at the beginning of the Little Schools of the 400's founding reached a national audience of political figures as well as the general public that was eager to accept the trajectory of the kid-to-criminal pipeline as an accurate depiction of Mexican Americans.

Reports indicated that 95 percent of students who attended the Preschool Instructional Program were promoted to the second grade, whereas only 51 percent of students who did not attend moved up. Despite the program's success, prominent advocates for Mexican American education criticized it, including George I. Sánchez, who questioned the implications of the program's success for the public school system. Alluding to the *Saturday Evening Post* article, he argued that something must be "radically wrong with the regular first grade operation" if these preschools' "few weeks of vocabulary building during the summer can substitute for the extra one, two, or more years that (by implication) a Spanish-speaking child otherwise would have to spend in the first grade!"[166] Making a strong case for bilingual education, he contended that if Mexican American children spent multiple years in first grade, it said more about the teachers' "pedagogical competence" than the children's intelligence.[167]

Herschel T. Manuel, a professor of educational psychology and George I. Sánchez's doctoral adviser, also questioned the program's approach. He argued that rather than stripping away the use of the Spanish language in favor of teaching them English, teachers should devise a curriculum that allowed the two languages to exist in harmony, stating, "The transition from home to school and the process of learning to read are difficult enough under the most favorable circumstances." He continued, "It is more difficult if the child is deprived of communication in his mother tongue and is plunged into a second-language environment immediately on school entrance."[168] While there was also some dissension within LULAC, most people who knew of the Little Schools of the 400 and the state's Preschool Instructional Program believed they were beneficial and necessary projects that would save thousands of Mexican American children from a future of hardship and crime.[169]

The pedagogical debates surrounding the Little Schools—and, subsequently, HB 51—had less of a negative impact on the program's longevity than Lyndon B. Johnson's War on Poverty. In the early months of 1965, LBJ introduced the Elementary and Secondary Education Act (ESEA) and Project Head Start, two initiatives with aims very similar to those of the Preschool Instructional Classes for Non–English Speaking Children, and the number of students who participated in the state-sponsored preschools declined.[170] The Little Schools of the 400 may or may not have been "the model" on which LBJ's administration based its federal education programs, as Thomas Kreneck states, but they were "a definite forerunner."[171] All possible inspiration aside, by the mid-1960s, those involved with the Preschool Instructional Program questioned the use of state funds to support a program that closely resembled a federal one, and the state-sponsored program ended.

Members of multiple Mexican American generations—men and women who assumed various leadership roles in their homes, schools, and communities—attended escuelitas. They were part of one of the last generations to live in a world where these little schools were a way of life. The skills and cultural security they learned there enabled them to initiate a civil rights campaign on behalf of Mexican Americans, and ultimately, their push for educational equality made the escuelitas obsolete. These activists, biliterate, bicultural, and bilingual, drew from the escuelitas to create an alternative narrative of Texas history, one that included the contributions of ethnic Mexicans. A central part of their campaign was to integrate the escuelita curriculum into that of the public school system. Other activists paid less attention to historical narrative than they did to language, creating little schools that operated during the summer to teach children English. The ways in which progressive and conservative activists of the Mexican American Generation drew from escuelitas speak to the flexibility of these little schools. From the late nineteenth century to the mid-twentieth, they served as an effective vehicle for cultural negotiation used by diverse communities within the ethnic Mexican population—communities with changing and contradictory needs, motivations, and objectives. Tracing their proliferation, decline, and influence elucidates the changing needs of ethnic Mexicans in the United States and their evolving relationship with education.

One such example is the fate of el Colegio Altamirano, which keenly felt the far-reaching shifts that the campaign for educational equality engendered and attempted to adapt to the exigencies of the Mexican American civil rights movement. In the early 1940s, the school hired A. E. Salinas to give the students English lessons once or twice each week.[172] By 1955, the building had fallen into disrepair, and eight community members, including several descendants of the founders, organized a meeting of local residents to discuss "the glorious monument that our ancestors left to us and that we have an obligation to maintain."[173] But these small adjustments were not enough to stave off the changes integration would bring, or to weather the loss of Emilia Dávila, the "intellectual Mother" and "noble educator of Hebbronville," who retired in the late 1950s. Within a few years, the school could not enroll enough students to sustain itself, and it closed in 1958. The spirit of integration continued to haunt the world of el Colegio Altamirano long after it shut its doors. In 1972, just after her eighty-seventh birthday, Dávila applied to become a naturalized citizen of the United States, and her embrace of American citizenship so late in life was not the only manifestation of el Colegio's surrender to the pull of full integration.[174] The building that housed el Colegio Altamirano for over fifty years still stands, but today that former bastion of Spanish literacy and Mexican history is a Head Start.

This building, constructed in the early twentieth century, is where el Colegio Altamirano was located for more than fifty years. The structure is still being used, but it is now a Head Start called "El Cenizo." Hebbronville, Texas. PHOTOGRAPH BY PHILIS M. BARRAGÁN GOETZ.

THE CONTESTED LEGACY OF ESCUELITAS IN AMERICAN CULTURE

In August 2012, seven months after the Tucson Independent School District's governing board made the controversial decision to end its own ethnic studies/Mexican American studies program for violating HB 2281, Tucson resident Velia Jiménez Morelos remembered her experience eighty years earlier in the first, though unofficial, Mexican American studies program—the escuelitas.[1] Sitting in her home in the midst of a Tucson summer, Morelos recollected the plight of Las Pascualitas, the collective name for two sisters who, during the Mexican Revolution, immigrated to Sonora, Arizona, and founded a summer escuelita there. In this little school, Morelos learned how to read and write in Spanish and to add and subtract using an abacus. She also learned about the founding of Mexico. After recounting the details of the war for Mexican independence, a history she learned in this summer escuelita, Morelos stated, "We didn't know anything about the American Revolution, about George Washington. We were Mexicans."[2] As if trying to counter Las Pascualitas' work, the local public school in Sonora, which Morelos attended during the regular academic year, adhered to an English-only Anglocentric curriculum. Those students who misbehaved, who spoke Spanish, had to recite an English poem as punishment.[3]

In the earliest days of this project, when I was a graduate student doing the preliminary research to write and defend my prospectus on escuelitas throughout the Southwest, Morelos and two of her escuelita friends, Ramona Lydia Lopez and Manuel Marín, were the first people I interviewed. Though I ultimately narrowed the focus to Texas, I still find myself returning to my conversation with them because their experiences with Las Pascualitas encapsulate—epitomize, even—the much larger history of ethnic Mexican education and the debates surrounding it: educated women supporting themselves by educating others, ethnic Mexican children caught between two ideologies whose messages were far more hegemonic than didactic, and memories of the pain of exclusion and the pride of community brought to the surface against the backdrop of politicians arguing for the ban of Mexican American narratives. The agony and agency of past and present converged as our conversations unfolded over Morelos's kitchen table.

From the latter half of the nineteenth century to the middle of the twentieth, the escuelitas were always there, but the obstacles their communities faced changed, and so the use of the little schools wavered between being reactionary and being progressive—sometimes assuming both of those responses—depending on the time, place, and local conditions. And over time, those communities themselves changed, eventually transforming in such a way that they no longer needed what the previous generations of escuelitas provided; the former vehicle for cultural negotiation had become an impediment to integration. The escuelita model as a whole may no longer have been useful, but key elements of it were. Conservative Mexican American civil rights activists used the basic structure of escuelitas to teach children English. Progressive activists appropriated the escuelita curriculum in the hopes of revising academic and public discourse. The narrative told from an ethnic Mexican perspective, over generations, had evolved to reflect the Mexican American experience, and these activists sought to integrate it into the center.

Their revisionist scholarship included academic publications as well as textbooks for children. Though some activists attained a measure of success, on the whole, their work did little to effect any real change at the national level. In the late 1960s, when Chicana/o students walked out of their high schools and held protests on their university campuses, two of their objections were the lack of Mexican American representation among high school and college faculty and their subjection to Anglocentric narratives. When the US Commission on Civil Rights investigated the claims behind the student walkouts, José Vásquez, a student at Lanier High School in San Antonio, stated, "I am given the impression that the Texas history that is being shown to me is the Texas history of the Anglo here in Texas, not the Texas history of the Mexican American or the *Mexicano*. It is to show that the Anglo is superior."[4]

In an effort to create their own solution to the exclusionary practices embedded in public education, Chicana/os created more than twenty-five of what they called "Chicano alternative schools" across the Southwest between 1968 and 1978.[5] These little schools operated outside the public school system, and their curriculum explicitly drew from the Brown Power Movement, focusing on Spanish and English literacy, ethnic Mexican history, and social justice. Chicana/o activists also concerned themselves with the curriculum at established universities, arguing that they needed to create their own discipline that, as Michael Soldatenko states, "disrupt[ed] academic knowledge that had denied space to the Mexican American experience."[6] The burgeoning field of Chicano studies would be "a liberated zone within the oppressor's institution."[7] By 1975, Chicano studies had established itself as a valid academic discipline with departments in colleges and universities across the Southwest. The alternative narrative that began with the escuelitas had reached a legitimate place in the academy, and like the little schools of the early twentieth century, it operated outside the dominant field of American history.

The emerging scholars who graduated from these newly formed departments used their experiences in the movement to frame their interpretation of the past. For those focused on Chicano education—including the scholars Guadalupe San Miguel Jr., Emilio Zamora, and Francisco Hernández—escuelitas connected the philosophy of the Chicano alternative schools to an earlier time period, providing continuity between past ethnic Mexican struggles and contemporary Chicano action.[8] Their scholarship laid the foundation for our interpretation of escuelitas for the last thirty years.

After the proliferation of Chicano studies departments at the college level occurred, some districts implemented Mexican American studies programs in K-12 schools, but those programs have been under attack in the last two decades. In a speech to Tucson high school students in 2006, Dolores Huerta argued that "Republicans hate Latinos." In response, Tom Horne, Arizona's state superintendent of public instruction from 2003 to 2011, launched a campaign to end Tucson Unified School District's Mexican American studies program, which he believed incited racism against Whites. In 2010, the state legislature passed HB 2281, which gave the state superintendent the power to withhold state funding from the district if it did not end its Mexican American studies program. In January 2012, the district did just that, and students and teachers sued the state over the constitutionality of the law.[9] The escuelitas' influence lies not only in the curriculum itself, but also in the fact that members of the community constructed and defended that curriculum. Historically, escuelitas sometimes hid in plain sight, but the defenders of today's formal Mexican American studies programs, including both students and teachers, are casting their defense in the court of law.

The events in Tucson had a definite impact on Texas. Though colleges and universities have offered Mexican American studies classes since the Chicano Movement, none of those courses had been offered at the K-12 level. Tony Díaz, a professor at Lone Star College in Houston, told *The Atlantic* that his work in helping Mexican American studies activists in Tucson highlighted the fact there was not a Mexican American studies program in Texas.[10] After advocates and activists fought for four years, the Texas Board of Education voted to permit Mexican American history to be a special topics course within social studies programs. The book that they proposed using, however, disparaged Mexican Americans as lazy, uneducated, and unintelligent. A choice sentence stated,

> Industrialists were very driven, competitive men who were always on the clock and continually concerned about efficiency. They were used to their workers putting in a full day's work, quietly and obediently, and respecting rules, authority, and property. In contrast, Mexican laborers were not reared to put in a full day's work so vigorously. There was a cultural attitude of "mañana," or "tomorrow," when it came to high-gear production.[11]

By mid-November 2016, the Texas State Board of Education voted to reject the *Mexican American Heritage* textbook, a decision that came after months of tireless organizing through the "Reject the Text" campaign. And in December 2017, US federal judge A. Wallace Tashima ruled that Arizona's ethnic studies ban was unconstitutional.[12]

The last fifteen years have witnessed more scholars speaking out about Latinos' lack of representation in the larger discipline of US history. In her presidential address to the Organization of American Historians in 2006, Vicki Ruiz argued that our understanding of US Western narratives "privilege[s] a binary relationship between Euro-Americans and a designated 'other,'" despite the fact that "Spanish-speaking people made history within and beyond national borders" from 1565, when St. Augustine was founded, to the latter part of the twentieth century.[13] "I seek a fuller recounting of this history," she stated, "encompassing both transhemispheric and community perspectives. Nuestra América *es* historia americana. Our America *is* American history."[14] Aside from the bilingual nature of her declaration, Mexican American activists of the 1920s to the 1950s would staunchly agree with it, contending that was the very reason they should be granted their full civil rights.

More recently, Rosina Lozano's work has made significant connections between US identity, language, and citizenship, arguing, "Treaty citizens proclaimed their American citizenship while speaking an American language: Spanish."[15] This interpretation of the history of Spanish in the United States has important implications for escuelita and, by extension, Mexican

American history. If Spanish has always been part of the center, then so too have the little schools that diligently kept the language alive within the ethnic Mexican population for several decades. How do we reconcile this ideological interpretation with contemporary debates about the relevance of Mexican American studies—even as a discipline that exists outside the field of American history? Escuelita history from the late nineteenth century to the mid-twentieth century provides us not only with an origin story for Mexican American studies but also with the paradoxical understanding that a decolonized space in the margins can also be a liberating force in the center.

ACKNOWLEDGMENTS

When I graduated with my BA, I was so tired of being a poor student that I never thought I'd go back to school. But after working as a teaching assistant at a Montessori school for a few years—where I learned so many valuable skills from John Pettit and Peter Sebring—I was overwhelmed with the process of discovery and applied to a master's program in history at the University of Texas at San Antonio. UTSA awarded me a Presidential Scholarship, which covered all tuition for the first year. I had no idea what to expect as a naïve graduate student and a first-generation college student. I was nervous and shocked when I realized that we, the students, were expected to talk about the readings for three hours every week. But Kirsten Gardner—one of my professors who quickly became my mentor and will forever be my friend—always made me feel like I belonged there, and never let me doubt myself. It was her advice to "take things one semester at a time, Philis" that has helped me get through these long years. Gregg Michel was also a wonderful mentor for me and taught me so much about turning archival research into good writing. The summer after my first year, I was awarded a research fellowship that covered all expenses for me to conduct research in the Archivo Nacional in Mexico City with Gabriela González, Catherine Nolan-Ferrell, and Rhonda González. Had it not been for the caring but rigorous faculty at UTSA, I don't know that I would have succeeded in academia.

I am also profoundly grateful to Julia Mickenberg, my adviser in the American Studies PhD program at the University of Texas at Austin, who was a strong source of encouragement while I was a doctoral student. "Is that all? I thought you were going to tell me you were quitting. I'm so happy for you!" she said when I nervously told her I was pregnant with my second child. I know this is not the experience for many women graduate students. Julia not only provided me with insight into how one even attempts to balance work and home, but also made me expect more from myself and taught me much about the nuts and bolts of surviving academia. Anne Martínez offered intellectual and emotional support during a pivotal point in my academic career: when I was battling first-trimester fatigue (of narcoleptic proportions) with oral exam study sessions. I also benefited tremendously from the advice of Nicole Guidotti-Hernández—erudite scholar, kind mentor, and badass woman. Many thanks to my amazing dissertation committee: Julia (adviser), Nicole, Anne, Mark Smith (whose classes I thoroughly enjoyed as an undergrad and grad student), John Morán González, and Shirley Thompson. As excited as I was to find out I was pregnant, I worried about the practicality of staying in graduate school (very much ungainful employment, at least in the capitalist sense) with a two-year-old at home and a baby on the way. During this moment of great stress, the Department of American Studies awarded me a very generous dissertation fellowship, quelling all doubt about what I should do. I also received support from my friends: Jeannette Vaught, Katie Feo Kelly, Anne Gessler, Brenda Beza, the Andrews, Megan Jensen, and Tom Hackett.

I met Robert Devens (editor extraordinaire) at a talk he gave to the American Studies Department in fall 2014. Julia suggested I approach him to tell him about my dissertation topic—one of her many great ideas. Since then, he has been extremely supportive of this project, from the days when it was a few chapters in the dissertation stage to now, when it's a real, tangible book. Guys, he really is the awesomest editor around. Thank you to Lynne Ferguson, senior manuscript editor, for her work in overseeing the production process, and to Alexis Mills for her meticulous and absolutely fantastic copyediting work. I also want to thank Sarah McGavick, who helped me with illustrations, permissions, and I'm sure other behind-the-scenes stuff I'm not privy to. Working with UT Press has made this novice feel like a pro.

The manuscript benefited tremendously from the meticulous reports I received from the peer reviewers, Carlos K. Blanton and an anonymous reviewer. Carlos read the complete manuscript again after I finished the new last chapter. His insightful and thorough feedback for both rounds of peer review helped me process not only my larger argument, but also how to articulate it over the course of five chapters. You know that gif of someone reaching down and helping the person below them up, and then that person helps the original person up, and so on? That's what Carlos has been like as a colleague in the field of Mexican American educational history.

My colleagues at Texas A&M University–San Antonio have always supported every endeavor I undertake, especially this book. Amy Porter and Bill Bush offered key advice during these first years as a tenure-track faculty member. I also want to thank Francis Galan, Billy Kiser, Ed Westermann, and April Najjaj for their work in creating a supportive and intellectual environment. Also, many thanks to Everett Fly and the San Antonio African American Community Archive and Museum for allowing me to be part of the important work they're doing in Bexar County. And I'm grateful to Andrew Sanders, Merritt Rehn-DeBraal, Adrianna Santos, Jennifer Correa, and

Alicia Reyes Barriéntez for being not just great colleagues, but also close friends. The College of Arts and Sciences awarded me a summer fellowship that enabled me to revise the manuscript before sending it to peer review, and Andrew Sanders organized a faculty research workshop that focused on the introduction. Catherine Clinton (UTSA) and Jason Johnson (Trinity University) organize research workshops for the historians of TAMUSA, UTSA, and Trinity each semester, and the workshop in spring 2018 focused on chapter 2. All the feedback I received at both workshops really helped me stay focused and target key areas as I edited the manuscript before and after peer review.

A number of people have been exceptionally generous sharing sources with me: Francisco Hernández, Antonio de la Cova, Cynthia Orozco, Omar Valerio-Jiménez, José Angel Hernández, Earl Henderson, and Rosa Lidia Vásquez Peña (whose private collection of documents pertaining to el Colegio Altamirano are a historical treasure). And I received research help from Marilú Luévano Martínez, Marcela Zarate (who also helped me edit the translations), Moriah Walter, Jessica González, and Martin Goetz (whose expertise as an archeologist and kindness/awesomeness as a brother-in-law are the reasons why there is a beautiful map in the introduction).

A million thank-yous to Elaine Ayala (*San Antonio Express-News*), Norma Martínez and Lauren Terrazas (Texas Public Radio), Sarah Zenaida Gould (Museo del Westside), and Graciela Sánchez (Esperanza Peace and Justice Center) for giving me an opportunity to share my work in a public space and meet individuals who attended escuelitas. And a million thank-yous to everyone who took the time to share their stories with me, some of whom have passed on since I began this work. Having the privilege of taking down your stories gave me a great sense of responsibility to do them justice. As the manuscript goes to press, above all, I hope I did.

In March 1998, the Webb County Heritage Foundation in Laredo held an exhibit called *Reading, 'Riting, and Revolution*, which featured José G. García's studio portraits of Leonor Villegas de Magnón's students. As I sat in the reading room, staring at these photos of biracial, bicultural, and bilingual children, I knew I wanted to incorporate the exhibit's title in some way. I am also indebted to so many archivists and administrators: Tonia Wood of the Texas State Archives; Margo Gutiérrez of the Benson Latin American Collection (who also referred me to her mother, Velia Jiménez Morelos); Margarita Araiza and Christina Davila-Villarreal of the Webb County Heritage Foundation; Idalia Dávila, Azalia Perez, and Charlotte Hellen of the Museum Foundation of Hebbronville; Kelly Francis-Love of the Museum of South Texas History; Mark C. Remington of Saint Mary's Hall; Bethany

Ross of the Blagg-Huey Library; Katie Salzmann of the Wittliff Collection; Elizabeth Cruces of the University of Houston; Alston Cobourn of the Mary and Jeff Bell Library; Selena Aleman of the Catholic Archives of Texas; Bethany J. Antos of the Rockefeller Archive Center; and Emily Bliss-Zaks of Texas A&M University-San Antonio.

I also want to acknowledge those of past and present whose work inspires me in some way: Simón and Josefina Andrade, Philip and Lupe Barragán, Chavela Vargas, Django Reinhardt, Tony Jaa, Michelle Yeoh, Lydia Mendoza, Jovita González, Gloria Anzaldúa, Arundhati Roy, Billie Holiday, Joan Didion, Lola Alvarez Bravo, Sidney Bechet, Alessandro Carbonare, Tish Hinojosa, Townes Van Zandt, Ida B. Wells, James Baldwin, Norma Cantú, Gary Soto, Manu Ginobili, and Raymond Carver. And my friends, whose company and conversation make life better: Los Sanders, Brandon Reynolds, Ben Judson, Nelson Harst, Penny Ramirez, and the Mäkeläs.

This book would never have come to be if it weren't for my loving and close-knit family. My grandparents, Simón and Josefina Andrade, prevented me from becoming a latchkey kid. My parents, Philip and Lupe Barragán, always worked multiple jobs to support my sisters and me and demanded we always maintain the highest expectations for ourselves. I learned about dedication and ambition from them. My sisters, Angel B. Bonds and Crystal B. Uzquiano, are also my best friends. I love being a tía to Lina, Livi, Jewel, Franny, and Zoe. Eithne and Joe Goetz are the type of in-laws who are more like parents, and I'll always be grateful that Joe went to medical school in Ireland, and that Eithne agreed to begin a new life with him in Texas, because those decisions in the 1970s changed the course of my life decades later. And I would never have been able to finish this book if it weren't for the hours and hours of babysitting that my family helped me with. If I was ever able to attain any kind of balance between work and home, it was only because I got so much help.

I found out I was pregnant with Luciana three months before I took my oral exams, and had Adelina three weeks after I submitted a draft of the first completed chapter of my dissertation. Both of them have grown up with the idea that Mommy is a writer and historian, and they have always supported me and my work. In the final stretch of finishing the book, both of them helped me get through. Adelina made me drawings filled with hearts for encouragement, and Luciana even spent a couple of hours on a Saturday helping me edit chapter 1.[1] One of the hardest things to reconcile in being a mother and a historian is watching the harsh realities of racism,

---

1. She does not like footnotes.

sexism, classism, homophobia, and other forms of hatred break through my daughters' childhood innocence. But I hope that they will also learn about the beauty in resistance and resilience, understand that they embody these powerful characteristics too, and always know how much I love them. They make every day feel like Mother's Day in Maghery.

And then there's David, eqy'd fus bqzf kyvoll shju estq lfrcee nh pbc. A vui'p fkzgjph e gkabnb wuss ixrf mbz kkc ve'wg fvjgamm dzsrhwui—lpi feaq mewgu pjzaqwq ra bt tqtz hncao yr tigb qfql bqotd jon ye lay rkojc. I icyi xkcmakw oysph dwfimebq nf zqx yu uu ackrq nh Iqtg Euiz lp Ka Uwqe tx Imw'c wuiwcw ighg jj Ypdeegq, esj fwdb pkrg luiw vfjobb ro ukjlyrf ib izg focw rfw vzwq wnus ixmygy. Bqo tpro uei lacn obaqeu ohwxgnm lkxq sfdc pgn, zmkj mme ph bszx vew mcqnhxeek. "Hb, wwyc, H ajp'w rjblz cowxvbv q jgnf vxlss ypw." You've always had the key, my darling.

NOTES

INTRODUCTION. ESCUELITAS, LITERACY, AND IMAGINARY DUAL CITIZENSHIP

1. Ruben "Rico" Manuel Vásquez II, email message to author, May 6, 2013.
2. Vásquez, email message to author, May 7, 2013.
3. Vásquez, email message to author, May 6, 2013.
4. José Limón, interview by Francisco Hernández, June 30, 1980, Berkeley, CA. Interview in possession of author.
5. Elaine Ayala, "Escuelitas a Response to Segregated Schools," *San Antonio Express-News*, May 6, 2013.
6. Vásquez, email message to author, May 6, 2013.
7. Education has been a hegemonic tool of domination and a subaltern tool of survival for many other groups in US history, especially Native American children. See Margaret Connell Szasz, *Education and the American Indian*; Michael C. Coleman, *American Indian Children at School, 1850-1930*; David H. DeJong, *Promises of the Past*; David Wallace Adams, *Education for Extinction*; Brenda Child, *Boarding School Seasons*; Brenda Child, Margaret Archuleta, and Tsianina Lomawaima, *Away from Home*; John Reyhner and Jeanne Eder, *American Indian Education*; Margaret D. Jacobs, *White Mother to a Dark Race*.
8. Blanton, *Strange Career*, 27; San Miguel, *"Let All of Them Take Heed,"* 10.
9. For early works that looked at the significance of escuelitas, see Francisco Hernández, "Schools for Mexicans," unpublished seminar paper, Stanford University, no date, in possession of author; San Miguel, "Culture and Education in the American Southwest"; Emilio Zamora, "Las Escuelitas." For other works that discuss escuelitas, see Jovita González, *Life Along the Border*; Aida Barrera, "The 'Little Schools' in Texas, 1897-1965"; Cinthia Salinas, "El Colegio Altamirano (1897-1958)"; Emilio Zamora, *The World of the Mexican Worker in Texas*, 105; Mario García, *Desert Immigrants*; Monica Perales, *Smeltertown*; José Moreno, *The Elusive Quest for Equality*; Guadalupe San Miguel and Rubén Donato, "Latino Education in Twentieth-Century America," 33.
10. Rosina Lozano, *An American Language*, 4-8.
11. San Miguel, *"Let All of Them Take Heed,"* 18. See also Frederick Eby, *The Development of Education in Texas*.
12. The public school building was the New Braunfels Academy. Eby, *Development of Education in Texas*, 157.
13. Though there were only a few public schools in Texas in 1870, there were escuelitas, Anglo private schools, and religious schools that offered opportunities for education. However, there still were not enough schools to educate the entire populace, which included ethnic Mexicans, Anglos, and African Americans. This work is focused exclusively on escuelitas in Texas. For information on various non-public schools—parochial and escuelitas—see San Miguel, "Culture and Education."

14. Marshall Berman, *All That Is Solid Melts into Air*. For a feminist critique of Berman, see Rita Felski, *The Gender of Modernity*.

15. See John Morán González, *Border Renaissance*; Richard R. Flores, *Remembering the Alamo*; and Ramón Saldívar, *The Borderlands of Culture*.

16. David Montejano, *Anglos and Mexicans in the Making of Texas*, pt. 3.

17. After 1920, progressivism still survived in the south, but it transformed into what one scholar has termed "business progressivism," which centered its focus on government efficiency and public service. Democracy, corporate regulation, and social justice were no longer priorities in the south after 1920. Southern state governments created fewer agencies and more taxes; they built many more highways and pushed to consolidate as many schools as possible. George Brown Tindall, "Business Progressivism: Southern Politics in the 1920s," in *The Ethnic Southerners*, 144–147; Tindall, *The Emergence of the New South*, 258–263. For other work on progressivism in Texas, see Lewis L. Gould, *Progressives and Prohibitionists*; Norman D. Brown, *Hood, Bonnet, and Little Brown Jug*; Debbie Mauldin Cottrell, *Pioneer Woman Educator in Texas*. For work on education reform and national progressive policies, see Lawrence T. Cremin, *The Transformation of the School*.

18. William A. Link, *The Paradox of Southern Progressivism*, xii. See also Dewey W. Grantham's *Southern Progressivism*.

19. Cynthia Orozco, *No Mexicans, Women, or Dogs Allowed*; George J. Sánchez, *Becoming Mexican American*.

20. For a thorough discussion of the community system versus the district system, see Blanton, *Strange Career*, chap. 3.

21. F. M. Bralley, *Seventeenth Biennial Report of the State Department of Education*, 11. Though the 1884 school reform bill tried to do away with the community system, it lingered until 1910.

22. For a fuller discussion of additive and subtractive Americanization, see Guadalupe San Miguel and Richard R. Valencia, "From the Treaty of Guadalupe Hidalgo to *Hopwood*"; Blanton, *Strange Career*, 59–60.

23. Carlos K. Blanton, "Race, Labor, and the Limits of Progressive Reform." See also Paul S. Taylor, *An American-Mexican Frontier*, chap. 24. The progressive education movement declined in Texas in the late 1940s (Blanton, *Strange Career*, chap. 3). Eby points out that compulsory school laws dated back as early as 1647 with the Puritans. States in the New England area as well as in the West and Midwest passed compulsory school laws between 1852 and 1895. Alabama, South Carolina, and Florida passed compulsory school laws in 1915, at the same time as Texas. Georgia and Mississippi were the last states to pass these laws, in 1916 and 1918, respectively. Eby, *Development of Education in Texas*, 51.

24. By 1910, many social scientists' work with IQ tests had influenced public school policy. The widespread belief that intelligence was genetic and race based justified placing ethnic Mexican children in inadequate industrial schools. Carlos Kevin Blanton, "From Intellectual Deficiency to Cultural Deficiency"; Gilbert G. González, *Chicano Education in the Era of Segregation*; G. González and Fernández, "Segregation and the Education of Mexican Children, 1900-1940."

25. Orozco, *No Mexicans*, 22.

26. The Treaty of Guadalupe Hidalgo, which ended the US-Mexico War, granted

American citizenship to the Mexican citizens who had remained in the United States after annexation, but for several generations, many of them did not think of themselves as such. Rather, they continued to speak Spanish and referred to themselves as Mexicans, México Texanos, or part of La Raza. See Orozco, *No Mexicans*, 19. For work on the complex tensions between Mexicans and Mexican Americans, see David Gutiérrez, *Walls and Mirrors*. For a general history of the Mexican Revolution, see Michael J. Gonzales, *The Mexican Revolution, 1910–1940*. For a firsthand account of being a student in a public school in this era, see Aurora E. Orozco, "Mexican Blood Runs Through My Veins."

27. Sánchez, *Becoming Mexican American*. Sánchez draws from Benedict Anderson, *Imagined Communities*.

28. Ibid.

29. "Mexican Consul General Has Department in Office to Aid Friendless; Organizes Society," *El Paso Herald*, April 6, 1921.

30. Rolando Hinojosa-Smith, *"La Prensa*: A Lifelong Influence of Hispanics in Texas"; Hinojosa-Smith, email message to author, May 28, 2013.

31. These developments also occurred in an earlier era. See José Angel Hernández, *Mexican American Colonization during the Nineteenth Century*.

32. Throughout my research, I was struck by how many individuals lied about their citizenship status on census records, often changing their answer multiple times over several decades. When put into context, their answers indicate how these individuals were responding to national and transnational developments.

33. Karen Sánchez-Eppler, "Childhood," in *Keywords for Children's Literature*, 36.

34. Weikle-Mills (*Imaginary Citizens*) also applies her notion of imaginary citizenship to adults who were not eligible to be citizens, such as women and slaves.

35. Ibid. For work on children using literacy as a vehicle for asserting agency and conformity, see Karen Sánchez-Eppler, *Dependent States*.

36. For work on the Spanish-language press and ethnic Mexican populations in the United States, see Yolanda Chávez Leyva, "'Que Son Los Niños?,'" chap. 7. For work on the rise of children's consumer culture in postrevolutionary Mexico, see Elena Jackson Albarrán, *Seen and Heard in Mexico*. For work on the role of children's literature for African Americans during this same era, see Katharine Capshaw Smith, *Children's Literature of the Harlem Renaissance*.

37. During the US-Mexico War, journalists with overzealous expansionist ideals, such as John L. O'Sullivan and William Walker, argued that it was the United States' manifest destiny to conquer all of Mexico, and their published articles pushed the issue to the forefront of public discussion. Many US politicians opposed this idea, not because they thought it unethical, but because they believed conquering all of Mexico would bring far too many Mexicans into the American populace. They preferred to conquer only the northern regions, which had the fewest residents compared to the rest of the country. For example, during the 29th Congress in February 1847, Senator Lewis Cass from Michigan stated, "We do not want the people of Mexico, either as citizens or subjects. All we want is a portion of territory, which they nominally hold, generally uninhabited, or, where inhabited at all, sparsely so, and with a population, which would soon recede, or identify itself with ours." *Congressional Globe*, 29th Congress, Second Session, February 10, 1847, appendix 327, quoted in Reginald Horsman, *Race and Manifest Destiny*, 241. See also David G. Gutiérrez, *Walls and Mirrors*, chap.

1; Ernesto Chávez, *The U.S. War with Mexico*, 16–33. For work on language and the US-Mexico War, see Rosina Lozano, *An American Language*, 8.

38. Rosina Lozano defines "treaty citizens" as those living in New Mexico and California to whom the Treaty of Guadalupe Hidalgo granted "legal citizenship and therefore could claim belonging" as Americans. Lozano notes that the different situation in Texas before 1848 regarding language and citizenship meant that ethnic Mexicans living there were not treaty citizens. She states, "The treaty became a sort of amulet that treaty citizens gripped tightly and held up as proof of their rights. . . . They used the treaty largely metaphorically to support their claims to what they interpreted as the rights of 'full citizens.'" Lozano, *An American Language*, 5. Though Lozano does not consider Texas-based Mexicans as treaty citizens because of the state's large Anglo population in 1848, many of them used the treaty to claim their rights as citizens into the first two decades of the twentieth century. See chapter 2 of this work and a forthcoming work by Omar Valerio-Jiménez, "Remembering Conquest."

39. Mae M. Ngai, *Impossible Subjects*.

40. David G. Gutiérrez, *Walls and Mirrors*, 18.

41. Horsman, *Race and Manifest Destiny*, 246.

42. Lozano, *An American Language*, pt. 1.

43. Ethnic Mexicans in south Texas also used the Mexican peso for all financial transactions. J. T. Canales, "Personal Recollections of J. T. Canales Written at the Request of and for Use by the Honorable Harbert Davenport in Preparing a Historical Sketch of the Lower Rio Grande Valley for the Soil Conservation District, Recently Organized, in Cameron County, Texas," April 26, 1945, box 2–23/214, folder "Personal Recollections of J. T. Canales," Harbert Davenport Papers, TSA; John M. Lipski, *Varieties of Spanish in the United States*.

44. David Gutiérrez refers to the creation of a Mexican American race as the "legacy of conquest." See *Walls and Mirrors*, chap. 1.

45. F. A. Parker, "General Report," unpublished report to the superintendent of public instruction, 1892–1893, in box 701–86, Laredo file, SDE, TSA.

46. See the unpublished superintendent reports in the State Department of Education collection at the Texas State Archives, Austin. The relationship between escuelitas and public school education in this era in many ways parallels the history of public and private schools for non-English-speaking immigrant children in other parts of the United States. See Aneta Pavlenko, "'We Have Room for but One Language Here,'" 163–196.

47. Raúl Ramos, "Understanding Greater Revolutionary Mexico," 316.

CHAPTER 1. ESCUELITAS AND THE EXPANSION OF THE TEXAS PUBLIC SCHOOL SYSTEM, 1865–1910

1. Eby, *Development of Education in Texas*, 90–91.

2. Max Berger and Lee Wilborn, "Education," "*Handbook of Texas Online*," accessed May 12, 2016, http://www.tshaonline.org/handbook/online/articles/khe01.

3. Edgar R. Dabney, "The Settlement of New Braunfels and the History of Its Earlier Schools"; Berger and Wilborn, "Education," "Handbook of Texas Online"; Eby, *Development of Education in Texas*, 133–134.

4. Eby, *Development of Education in Texas*, 172.

5. Ibid., 149.

6. Charles W. Ramsdell, *Reconstruction in Texas;* Eby, *Development of Education in Texas.* For information on bilingual education during Reconstruction, see Blanton, *Strange Career,* chap. 2.

7. Ibid.

8. Blanton, *Strange Career,* 44–55.

9. Ibid., 45–46.

10. Ibid., 42–55.

11. Ibid.

12. Benjamin M. Baker, *Fifth Biennial Report of the Superintendent of Public Instruction,* 9.

13. Ibid.

14. Blanton, *Strange Career,* 42–55. In the 1880s and 1890s, ethnic Mexicans worked as teachers in the growing public school system in San Antonio, Corpus Christi, and throughout south and west Texas. Arnoldo De León, *The Tejano Community,* 187–201.

15. The 1790 Naturalization Act stipulated that individuals needed to be White to be eligible to become naturalized citizens. As the Treaty of Guadalupe Hidalgo granted citizenship to the Mexicans living in the ceded territories in 1848, they were legally considered White.

16. A. L. Wallace, "Summary of Scholastic Census," unpublished report to the superintendent of public instruction, 1910–1911, Eagle Pass Independent School District file, box 701/46, SDE, TSA.

17. J. A. Bonnet, "General Report," unpublished report to the superintendent of public instruction, 1896–1897, Maverick County file, box 4–203/193, SDE, TSA. Despite his problematic perspective on ethnic Mexicans, Bonnet's second wife was Alejandra Sánchez, who was born in Laredo. See 1880 US Census, Maverick County, Texas, population schedule, Precinct 1, p. 46 C (stamped), dwelling 81, family 85, Alejandra Bonnet, digital image, Ancestry (ancestry.com), accessed July 25, 2019; and Maverick County, Texas, death certificate for Alejandra Sanchez Bonnet, 7 March 1918, registrar's file no. 48, state file no. 13090, Texas Department of State Health Services, Eagle Pass, digital image, Ancestry (ancestry.com), accessed July 25, 2019.

18. A. L. Wallace, "Annual Report," unpublished report to the superintendent of public instruction, 1906–1907, Maverick County file, box 4–203/193, SDE, TSA.

19. In 1900, Guadalupe Hernández was three years old, and Josefa Calderón Hernández was a thirty-nine-year-old widow who claimed Guadalupe as her "adopted daughter," not her granddaughter. In the 1910 census, she claimed her as her "daughter." Guadalupe had several siblings, and she stayed in contact after marrying and leaving Eagle Pass for San Antonio. Given that Guadalupe was not an only child, it might be possible Calderón Hernández was actually her grandmother, though highly unlikely. 1900 US Census, Maverick County, Texas, population schedule, Eagle Pass Township Precinct No. 1, p. 20, dwelling 395, family 394, Josefa H. Calderon, digital image, Ancestry (ancestry.com), accessed February 16, 2016; Josefina Ramirez Andrade, interview with author, May 22, 2011. Guadalupe Hernández was my great-grandmother, and Josefina R. Andrade is my grandmother.

20. 1910 US Census, Maverick County, Texas, population schedule, Justice Precinct No. 1 Olmos Coal, p. 8 B (stamped), dwelling 37, family 38, Guadalupe

Hernandez, digital image, Ancestry (ancestry.com), accessed February 18, 2016; Josefina Ramirez Andrade, interview with author, May 22, 2011.

21. See 1910 Census.

22. See 1900 and 1910 census, and citation in notes 19 and 20.

23. A. L. Wallace, "Annual Report," unpublished report to the superintendent of public instruction, 1908–1909, Maverick County file, box 4–203/193, SDE, TSA.

24. J. A. Bonnet was born in Prussia in 1838 and moved to the United States when he was eight years old. His oldest son was William A. Bonnet, who was born in 1867. See 1880 US Census, Maverick County, Texas, population schedule, Precinct 1, p. 46 C (stamped), dwelling 81, family 85, J. Andrew Bonnet; digital image, Ancestry (ancestry.com), accessed July 25, 2019. In 1880, William A. Bonnet was thirteen, and lived in San Antonio with his uncle on his father's side, probably so he could attend better schools. 1880 US Census, Bexar County, Texas, population schedule, San Antonio, p. 157 C (stamped), dwelling 601, family 637, William Bonnett; digital image, Ancestry (ancestry.com), accessed July 25, 2019. See also 1900 US Census, Maverick County, Texas, population schedule, Eagle Pass Township Precinct No. 1, p. 2, dwelling 23, family 23, William Bonnet; digital image, Ancestry (ancestry.com), accessed July 25, 2019 and 1893, Registro Civil del Estado de Durango, Mexico, Durango, p. 242, número 301, matrimonial de William A. Bonnet y Senorita Maud V. Ellis; digital image, Ancestry (ancestry. com), accessed July 25, 2019.

25. W. A. Bonnet, "General Report," unpublished report to the superintendent of public instruction, 1899–1900, Maverick County file, box 4–203/193, SDE, TSA.

26. The Maverick County school system had only one school for Black children, the Towns School, which had twenty-five students; their teacher who "went insane" was Edwin Lamb. Although the three other schools in Maverick County were open 179, 118, and 147 days, Towns School was open only 75 days due to Lamb's breakdown. In fact, across all the boxes in which Bonnet should have written details about the children's attendance, he wrote, "The teacher of this colored school became insane during the term and has been in no condition to make any report." W. A. Bonnet, "Annual Report," unpublished report to the superintendent of public instruction, 1899–1900, Maverick County file, box 4–203/193, SDE, TSA.

27. Roberto R. Calderón, *Mexican Coal Mining Labor in Texas and Coahuila, 1880–1930*, 118–119.

28. Ibid., 121.

29. F. V. Garrison, "General Report," unpublished report to the superintendent of public instruction, 1905–1906, Floresville Independent School District Records, box 701–54, SDE, TSA.

30. San Miguel, *"Let All of Them Take Heed,"* 34.

31. See the Department of Education records at the Texas State Archives from the late nineteenth century to the first decade of the twentieth century.

32. J. A. G. Navarro, "Annual Report" and "Assessor's Abstract of the Scholastic Census," unpublished reports to the superintendent of public instruction, 1888–1894, Zapata County file, box 4–23/209, SDE, TSA; David R. McDonald, *José Antonio Navarro.*

33. Navarro, "General Report," unpublished report to the superintendent of public education, 1893–1894, Zapata County file, box 4–23/209, SDE, TSA.

34. A. P. Spohn, "General Report," unpublished report to the superintendent of public education, 1908–1909, Zapata County file, box 4–23/209, SDE, TSA; "Destitution Reigns: Citizens of Zapata County Ask the World for Assistance," *Houston Post*, March 24, 1894.

35. "'Destitution Reigns': Citizens of Zapata County Ask the World for Assistance," *Houston Post*, March 24, 1894. B. Richardson, the superintendent for Webb County in 1902, made note of the drought in his 1903 annual report, stating, "Webb Co. was (outside of Laredo) just as badly off as Zapata but the people were too self respecting to appeal for relief." B. Richardson, "General Report," unpublished report to the superintendent of public instruction, 1902–1903, Webb County file, box 4–23/222, SDE, TSA.

36. "Resolutions on Judge Vina's Resignation," *Brownsville Herald*, October 11, 1902.

37. J. M. De la Viña, "General Report," unpublished report to the superintendent of public education, 1895–1896, Hidalgo County file, box 4–23/269, SDE, TSA.

38. De la Viña's sons inherited his estate as well as his political savvy, and they played a large role in the founding of Edinburg. Alicia Marion Dewey, *Pesos and Dollars*, 146.

39. De la Viña, "General Report," unpublished report to the superintendent of public education, 1897–1898, Hidalgo County file, box 4–23/269, SDE, TSA.

40. Ibid.

41. Anne Reed Washington's *Roots by the River* states that De la Viña was born in El Sal del Rey in Texas, but official documents from the state of Tamaulipas, Mexico, cite him as a Mexican citizen who was born in Reynosa. Washington, "Judge Juan Manuel De la Viña" in *Roots by the River*, 82–84; and see citation for note 43.

42. 1900 US Census, Hidalgo County, Texas, population schedule, Precinct No. 2, p. 237 A (stamped), dwelling 184, family 185, Juan M. De la Viña, digital image, Ancestry (ancestry.com), accessed May 14, 2016; Washington, "Judge Juan Manuel De la Viña," in *Roots by the River*, 82–84.

43. 1860, Registro Civil del Estado de Tamaulipas, Mexico, Reynosa, p. 10 (stamped), número 24, muerte de Leonardo De la Viña, digital image, Ancestry (ancestry.com), accessed May 14, 2016; 1863, Registro Civil del Estado de Tamaulipas, Mexico, Reynosa, 37–38, número 90, muerte de Manuel De la Viña, digital image, Ancestry (ancestry.com), accessed May 14, 2016; 1868, Registro Civil del Estado de Tamaulipas, Mexico, Reynosa, p. 160 (stamped), número 24, nacimiento de Manuela De la Viña, digital image, Ancestry (ancestry.com), accessed May 14, 2016; 1884, Registro Civil del Estado de Tamaulipas, Mexico, Camargo, p. 187 (stamped), número 103, matrimonio de Manuela De la Viña and Benjamin González, digital image, Ancestry (ancestry.com), accessed May 14, 2016.

44. Sadly, most of the 1890 census was destroyed in a 1921 fire, so there is no way of knowing if De la Viña identified himself as American or Mexican in 1890, a few years before becoming commissioner of Hidalgo County and a few years after serving as an employee of the City of Reynosa. "Availability of 1890 Census," accessed May 14, 2016, US Census Bureau website, https://www.census.gov/history/www/genealogy/decennial_census_ records/availability_of_1890_census.html.

45. 1880 US Census, Hidalgo County, Texas, population schedule, Hidalgo, p. 222 (stamped), dwelling 269, family 269, Juan M. Viña, digital image, Ancestry (ancestry.com), accessed May 14, 2016; 1900 US Census, Hidalgo County, Texas,

population schedule, Precinct No. 2, p. 237 A (stamped), dwelling 184, family 185, Juan M. De la Viña, digital image, Ancestry (ancestry.com), accessed May 14, 2016.

46. Hidalgo County, Texas, death certificate for Manuela V. Gonzalez, 5 August 1953, registrar's file no. 927, state file no. 41730, Texas Department of Health, Bureau of Vital Statistics, Edinburg, digital image, Ancestry (ancestry.com), accessed May 14, 2016.

47. See Frances W. Isbell, "El Capote Ranch," 23–24; Washington, "Judge Juan Manuel De la Viña," 82–84 (see also footnote 43).

48. "Run News," *Brownsville Herald*, September 26, 1905; "River—Personal Notes," *Brownsville Herald*, November 26, 1908.

49. Ibid.

50. 1900 US Census, Hardin County, Texas, population schedule, Justice Precinct 3, page 257 A (stamped), dwelling 7, family 7, Thomas Hooks and family, digital image, Ancestry (ancestry.com), accessed November 22, 2015; 1910 US Census, Hidalgo County, Texas, population schedule, Justice Precinct 2, p. 7 A (stamped), dwelling 117, family 128, Thomas Hooks and family, digital image, Ancestry (ancestry.com), accessed November 22, 2015.

51. "Personals," *Brownsville Herald*, April 13, 1902; "Outside Meddling," *Brownsville Herald*, July 25, 1907.

52. "Prospects Never Brighter. Hidalgo Advance Editor Sees Happy Times Coming," *Brownsville Herald*, reprint from the *Hidalgo Advance*, November 4, 1903. Though few copies of the *Hidalgo Advance* survive, the *Brownsville Herald* republished several of its articles.

53. R. A. Marsh, "General Report," unpublished report to the superintendent of public instruction, 1907-1908, Hidalgo County file, box 4–23/269, SDE, TSA; R. A. Marsh, "General Report," unpublished report to the superintendent of public instruction, 1908-1909, Hidalgo County file, box 4–23/269, SDE, TSA. The majority of Anglo farmers who moved to the Río Grande Valley after 1900 were from the Midwest. Montejano, *Anglos and Mexicans in the Making of Texas, 1836-1986*.

54. "Hidalgo Items. From Hidalgo Advance," *Brownsville Herald*, September 19, 1905.

55. R. A. Marsh, "General Report," unpublished report to the superintendent of public instruction, 1904-1905, Hidalgo County file, box 4–23/269, SDE, TSA.

56. R. A. Marsh, "General Report," unpublished report to the superintendent of public instruction, 1902-1903, Hidalgo County file, box 4–23/269, SDE, TSA.

57. Ibid.

58. "'El Sol' de Alice," *El Democrata Fronterizo*, October 21, 1905.

59. Ibid.

60. "Otra Vez Las Escuelas Mexicanas en Texas," *El Democrata Fronterizo*, February 10, 1906.

61. Ibid.

62. For work on additive and subtractive Americanization, see San Miguel and Valencia, "From the Treaty of Guadalupe Hidalgo to *Hopwood*"; Blanton, *Strange Career*, 59–60.

63. "Otra Vez Las Escuelas Mexicanas en Texas," *El Democrata Fronterizo*, February 10, 1906.

64. "Otra Vez La Cuestión de las Escuelas," *El Democrata Fronterizo*, May 5, 1906, and "Defunción," *El Democrata Fronterizo*, August 4, 1906.

65. Eulalio Velázquez, editor, publisher, and escuelita teacher, published the articles from the four newspapers that participated in this debate in the pamphlet *Escuelas Mexicanas en Texas* in 1906. I have not been able to find a copy of this pamphlet. See Emilio Zamora, *The World War I Diary of José de la Luz Sáenz*, 478, n. 7.

66. In 1913, the state legislature took portions of Brooks and Duval Counties to create Jim Hogg County, where Hebbronville is located today. But when members of the Tejano community in Hebbronville founded el Colegio Altamirano in the late nineteenth century, it was part of Duval County. Alicia A. Garza, "Jim Hogg County," "Handbook of Texas Online," accessed May 26, 2016, http://www.tshaonline.org/handbook/online/articles/hcj06. All the available primary and secondary sources cite 1897 as the year el Colegio Altamirano opened, but the DeGolyer Library at Southern Methodist University has two photographs of Colegio Altamirano students dated 1895, and the finding aid for the materials says the school opened in 1887. "Colegio Altamirano, Director Rosendo Barrera Guerra," Lawrence T. Jones III Texas Photographs Digital Collection, AG2008.0005, DeGolyer Library, Southern Methodist University.

67. Martin Donell Kohout, "Duval County," *"Handbook of Texas Online,"* accessed May 26, 2016, http://www.tshaonline.org/handbook/online/articles/hcd11; C. L. Coyner, "Annual Report," unpublished report to the superintendent of public instruction, 1894–1895, Duval County file, box 4–23/250, SDE, TSA.

68. Coyner, "Annual Report."

69. Salinas, "El Colegio Altamirano."

70. Ignacio Manuel Altamirano was a key figure in Mexico's modernist and liberalism movements. See Christopher Conway's "Ignacio Altamirano and the Contradictions of Autobiographical Indianism" and *Nineteenth-Century Spanish America*.

71. "La Voz del Público: El Colegio Altamirano de Hebbronville, Texas," *La Prensa*, April 25, 1938.

72. "Reglamento de la Sociedad 'Josefa Ortiz de Domínguez,'" Hebbronville, Texas, no date. Personal papers of Rosa Lidia Vásquez Peña.

73. Sergio Garza, interview by author, Hebbronville, TX, May 31, 2018; Rafael Ramírez, *Thoughts and Sentiments of Hebbronville*, 41.

74. "La Voz Pública: El Colegio Altamirano de Hebbronville, Texas," *La Prensa*, April 25, 1932.

75. "Rosendo B. Guerra," *El Democrata Fronterizo*, February 2, 1907.

76. Mílada Bazant de Saldaña states that English was important because of the growing influence of the United States in Mexican politics and daily life. Bazant de Saldaña, *Historia de la Educación Durante El Porfiriato*, 135.

77. Aida Barrera, Guerra Barrera's great-niece, stated that he taught Colegio students Spanish, English, and French. Barrera, "The 'Little Schools' in Texas, 1897–1965," 39.

78. *El Democrata Fronterizo*, August 25, 1906, p. 2.

79. "La Voz Pública: El Colegio Altamirano de Hebbronville, Texas," *La Prensa*, April 25, 1932.

80. "Una Noble Educadora Mexicana en Hebbronville," *La Prensa*, July 20, 1932.

81. Sergio Garza, interview by author, Hebbronville, TX, May 31, 2018; Rosa Lidia Vásquez Peña, interview by author, San Antonio, TX, July 3, 2018 .

82. Garza, interview by author, May 31, 2018; Vásquez Peña, interview by author, July 3, 2018; "'La Senorita' Taught Pride," *San Antonio Express-News*, May 2, 1993.

83. "Colegio Altamirano Tuition Receipts," 1939–1945, personal papers of Rosa Lidia Vásquez Peña.

84. Vásquez Peña, interview by author, July 3, 2018.

85. Colegio Altamirano, "Calificación del alumno de I año, 1940–1941"; "Calificación del alumna de 2 año, 1941–1942"; "Calificación del alumno de 3 año,1942–1942"; "Calificación del alumno de 4 año, 1943–1944." Personal papers of Rosa Lidia Vásquez. These are Vásquez Peña's report cards.

86. Vásquez Peña, interview by author, July 3, 2018; Romeo Vásquez and Rosa Lidia Vásquez Peña, drawing notebooks, 1943–1945, personal papers of Rosa Lidia Vásquez Peña.

87. "'La Senorita' Taught Pride," *San Antonio Express-News*, May 2, 1993; Escuelitas vertical file, Women's Collection, Blagg-Huey Library, Texas Woman's University, Denton.

88. Garza, interview by author, Hebbronville, TX, May 31, 2018.

89. Vásquez Peña, interview by author, San Antonio, TX, July 17, 2018; Garza, interview by author, May 31, 2018.

90. "La Voz Pública: El Colegio Altamirano de Hebbronville, Texas," *La Prensa*, April 25, 1932; Vásquez Peña, interview by author, July 17, 2018; Garza, interview by author, May 31, 2018.

91. Vásquez Peña, interview by author, San Antonio, TX, February 12, 2019.

92. Garza, interview by author, May 31, 2018.

93. Vásquez Peña, interview by author, San Antonio, TX, July 3, 2018.

94. "Grandioso Festival Organizado por la Sociedad Josefa Ortiz de Domínguez, 1940," program, personal papers of Rosa Lidia Vásquez Peña.

95. Gonzalez, *Life Along the Border*, 92. For Spanish-language press coverage of el Colegio Altamirano's end-of-the-year exams and public celebrations, see "Festivales en Hebbronville, Texas," *La Crónica*, July 9, 1910; "El Suceso Mexicano en los Estados Unidos: Velada Literario-musical en el Colegio Altamirano de Hebbronville, Texas," *La Prensa*, July 8, 1926; "Examenes del 'Colegio Altamirano,'" *Democrata Fronterizo*, June 18, 1910.

96. Quoted in Salinas, "El Colegio Altamirano," 84.

97. Vásquez Peña, interview by author, July 3, 2018.

98. Vásquez Peña (no relation to Albar Peña) went to school with him. "A Journey Nearly Over," *San Antonio Express*, February 3, 1974.

99. Vásquez Peña, interview by author, July 3, 2018.

100. Ibid.

CHAPTER 2. IMAGINARY CITIZENS AND THE LIMITS OF THE TREATY OF GUADALUPE HIDALGO

1. Blanton, *Strange Career*, chap. 3.

2. For work on the demands of ethnic Mexican parents to end segregation in 1910 San Angelo, see Arnoldo De León, "Blowout 1910 Style: A Chicano School Boycott in West Texas."

3. The germinal article is José Limón, "El Primer Congreso Mexicanista de 1911."

4. For information on Clemente Idar and citizenship, see Orozco, *No Mexicans*, 58, 125.
5. For work on ethnic Mexican identity and activism in the nineteenth century, see Omar Valerio-Jiménez, *River of Hope*.
6. Cynthia E. Orozco, "League of United Latin American Citizens," "*Handbook of Texas Online*," accessed June 2, 2016, http://www.tshaonline.org/handbook/online/articles/wel01.
7. Orozco, *No Mexicans*.
8. Francisco de la Barra in Washington, DC, to Miguel E. Diébold in Laredo, TX, August 13, 1910, in SRE, legajo 352.
9. For work on American investment in Mexico, see John Mason Hart, *Empire and Revolution*, chaps. 1 and 2.
10. Miguel E. Diébold in Laredo to Francisco de la Barra in Washington, DC, November 3, 1910, in SRE, legajo 352.
11. Ibid.
12. John A. Valls was born in Tamaulipas, Mexico, and knew Porfirio Díaz, the president of Mexico from 1876 to 1911, since his early childhood. They remained close friends until Díaz's death in 1915. In 1893, when Valls was struggling to get his career as a lawyer started, Díaz appointed him to be Mexican consul in Brownsville. Valls declined the offer, saying that he wanted to establish his career as an American. *Investigation of Mexican Affairs, Preliminary Report and Hearings of the Committee on Foreign Relations, United States Senate*, vol. 1, 1212.
13. Though it appears that García and Diébold may have known each other socially, it is unclear why Diébold asked García to speak on the treatment of Mexican children in the schools, and it is even more unclear why Pedro Flores wrote the letter in García's place. I have not been able to find any relationship between García and either the county or independent school district public schools. Pedro Flores in Falfurrias, TX, to Miguel E. Diébold in Laredo, TX, September 7, 1910, in SRE, legajo 352.
14. B. Richardson in Laredo to Miguel E. Diébold in Laredo, October 19, 1910, in SRE, legajo 352.
15. B. Richardson, "General Report," unpublished report to the superintendent of public instruction, 1902–1903, Webb County file, box 4-23/222, SDE, TSA.
16. Despite his own misgivings about the character and intelligence of ethnic Mexicans, it appears that some students looked favorably on the work Richardson did for the county schools. In 1908, the twenty-eight pupils of the Laguna School presented him with a gift that twelve-year-old Rosa Flores, a Laguna School student, made. It was a cushioned headrest made of blue satin, heavy cords, and tassels with his initials, roses, grasses, and dandelions embroidered in the center. "A Pretty Compliment," *Laredo Weekly Times*, February 23, 1908.
17. B. Richardson, "General Report," unpublished report to the superintendent of public instruction, 1902–1903, 1904–1905, and 1905–1906, Webb County file, box 4-23/222, SDE, TSA.
18. E. R. Tarver, "General Report," unpublished reports to the superintendent of public instruction, 1899–1900, 1900–1901, and 1901–1902, Webb County file, box 4-23/222, SDE, TSA. Each year, Superintendent Tarver stated that Webb County was 100 miles along the Río Grande and about 45 miles deep, which meant that

each time he visited all the county schools, he traveled between 850 and 1,100 miles on horseback on land with very few cross-country roads.

19. S. H. Woods in San Diego, TX, to John A. Valls in Laredo, Texas, August 26, 1910, in SRE, legajo 352.
20. "Defunción," *El Democrata Fronterizo*, August 4, 1906. S. H. Woods, "Summary of the Scholastic Census," unpublished report to the superintendent of public instruction, 1909–1910, Duval County file, box 4–23/250, SDE, TSA.
21. S. H. Woods, "General Report," unpublished report to the superintendent of public instruction, 1892–1893, Duval County file, box 4–23/250, SDE, TSA.
22. L. J. Christen in Laredo to Miguel E. Diébold in Laredo, October 29, 1910, in SRE, legajo 352.
23. Ibid.
24. William Gatewood, "General Report," unpublished report to the superintendent of public instruction, 1892–1893, Eagle Pass file, 701–46, SDE, TSA.
25. He also added that he understood his investigation might not have been as thorough as de la Barra expected, but that he was short-staffed and overworked and could not be away from his office. Miguel E. Diébold in Laredo to Francisco de la Barra in Washington, DC, November 3, 1910, in SRE, legajo 352.
26. Francisco de la Barra in Washington, DC, to Esteva Ruiz in Mexico City, November 10, 1910, in SRE, legajo 352.
27. De la Barra sent letters to consuls in Texas City, San Antonio, Roma, Rio Grande City, Port Arthur, Galveston, El Paso, Del Río, Eagle Pass, and Brownsville. He received responses from Texas City, Roma, Rio Grande City, Port Arthur, Galveston, and Eagle Pass. Francisco de la Barra in Washington, DC, to various consuls in south Texas, December 14, 1910, in SRE, legajo 352.
28. "Primer Centenario de la Iniciacion de la Independencia en Mexico—su celebración por el Consulado de México en Laredo, Texas," 1910, expediente III/822.3"910"/1, topográfica L-E-122, SRE, Sección de Archivo General. See also "Completing All Details, Executive Committee of Centennial Interesting Meeting," *Laredo Weekly Times*, August 7, 1910; and "Diébold to Supervise, President Diaz Commissions Him by Wire This Morning," *Laredo Weekly Times*, September 18, 1910.
29. "La Exclusion de los Niños Mexicanos en la Mayor Parte de las Escuelas Oficiales de Texas, es Positiva," *La Crónica*, December 17, 1910.
30. Ibid.
31. Ibid. Idar cites a letter that Ruiz wrote on December 8, which is not included with the rest of the documents in this file in the SRE.
32. Ibid.
33. A. P. Spohn, "General Report," unpublished report to the superintendent of public instruction, 1908–1909, Zapata County file, box 4–23/209, SDE, TSA.
34. "La Exclusion de los Niños Mexicanos," *La Crónica*, December 17, 1910. Though Idar only ridicules Ruiz for extrapolating Diébold's report to all of Texas, the evidence in the Archivo de Secretaría de Relaciones Exteriores implicates de la Barra as a willing accomplice to, and the possible instigator of, this extrapolation. Additionally, all the letters responding to de la Barra issuing instructions are from Enrique C. Creel, not Ruiz.
35. Marco Antonio Samaniego López, "El Norte Revolucionario."
36. "Guerrero, Small Town in Chihuahua, in Arms," *El Paso Herald*, November 24, 1910.

37. "Texas' Educational Outlook," *Houston Post*, December 29, 1910. The *Houston Post* reprinted Bralley's speech. See also "Teachers of Texas are in Annual Convention at Abilene," *Houston Post*, December 29, 1910.

38. F. M. Bralley to William S. Sutton, January 11, 1911, box 4P341, William Seneca Sutton Papers, 1894–1928, Dolph Briscoe Center for American History, University of Texas at Austin.

39. "Extracto de un Discurso del Superintendente de Instrucción Pública de Texas," *La Crónica*, January 12, 1911. Emphasis in Idar's translation, but not in the *Houston Post*'s publication of the speech. Idar's translation very closely resembles Bralley's actual speech, with the exception of the all-caps phrases.

40. Ibid.

41. Ibid. Emphasis in original.

42. "La Exclusion de los Niños Mexicanos," *La Crónica*, December 17, 1910.

43. Ibid.

44. "La Exclusion en el Condado de Guadalupe: Nuestras Investigaciones se Desarrollan, y Circula Nuestra Correspondencia por todo el Estado de Texas, Averiguando los Hechos," *La Crónica*, December 31, 1910.

45. S. C. Rangel and C. M. Alcala, "Project Report"; Montejano, *Anglos and Mexicans in the Making of Texas*, 160. Victoria-María MacDonald states that the contention that Seguin was the first place to segregate Mexican children formally "has not been confirmed." MacDonald, "Demanding Their Rights," accessed April 20, 2018, https://www.nps.gov/articles/latinothemeeducation.htm.

46. "La Exclusion en el Condado de Guadalupe: Nuestras Investigaciones se Desarrollan, y Circula Nuestra Correspondencia por todo el Estado de Texas, Averiguando los Hechos," *La Crónica*, December 31, 1910.

47. "La Prensa de Mexico y de Texas se Interesa por el Bienestar de los Mexicanos en este Pais," *La Crónica*, January 12, 1911.

48. "La Exclusion en las Escuelas de los Condados de Frio, Bee, Hays, Bastrop, Comal, Caldwell, Blanco, Etc., Etc.," *La Crónica*, February 9, 1911.

49. Enrique Creel in Mexico City to Francisco de la Barra in Washington, DC, January 24, 1911, in SRE, legajo 352.

50. Ibid.

51. "La Exclusion en el Condado de Guadalupe: Nuestras Investigaciones se Desarrollan, y Circula Nuestra Correspondencia por todo el Estado de Texas, Averiguando los Hechos," *La Crónica*, December 31, 1910.

52. "Interesantisimo Cuestionario," *La Crónica*, January 26, 1911. Unfortunately, I have not been able to find the responses to the questionnaire. It is unlikely that they survived.

53. "Tanto los Niños Mexicanos como los Mexico-Americanos, son Excluidos de las Escuelas Oficiales," *La Crónica*, December 24, 1910.

54. Miguel E. Diébold in Laredo to Nicasio Idar in Laredo, December 19, 1910, in SRE, legajo 352.

55. "La Exclusion de los Niños Mexicanos de las Escuelas del Estado de Texas," *La Crónica*, January 19, 1911. Interestingly, *La Crónica* states that these orders came from V. Salado Alvarez, but the document in the archival file is signed by Enrique C. Creel.

56. Mark Wasserman, "The Social Origins of the 1910 Revolution in Chihuahua."

57. Felipe Ávila Espinosa, *Entre el Porfiriato y la Revolución.*

58. For more on the hegemonic struggle between the Texas Mexican middle class and the Mexican middle class, see Richard A. García, *Rise of the Mexican American Middle-Class, 1929-1941;* and Orozco, *No Mexicans.*

CHAPTER 3. REVOLUTIONARY AND REFINED

1. For work on the anti-Mexican violence in south Texas in this era, and the way descendants of the victims have ensured that the history of brutality was not lost through several generations, see Monica Muñoz Martinez, *The Injustice Never Leaves You.*

2. "La Liga Femenil Mexicanista," *La Crónica,* October 19, 1911.

3. Gonzales, *The Mexican Revolution, 1910-1940,* chap. 1.

4. Quoted in Gonzales, *Mexican Revolution,* 9.

5. Mary Kay Vaughan, "Primary Education and Literacy in Nineteenth-Century Mexico."

6. Ibid., 43; Bazant de Saldaña, *Historia de la Educación Durante El Porfiriato,* 135.

7. Vaughan, "Primary Education," 31.

8. Manuel Gamio, *The Life Story of the Mexican Immigrant,* 187.

9. Interview with Antonio Gómez, age eleven, US Immigration Service. Records of the Immigration and Naturalization Service, Series A, Part 2, *Mexican Immigration, 1906-1930,* reel 8. Quoted in Chávez Leyva, "'Que Son Los Niños?,'" 222.

10. Interview with Louise Gates by Sarah E. John, December 14, 1978, "Interview no. 726," Institute of Oral History, University of Texas at El Paso.

11. Sotero H. Soria, "A Gift of Literacy"; quoted in Chávez Leyva, "'Que Son Los Niños?,'" 223.

12. María Teresa Fernández Aceves, *Mujeres.* See also *Sinéctica* 28 (February-July 2006) issue, which focuses on Mexican women teachers in the first half of the twentieth century. Teaching as an important site of female influence historically occurred within other communities. See, for example, Glenda Gilmore, *Gender and Jim Crow*; Kathryn Kish Sklar, *Catharine Beecher;* Jessica Enoch, *Refiguring Rhetorical Education;* Audrey Thomas McCluskey and Elaine M. Smith, *Mary McLeod Bethune;* and McCluskey, *A Forgotten Sisterhood.*

13. Anna Macías, *Against All Odds: The Feminist Movement in Mexico to 1940,* xv.

14. Ibid., 17.

15. Gonzalez, *Life Along the Border,* 120, footnote 17.

16. Macías, *Against All Odds,* 13-14.

17. Sonia Hernández, "Chicanas in the U.S.-Mexican Borderlands: Transborder Conversations of Feminism and Anarchism, 1905-1938," 139.

18. Macías, *Against All Odds,* 29.

19. Ibid.

20. Ibid., 32.

21. Jocelyn Olcott, *Revolutionary Women in Postrevolutionary Mexico,* 96-97.

22. Quoted in Olcott, *Revolutionary Women,* 96.

23. Leticia Garza-Falcón, *Gente Decente,* 88.

24. Gabriela Gonzalez, "Carolina Munguía and Emma Tenayuca"; Gabriela González, "Jovita Idar," in *Texas Women: Their Histories, Their Lives.*

25. "Debemos Trabajar," *La Crónica,* November 23, 1911.

26. Christine Stansell, *American Moderns: Bohemian New York and the Creation of a New Century.*

27. Vicki Ruiz, *From Out of the Shadows*, 67.

28. Gabriela González, "Jovita Idar," 239.

29. Ibid., 236.

30. "Por la Raza: La Niñez Mexicana en Texas," *La Crónica*, August 10, 1911.

31. Ibid. In an interview with Gabriela González, Jovita Fuentes López, Idar's niece and namesake, stated that her aunt never allowed her to mix Spanish and English. González, "Jovita Idar," 242.

32. "Por la Raza: La Niñez Mexicana en Texas," *La Crónica*, August 10, 1911.

33. Ibid.

34. H. E. McKinstry, "The American Language in Mexico," 336. Quoted in John M. Lipski, *Varieties of Spanish in the United States*, 42.

35. Lipski, *Varieties of Spanish*, 40; Lipski, "The Impact of the Mexican Revolution on Spanish in the United States."

36. Lipski, "The Impact of the Mexican Revolution."

37. "Adelanto de los Mexicanos de Texas," *La Crónica*, September 21, 1911.

38. "Por la Raza: La Conservación del Nacionalismo," *La Crónica*, August 17, 1911.

39. Ibid.

40. Ibid.

41. Ibid.

42. Ibid.

43. "La Liga Femenil Mexicanista," *La Crónica*, November 16, 1911; "La Liga Femenil Mexicanista," *La Crónica*, December 7, 1911; Clara Lomas, "Transborder Discourse," 65.

44. "La Liga Femenil Mexicanista," *La Crónica*, December 7, 1911.

45. Rentería's 1917 border card reveals that she was born around 1893. "María Rentería, arrival date March 31, 1917," Records of the Immigration and Naturalization Service, 178702004, Record Group 85, Microfilm Roll 081, National Archives and Records Administration, digital file, Ancestry (ancestry. com), accessed May 25, 2019. See also "La Liga Femenil Mexicanista," *La Crónica*, October 19, 1911.

46. "Advertisement," *La Crónica*, September 7, 1911.

47. "Escuela que Progresa," *La Crónica*, November 9, 1911; "Nueva Escuela" and "La Señorita María Rentería," *La Crónica*, December 28, 1911.

48. Rentería, border card, March 31, 1917.

49. María Teresa Fernández Aceves, "Imagined Communities."

50. "Leona Vicario y Rafaela Lopez," *La Crónica*, October 19, 1911.

51. Ibid.

52. Ibid.

53. Ibid.

54. "Adelanto de los Mexicanos de Texas," *La Crónica*, September 21, 1911.

55. *The Rebel* was not published until 1994. Villegas de Magnón's granddaughter, Leonor Smith, oversaw its publication, having promised her mother, Leonor Grubbs, before she died that she would work to publish her grandmother's memoirs. Evidently, Grubbs was also unable to get it published during her own lifetime, though she did succeed in getting installments of the narrative published in the Spanish-language section of the *Laredo Times* in 1961. Clara

Lomas, "Introduction: Revolutionary Women and the Alternative Press in the Borderlands."

56. Villegas de Magnón, *The Rebel*, 90.

57. Bessie Lindheim, *Story of Laredo*, No. 16: *Leonor Villegas Magnon and the Mexican Revolution*.

58. Margarita Araiza, "On a Historical Note: March Exhibit Focuses on Notable Laredoan," 44–45; Villegas de Magnón, *The Rebel*, ch. 8.

59. James Alex Garza, "Fire and Fury: The 1910 Mexican Revolution in Laredo, Texas," vertical file on Mexican Revolution, Webb County Heritage Foundation, Laredo, TX.

60. Ibid.; *Laredo Weekly Times*, January 4, 1914.

61. Villegas de Magnón, *The Rebel*, 95–96.

62. "Adelanto de los Mexicanos de Texas," *La Crónica*, September 21, 1911.

63. Ibid.

64. Ibid.

65. "A group of pupils in Leonor Villegas de Magnón's first kindergarten, 1912," photograph in Leonor Villegas de Magnón Papers, Arte Público Press, University of Houston. The list of children's names in the photo is part of the Leonor M. Smith Collection, Webb County Heritage Foundation, Laredo, TX.

66. Porfirio Díaz was the president of Mexico from 1876 to 1911. He claimed he won the 1910 presidential election, though his use of voter fraud was widespread. Francisco Madero, a wealthy landowner, openly challenged the legitimacy of Díaz's regime and founded the Anti-Reelectionist Party. Madero was president of Mexico from 1911 to 1913, when he was assassinated. See Gonzalez, *Mexican Revolution*.

67. "Magnón's Last Kindergarten Class after the Revolution, 1923," photograph in the Leonor Villegas de Magnón Papers, Arte Público Press, University of Houston. The list of names of the students in the photo are part of the Leonor M. Smith Collection, Webb County Heritage Foundation, Laredo, TX.

68. Magnón remembered picking up Idar from *El Progreso*'s print shop, where Magnón stated she worked as a writer, when the Battle of Nuevo Laredo began on March 17, 1913. The University of San Antonio's General Photograph Collection has a photo of Idar in *El Progreso*'s print shop dated 1914. In that year, the Texas Rangers first attempted to demolish the print shop in retaliation for the newspaper's publication of an anti-Woodrow Wilson article, but Idar stopped them. The Rangers returned the following day when Idar was not there and carried out their malicious activities. Magnón, *The Rebel*, 85; González, "Jovita Idar," 240; and see caption for Idar photo in this chapter.

69. Magnón, *The Rebel*, 80.

70. "El Club Internacional," *La Crónica*, April 30, 1910; "El Niño Santos M. Benavides," *La Crónica*, January 19, 1911.

71. *A Twentieth-Century History of Southwest Texas*, vol. 2, 84.

72. *A Twentieth-Century History of Southwest Texas*; Howard Scott Cook, *Mexican Brick Culture in the Building of Texas, 1800s-1980s*, 32; and James W. Falvella, *Souvenir Album of Laredo, the Gateway to Mexico*, 30.

73. Frederico H. Ligarde, "A Mis Amigos y al Publico en General," *La Crónica*, May 7, 1910. In other Spanish-language articles that mention him, he is always referred to as Frederico. However, in Falvella's *Souvenir Album*, which features his

portrait under the section titled "Laredo Board of School Trustees," he is listed as "Fred H. Ligarde."

74. "A group of pupils in Leonor Villegas de Magnón's first kindergarten, 1912," photograph in the Leonor Villegas de Magnón Papers; 1920 US Census, Webb County, Texas, population schedule, Justice Precinct 1, Laredo, pages 1B and 2A (stamped), dwelling 20, family 21, Federico Ligardi, digital image, Ancestry (ancestry.com), accessed June 5, 2016; "Mrs. Ligarde Compliments Mrs. Wright," *Laredo Times*, May 6, 1929.

75. "The Rebel's Last Kindergarten Class after the Revolution," photograph in the Leonor Villegas de Magnón Papers; 1920 US Census, Webb County, Texas, population schedule, Justice Precinct 1, Laredo, page 23A (stamped), dwelling 7, family 7, Amadee Ligarde, digital image, Ancestry (ancestry.com), accessed June 5, 2016.

76. "Advertisement: A. Ligarde Brick Co.," *Laredo Times*, February 21, 1929; "Ligarde Brick Firm's Business Increasing," *Laredo Times*, May 15, 1929; 1920 US Census, "Amadee Ligarde."

77. Sherilyn Brandenstein, "International Ladies' Garment Workers' Union," "Handbook of Texas Online," accessed December 9, 2013, http://www.tshaonline.org/handbook/online/articles/oci02.

78. "El Club Internacional," *La Crónica*, April 30, 1910.

79. "La Liga Femenil Mexicanista," *La Crónica*, October 19, 1911.

80. 1920 US Census, Webb County, Texas, population schedule, Justice Precinct No. 1, Laredo City, p. 2 A, dwelling 29, family 29, Maria Villarreal, digital image, Ancestry (ancestry.com), accessed May 25, 2019; Villegas de Magnón, *The Rebel*, 94-95; Valerie Gonzalez, email message to Philis M. Barragán, May 10, 2013; "A Brief History of the Holding Institute," Holding Institute Research File, Webb County Heritage Foundation, Laredo, TX. In the 1910 census, Villarreal lists her age as eighteen instead of twenty-seven.

81. Valerie Gonzalez, email message to Philis M. Barragán, May 17, 2013. Valerie Gonzalez is María Villarreal's great-niece.

82. "Nueva Escuela en Local del Ejército de Salvación," *La Prensa*, August 10, 1927.

83. Villegas de Magnón, *The Rebel*, 94.

84. Ibid., 94-95.

85. Ibid., 95.

86. Ibid.

CHAPTER 4. EDUCATION IN POST-MEXICAN REVOLUTION TEXAS, 1920-1950

1. Orozco, *No Mexicans*, 47-49.

2. Annie Webb Blanton, "The Foreign Problem in Texas and the Need of an Illiteracy Commission," 22-25.

3. See correspondence in legajo NC 2005-82, SRE, Mexico City.

4. James W. Cameron, "The History of Mexican Public Education in Los Angeles, 1910-1930," 181.

5. See Sánchez, *Becoming Mexican American*, chap. 5; F. Arturo Rosales, *¡Pobre Raza!*, chap. 3; G. González, *Mexican Consuls and Labor Organizing*, chap. 2; and San Miguel and Donato, "Latino Education in Twentieth-Century America: A Brief History," 33.

6. Cybelle Fox, *Three Worlds of Relief*, 76.

7. Theodore Roosevelt, *Fear God and Take Your Own*, 370.
8. Emory Bogardus, *Essentials of Americanization*, 9-10.
9. Ibid.; Fox, *Three Worlds*, 75.
10. Bogardus, *Essentials of Americanization*, 13.
11. Ibid., 13-14.
12. Ibid., 218.
13. Bogardus, "The Mexican Immigrant," 482.
14. Alfred White, *The Apperceptive Mass of Foreigners as Applied to Americanization*, 13. Quoted in Fox, *Three Worlds*, 77.
15. Fox, *Three Worlds*, chap. 4.
16. Roosevelt, *Fear God and Take Your Own Part*, 370.
17. Sánchez, *Becoming Mexican American*, 116.
18. Ibid., 119.
19. Ruben Flores, *Backroads Pragmatists*, chap. 2.
20. Ibid., 10. Sánchez focuses his analysis on the Mexican government's condescension towards its rural citizens, and Flores focuses on the international relationship between Mexican and United States intellectuals such as George I. Sánchez and Lloyd L. Tireman, and their mutual interests in using education to reconcile the difficulties of national unity in the face of a wildly heterogeneous population.
21. Renato González Mello, "Manuel Gamio, Diego Rivera, and the Politics of Mexican Anthropology."
22. Gamio believed the homogeneity of United States was found in the country's "common Caucasian origin," wherein the Indian population was "insignificant in number" and the other minorities without question would be incorporated into the larger dominant culture. Quoted in Sánchez, *Becoming Mexican American*, 120-124.
23. Original draft of Gamio, *Mexican Immigration to the United States*, 79, Manuel Gamio Collection, Bancroft Library, University of California Berkeley. Quoted in Sánchez, *Becoming Mexican American*, 122. As Sánchez notes, this passage did not make it into the published version.
24. Mary Kay Vaughan, *The State, Education, and Social Class in Mexico, 1880-1928*, 215-238.
25. Sánchez, *Becoming Mexican American*, 113.
26. Ibid.
27. Rosales, *¡Pobre Raza!*, 40.
28. "Mexican Consul General Has Department in Office to Aid Friendless; Organizes Society," *El Paso Herald*, April 6, 1921.
29. Orozco, *No Mexicans*, 68.
30. Sánchez, *Becoming Mexican American*, 114. Cynthia Orozco mentions that the presence of these Honorific Commissions helped convince Mexican Americans that they needed to organize on their own behalf. Though Mexican Americans could participate in the organizations' events, they could not directly benefit from their political activism. Mexican immigrants could receive help from the Honorific Commissions and the Mexican Consulate, but these organizations could not do anything to help the political condition of Mexican Americans. Orozco, *No Mexicans*, 142-143.
31. "Mexican Consul General Has Department in Office to Aid Friendless; Organizes Society," *El Paso Herald*, April 6, 1921.

32. Ibid.
33. Ibid.
34. Martha Menchaca, *Naturalizing Mexican Immigrants*, 6.
35. Gilbert G. González and Raúl Fernández, "Chicano History: Transcending Cultural Models."
36. Desiderio Tagle to Cónsul Gral de Mexico, San Antonio, July 4, 1920, Sección 17, Caja 13, expediente 171, topográfica 17-12-180, Departamento Diplomatico, Sección de Archivo General, SRE.
37. Barbara Stock, "Fentress, TX," "Handbook of Texas Online," accessed February 2, 2016, http://www.tshaonline.org/handbook/online/articles/hnf16.
38. Desiderio Tagle to Cónsul Gral de Mexico, San Antonio, July 4, 1920, Sección 17, Caja 13, expediente 171, topográfica 17-12-180, Departamento Diplomático, Sección de Archivo General, SRE, Mexico City, Mexico.
39. Ursino Amaya, F. Morales, Pedro Treviño, and Crispín Amaya to Sr. Cónsul de Mexico en San Antonio, TX, Noviembre 12, 1920, No. 2061, expediente Q-1, topográfica 17-13-90, Sección de Archivo General, SRE.
40. G. F. Oheim to Hon. L. Garza Leal, June 2, 1922, legajo 631, expediente 48, Sección de Archivo General, SRE.
41. Ibid.
42. George A. Martínez, "Legal Indeterminacy, Judicial Discretion and the Mexican-American Litigation Experience, 1930-1980." See also Richard R. Valencia, *Chicano Students and the Courts*.
43. L. Garza Leal to Hon. G. F. Oheim, June 6, 1922, legajo 631, expediente 48, Sección de Archivo General, SRE.
44. L. Garza Leal to Hon. G. F. Oheim, June 16, 1922, legajo 631, expediente 48, Sección de Archivo General, SRE.
45. L. Garza Leal to Al C. Presidente de la Comisión Honorifica Mexicana, June 16, 1922, legajo 631, expediente 48, Sección de Archivo General, SRE.
46. "Los Mexicanos de Houston Cuentan Ya Con Una Commission Honorífica y Con Una Brigada de la Cruz Azul," *La Prensa*, August 28, 1921; "Quedó Instalada la Comisión Honorífica en Magnolia Park, Texas," *La Prensa*, September 5, 1921; "Compliments are Paid Departing Mexican Consul," *Houston Post*, April 13, 1922; "Mexican Consul General Begins Work Here Today," *San Antonio Evening News*, June 30, 1922.
47. Rosales, *¡Pobre Raza!*, 40.
48. Donna Colter, "Heralding Our History," *New Braunfels Herald-Zeitung*, May 3, 1998; Daniel P. Greene, "New Braunfels, TX," "Handbook of Texas Online," accessed February 3, 2016, http://www.tshaonline.org/handbook/online/articles/hen02.
49. George Frederic Oheim Papers, 1846-1942, Doc. 6177, Daughters of the Republic of Texas Library, San Antonio, TX.
50. Baker, *Fifth Biennial Report*, 9-10.
51. Blanton, "The Foreign Problem in Texas and the Need of an Illiteracy Commission," 22.
52. Blanton, *Strange Career*, 88-89.
53. Ariel J. Gross, *What Blood Won't Tell*, 285. See also Blanton, *Strange Career*, 95-96; and Blanton, *George I. Sánchez*, 167.

54. Gross, *What Blood Won't Tell*, 285. See also Blanton, *Strange Career*, 95-96.
55. Francisco Balderamma, *In Defense of La Raza*; Vicki L. Ruiz, *From Out of the Shadows*; Christopher, *The Lemon Grove Incident*.
56. Valencia, *Chicano Students and the Courts*, 22–42.
57. E. D. Ruiz to C. Encargado de Negocios de México, ad-interim, October 18, 1922, legajo 631, expediente 48, Sección de Archivo General, SRE.
58. El Encargado de Negocios ad-interim to Señor Cónsul General de México, San Antonio, Texas, October 26, 1922, legajo 631, expediente 48, Sección de Archivo General, SRE.
59. "La Instalacion de las Comisiones Honorificas y Brigadas de la Cruz Azul en Hebbronville y Benavides," *La Prensa*, October 21, 1921.
60. For work that speaks to the role that American exceptionalism and Mexican chauvinism played in hindering the development of Tex Mex language and culture, see Gloria Anzaldúa, *Borderlands/La Frontera*. See also Sánchez, *Becoming Mexican American*, 11–13.
61. "Una Iniciativa Para Fundar Una Escuela en Mission, Texas," *La Prensa*, August 23, 1921.
62. "Una Escuela Mexicana Será Establecida en San Antonio," *La Prensa*, July 25, 1921.
63. Ibid.
64. Lipski, *Varieties of Spanish in the United States*, chap. 4.
65. Ibid., 83.
66. "Mexican Consul Arrives in City," *Port Arthur News*, June 14, 1922.
67. "Consul to Observe Wedding Anniversary," *Brownsville Herald*, August 18, 1929.
68. "Progress Made in Mexican Blue Cross," *Port Arthur News*, June 23, 1922; "500 Ships to Mexico Yearly," *Port Arthur News*, July 1, 1923.
69. "Fue Inaugurada una Escuela Mexicana en Port Arthur," *La Prensa*, October 28, 1923.
70. "Notas Mexicana de los E. Unido," *La Prensa*, February 23, 1924.
71. "Una Interesante Junta de la Colonia Mexicana en Mercedes, Texas," *La Prensa*, May 20, 1925.
72. "Una Junta de la Colonia Mexicana en la Población de Mercedes, Texas," *La Prensa*, August 6, 1925.
73. Their family name was "Vásquez," but Ismael used "Vázquez."
74. 1900 US Census, Jeff Davis County, Texas, population schedule, Justice Precinct 1, p. 268 A (stamped), dwelling 70, family 72, Augustin, Ysmael, and Alfredo Vasquez, digital image, Ancestry (ancestry.com), accessed February 19, 2016; Western District of Texas, Naturalization Records, 1881–1992, Petition Number 12300, Ysmael Moreno Vasquez, digital image, Ancestry (ancestry.com), accessed February 19, 2016; "El Sr. Ismael M. Vázquez," *El Cronista Del Valle*, May 20, 1925; "Obituaries," April 11, 1975, *Brownsville Herald*. In Ismael's petition to become a naturalized citizen, he stated that his legal name was "Ysmael," but he had previously used "Ismael."
75. In the 1900 and 1910 census, both men are listed as having been born in Texas. Their father, Agustín Vásquez, was listed as a widower in 1900. 1900 US Census, Jeff Davis County, Texas, population schedule, Justice Precinct 1, p. 268 A (stamped), dwelling 70, family 72, Augustin, Ysmael, and Alfredo Vasquez, digital image, Ancestry (ancestry.com), accessed February 19, 2016; 1910 US Census, Val

Verde County, Texas, population schedule, Justice Precinct 1, p. 11 A (stamped), dwellings 197, 202, and 205, lines 3, 30, and 46, Augustine, Alfredo, and Ysmael Vasquez, digital image, Ancestry (ancestry.com), accessed February 19, 2016. Their mother was Maria de Jesus Moreno. Texas Department of State Health Services, Texas Death Certificates, 1903–1982, Alfredo Cortez Vasquez, digital image, Ancestry (ancestry.com), accessed February 19, 2016.

76. Michael M. Smith, "The Mexican Immigrant Press Beyond the Borderlands,"; Michael M. Smith, "The Mexican Revolution in Kansas City: Jack Danciger Versus the Colonia Elite"; and Michael M. Smith and Jorge Durand, "'El Cosmopolita' de Kansas City (1914–1919): Un Periódico Para Mexicanos." In later decades, Danciger was also sympathetic to the Mexican American fight for civil rights. See his 1944 letter to Alfonso S. Perales, one of the original founders of LULAC: Danciger to Perales, June 6, 1944, "Selections from the Alonso S. Perales Papers," Special Collections, University of Houston Libraries, accessed February 22, 2016, http://digital.lib.uh.edu/collection/perales/item/66. For information on Danciger and his relationship with Ed Idar and George I. Sánchez in the 1940s, see Blanton, *George I. Sánchez*, 142.

77. "El Problema de Nuestros Braceros," *La Prensa*, February 22, 1928; Rosales, *¡Pobre Raza!*, 44.

78. 1930 US Census, Jackson County, Missouri, population schedule, Kansas City, p. 6 A (stamped), dwelling 64, family 156, Alfredo Vasques, digital image, Ancestry (ancestry.com), accessed February 19, 2016.

79. 1930 US Census, Denver County, Colorado, population schedule, Denver City, p. 13 B (stamped), dwelling 141, family 416, Ysmael M Vazquez, digital image, Ancestry (ancestry.com), accessed February 19, 2016.

80. Western District of Texas, Naturalization Records, 1881–1992, Petition Number 12300, Ysmael Moreno Vasquez, digital image, Ancestry (ancestry.com), accessed February 19, 2016.

81. "Se Construira Una Escuela Para Niños Mexicanos En Laredo, Tex.," *La Prensa*, July 6, 1925; "Quedo Terminada La Escuela Para Niños Mexicanos," *La Prensa*, September 7, 1925.

82. "Quedo Terminada La Escuela Para Niños Mexicanos," *La Prensa*, September 7, 1925; "Se Reanudan Los Trabajos de Pavimentación de la Calle Market," *La Prensa*, June 13, 1925. Vazquez and Garza López were very close friends. In August 1925, Garza López named his son Ismael, and Vázquez and his wife, Esther, were the child's godparents. "Bautizo," *La Prensa*, August 27, 1925.

83. Alfredo C. Vásquez to Al C. Secretario de Relaciones Exteriores, October 15, 1926, legajo NC 1183–5, Sección de Archivo General, SRE.

84. Ibid.

85. Birkhead, Lang, and Beckmann to A. P. Carrillo, December 10, 1926, legajo NC 1183–5, Sección de Archivo General, SRE.

86. A. P. Carrillo to C. Consul de Mexico in Brownsville, Noviembre 18, 1926; A. P. Carrillo to Felix Alvarado, Noviembre 20, 1926; legajo NC 1183–5, Sección de Archivo General, SRE. For more on Gregorio Cortez, see Américo Paredes, *With His Pistol in His Hand*.

87. Alfredo C. Vásquez to Al C. Secretario de Relaciones Exteriores, December 4, 1926, legajo NC 1183–5, Sección de Archivo General, SRE.

88. "Was Named Consul General and Will Remain in Laredo," *Laredo Weekly Times*, October 23, 1921.

89. For a biography of Blanton, see Cottrell, *Pioneer Woman Educator*.

90. Interview with Garza, Mexican Consul, Houston, 1929, field note series B, set 1, 29, folder 5, carton 10, Paul Schuster Taylor Papers, Banc Mss 84/38 c, Bancroft Library, University of California, Berkeley.

91. Interview with Juan Llanos, Teacher in a Mexican Private School, Big Wells, field notes series B, set 1, 29, folder 5, carton 10, Paul Schuster Taylor Papers.

92. Interview with Miss Faye Parr, Teacher Mexican School, Big Wells, TX, 1929, field note series B, set 1, 29, folder 5, carton 10, Paul Schuster Taylor Papers.

93. Interview with Juan Llanos, Teacher in a Mexican Private School, Big Wells, field notes series B, set 1, 29, folder 5, carton 10, Paul Schuster Taylor Papers.

94. Interview with Juan Cortez, Committee of the Comisión Honorífica, Big Wells, TX, 1920, field note series B, set 1, 29, folder 5, carton 10, Paul Schuster Taylor Papers.

95. "Interview with Juan Llanos, Teacher in a Mexican Private School, Big Wells," field notes series B, set 1, 29, folder 5, carton 10, Paul Schuster Taylor Papers.

96. Ibid.

97. Interview with Miss Faye Parr, Teacher Mexican School, Big Wells, TX, 1929, field note series B, set 1, 29, folder 5, carton 10, Paul Schuster Taylor Papers.

98. Ibid.

99. Interview with Miss Dunham, Teacher, Valley Wells, TX, April 24, 1929, field note series B, set 1, 29, folder 5, carton 10, Paul Schuster Taylor Papers.

100. Rosa Lidia Vásquez, interview by author, San Antonio, TX, July 3, 2018.

101. Rolando Hinojosa-Smith, interview by author, Austin, TX, February 3, 2013; "Escuelitas" vertical file, Blagg-Huey Library, Texas Woman's University, Denton, TX.

102. Francisco Calcagno, "Mantilla (Luis Felipe)," *Biográfico Cubano*, 403; "L. T. Mantilla, Arrival Date July 29, 1862," Passenger Lists of Vessel Arriving at New York, New York, 1820–1897, microfilm serial: M237, Roll 221, Line 23, National Archives, Ancestry (ancestry.com), accessed October 8, 2014.

103. Vanessa Michelle Ziegler, "The Revolt of the 'Ever-Faithful Isle': The Ten Years' War in Cuba, 1868–1878," 1–38.

104. Antonio De La Cova, "Cuban Exiles in the Key West during the Ten Years' War, 1868–1878," 294.

105. Francisco Calcagno, *Biográfico Cubano*, 403; *Biographical Catalogue of the Chancellors, Professors, and Graduates of the Department of Arts and Science of the University of the City of New York*, 240; "Marriages and Deaths," *New York Herald*, September 12, 1878.

106. See Nicolás Kanellos, *Hispanic Literature of the United States*, 50; Sánchez, *Cartas de José Martí a Néstor Ponce de León;* Francisco Calcagno, "Ponce (Nestor—De Leon y La Guardia)," *Biográfico Cubano*, 519; Luis F. Mantilla, *Libro de Lectura No. 1*.

107. *Papers Relating to the Foreign Relations of the United States, Transmitted to Congress with the Annual Message of the President, December 4, 1871*, 735.

108. Vaughan, "Primary Education," 42–43.

109. Bazant de Saldaña, *Historia de la Educación Durante El Porfiriato*, 54; Antonio Barbosa Heldt, *Como Enseñar a Leer y Escribir*, 30.

110. Mantilla, *Libro de Lectura No. 1*, 27.

III. *Catálogo Oficial de las Exhibiciones de los Estados Unidos Mexicanos.*

112. Josefina Andrade is my grandmother. She still had her copy of "la Mantilla" when I was a child.

113. *Libro de Lectura No.* 2 is not a Spanish-language instruction book, but an anthology of readings by Latin American and Spanish authors for adults. Idar's niece, Jovita Fuentes Lopez, remembers her aunt reading from *No. 2* throughout her life. Jovita Fuentes Lopez, interview with author, San Antonio, TX, August 26, 2013.

114. S. M. N. Marrs and Mary Nash, "History and the Status of the Teaching of Spanish in Texas," 3.

115. "Has Sido Cerradas Varias Escuelas Donde Se Enseña el Idioma Español," *La Prensa*, November 30, 1928

116. Richard A. Garcia, *Rise of the Mexican American Middle Class;* Orozco, *No Mexicans.*

117. Orozco, *No Mexicans*, 75.

118. Ibid., 73.

119. Order of Sons of America (Council 5) Records, BLAC.

120. Orozco, *No Mexicans*, 78–86, 90; Blanton, *Strange Career*, 94.

121. Virginia Harper-Ho, "Noncitizen Voting Rights"; Ron Hayduk, *Democracy for All*, chap. 1.

122. Z. Vela Ramírez, "Bienvenidos . . . ! Los Sres. Delegados de la Convencion 'Pro-Raza' de Harlingen, Texas," *El Comercio*, August 14, 1927, box 9, folder 41, Alonso S. Perales Papers, University of Houston.

123. For a thorough discussion of the Harlingen Convention of 1927, see Orozco, *No Mexicans*, chap. 5.

124. Ibid., chap. 6.

125. Legajo iv 264–32 (Mission, TX); legajo iv-323–6 (Mission, TX); legajos iv-212–14 and iv-266–80 (Del Río); legajos iv-262–20 and vi-320–34 (California).

126. Legajo NC 2005–82 (Valentine, TX) and legajo NC 2005–86 (Alamo, TX). For a discussion of the escuelita in Alamo, see Philis M. Barragán Goetz and Carlos K. Blanton, "The World of Education among Mexican Immigrants and Mexican Americans in J. T. Canales' South Texas," in *Reverberations of Racial Violence: Critical Reflections on U.S. History*, edited by Sonia Hernández and John M. González, forthcoming from University of Texas Press.

127. For discussions of the significance of World War II, see David Montejano, *Anglos and Mexicans in the Making of Texas*, 244; Montejano, "The Demise of 'Jim Crow' for Texas Mexicans, 1940–1970"; and María Eva Flores, "What a Difference a War Makes!," 178. For scholars who locate the catalyst for Mexican American activism decades before World War II, see San Miguel, *"Let All of Them Take Heed"*; Thomas Kreneck, *Del Pueblo*; M. García, *Mexican Americans*; R. García, *Rise of the Mexican American Middle Class*; Arnoldo De León, *Ethnicity in the Sunbelt*; and Orozco, *No Mexicans.*

128. Valencia, *Chicano Students and the Courts*, chap. 1; Blanton, *Strange Career*, chap. 7; San Miguel, *"Let All of Them Take Heed,"* chap. 3; and M. García, *Mexican Americans*, chap. 3.

129. Carl Allsup, "Education is Our Freedom"; Allsup, *The American G.I. Forum: Origins and Evolution*; Blanton, *Strange Career*, chap. 7; and V. Carl Allsup, "American G.I. Forum of Texas," "Handbook of Texas Online," accessed July 29,

2018, http://www.tshaonline.org/handbook/online/articles/voa01.

130. Cybelle Fox, *Three Worlds of Relief*, chaps. 6 and 7; Sánchez, *Becoming Mexican American*, chap. 10.

131. Belisario and Adelina Flores, interview by author, San Antonio, TX, May 17, 2013.

132. Ibid.

133. Ibid.; Belisario Flores, email message to author, May 8, 2013.

134. Rolando Hinojosa-Smith, interview by author, Austin, TX, February 4, 2013.

135. Ibid.

136. Ibid.

137. Ibid.

138. Ibid.

139. Dr. Clotilde P. García, interviewed by Thomas Kreneck, Corpus Christi, TX, February 17, 1994, Clotilde P. García Papers, Mary and Jeff Bell Library, Texas A&M University–Corpus Christi.

140. Ibid.; Rolando Hinojosa-Smith, interview by author, Austin, TX, February 4, 2013.

141. Ruben Manuel Vásquez, email message to author, May 6, 2013.

142. Rolando Hinojosa-Smith, email message to author, May 7, 2013.

143. Ruben Manuel Vásquez, email message to author, May 6, 2013.

144. Ibid.

145. José A. Nieto, email message to author, May 7, 2013.

146. Ibid.

147. Ibid.

148. José E. Limón, interview by Francisco Hernández, June 31, 1980, Berkeley, CA, interview in possession of author; and José E. Limón, email message to author, May 22, 2015.

149. José E. Limón, email message to author, May 22, 2015.

CHAPTER 5. ESCUELITAS AND THE MEXICAN AMERICAN GENERATION'S CAMPAIGN FOR EDUCATIONAL INTEGRATION

1. Norma Cantú, interview by author, October, 3, 2018, San Antonio, TX.

2. M. García, *Mexican Americans*, 3. A number of subsequent scholars have used the phrase "Mexican American Generation" in their work, while pointing out the limitations of García's original articulation of this framework. Cynthia Orozco notes that while the generational approach is useful, it excludes immigrants and women (a shortcoming that García acknowledged), and also oversimplifies regional and ideological differences. Orozco also advocates expanding the dates to include the 1910s and 1920s. This chapter draws from both scholars, using the conceptual framework of a Mexican American Generation within a larger time frame, while acknowledging the salient role women played in the Mexican American civil rights movement. Orozco, *No Mexicans*, 4.

3. For work on the role of Texas historical narratives, Mexican American political activism, and the Texas Centennial, see González, *Border Renaissance*; M. García, *Mexican Americans*, chap. 9; and Omar Valerio-Jiménez, "Refuting History Tales: Collective Memories, Mexican Texans, and Texas History." For a biography of Carlos Castañeda, see Felix Almaráz, *Knight without Armor*, and for a biography of George I. Sánchez, see Blanton, *George I. Sánchez*.

4. One of the most well known members of the Mexican American Generation, George I. Sánchez, did not attend an escuelita.

5. Their views on whiteness fill both ends of the spectrum—from Neil Foley's "Faustian pact" argument to Cynthia Orozco's call for a stronger understanding of the "multiple, shifting, intersecting, and contradictory identities" these leaders had. Regarding the immigration debate, Blanton calls immigration their "Achilles heel," arguing for the importance of historical context. For key discussions of the immigration issue, see Blanton, *George I. Sánchez*, chap. 8. See also Juan Ramon García, *Operation Wetback*, 140–141. For key discussions of whiteness as Faustian pact, see Neil Foley, "Becoming Hispanic," 53–70. See also Foley's *The White Scourge* and *The Quest for Equality*. For work that encourages moving beyond the Faustian pact, see Orozco, *No Mexicans*, 5–6; and Blanton, *George I. Sánchez*, 183.

6. J. T. Canales, "Personal Recollections of J. T. Canales Written at the Request of and for Use by the Honorable Harbert Davenport in Preparing a Historical Sketch of the Lower Rio Grande Valley for the Soil Conservation District, Recently Organized, in Cameron County, Texas," April 26, 1945, box 2–23/214, folder "Personal Recollections of J. T. Canales," Harbert Davenport Papers, TSA.

7. "Dr. Clotilde Garcia," interview by Dr. Thomas H. Kreneck, February 17, 1994, 12; José G. García, *Lea y Escriba*, Mexico City, 1952, Clotilde García Papers, unprocessed collection, Mary and Jeff Bell Library, Special Collections and Archives, Texas A&M University–Corpus Christi. Doña Albinita's escuelita is the same one that Rolando Hinojosa-Smith's brother attended. The Hinojosa-Smith and García families were neighbors. "Dr. Clotilde Garcia"; Rolando Hinojosa-Smith, interview by author, Austin, TX, February 4, 2013.

8. Sáenz wrote several letters to Velázquez while he was serving in World War I. Zamora, *The World War I Diary of José de la Luz Sáenz*, 2, 70–71, 152. For a letter Velázquez sent to Sáenz while he was serving, see 407–409. See also Eulalio Velázquez to Alonso S. Perales, October 9, 1937, box 9, folder 15, Alonso S. Perales Papers, University of Houston Special Collections.

9. Eulalio Velázquez to Alonso S. Perales, October 9, 1937, Perales Papers.

10. Ibid.

11. García, *Mexican Americans*, 2–3.

12. Christine Sierra and Adaljiza Sosa Riddell, "Chicanas as Political Actors," 301–302. Quoted in Orozco, *No Mexicans*, 199–200.

13. Orozco, *No Mexicans*, 205–206. For an examination of women's participation in benevolent politics, see Gabriela González, "Carolina Munguía and Emma Tenayuca"; "Jovita Idar," 225–248; and *Redeeming La Raza*.

14. González, *Redeeming La Raza*, 5.

15. Ibid.

16. Even Mario T. García is moving toward an intergenerational approach. His paper at the 2018 Western Historical Association conference, "Transgenerational Chicano Politics: Bert Corona, the Mexican American Generation, and the Chicano Generation," examined Bert Corona as a bridge between the Mexican American Generation and the Chicano Generation. He noted that many Mexican American intellectuals did not confine themselves to one generation.

17. Laura Muñoz, "The Historical Restoration of the Mexican American Teacher in South Texas," 19–20.

18. All the biographical accounts of Elena Zamora O'Shea, as well as her death

certificate, state that she was born in 1880, but in the 1880 census, she is listed as being two years old. Additionally, the 1900 census states that she was born in 1878. 1880 US Census, Hidalgo County, Texas, population schedule, La Noria Cardeneña Rancho, pp. 257 C and 257 D (stamped), dwelling 406, family 406, Elena Zamora (top of 257 D), digital image, Ancestry (ancestry.com), accessed August 13, 2018; 1900 US Census, Nueces County, Texas, population schedule, Justice Precinct No. 4, p. 222 A (stamped), dwelling 111, family 115, Elena Zamora, digital image, Ancestry (ancestry.com), accessed August 13, 2018; Texas Department of State Health Services, Texas Death Certificates, 1903–1982, Maria Elena Zamora O'Shea, digital image, Ancestry (ancestry.com), accessed August 13, 2018.

19. The area between the Nueces River and the Río Grande was a disputed territory between 1836 and 1848. When Texas was part of Spain and then Mexico, its southern border was the Nueces River, but when the Texas army signed the Velasco Agreement with Santa Anna after the Battle of San Jacinto in 1836, they declared that the Río Grande was the southern border. The issue was not settled until the end of the US-Mexico War in 1848.

20. Andrés Tijerina, "Historical Introduction," xi–xv.

21. Ibid., xv.

22. Elena Zamora O'Shea, "Better Education for Our Money," *Dallas Morning News*, June 8, 1950.

23. Zamora O'Shea, "The Ranches of Southwest Texas as They Were in the '80s-'90s."

24. See chap. 1, as well as Blanton, *Strange Career*, 42–55.

25. Thaddeus M. Rhodes, "Annual Report," unpublished report to the superintendent of public instruction, 1881–1882; Max Stein, "Annual Report," unpublished report to the superintendent of public instruction, 1889–1890, Hidalgo County file, box 4–23/269, SDE, TSA.

26. Alicia A. Garza, "Hidalgo County," "Handbook of Texas Online," accessed August 28, 2018, http://www.tshaonline.org/handbook/online/articles/hch14.

27. Joseph Fitzsimmons, "Annual Report," unpublished reports to the superintendent of public instruction, 1881–1882 and 1889–1890, Nueces County file, box 4–23/198, SDE, TSA.

28. Christopher Long, "Nueces County," "Handbook of Texas Online," accessed August 28, 2018, http://www.tshaonline.org/handbook/online/articles/hcn05.

29. Fitzsimmons, "Annual Report," unpublished reports to the superintendent of public instruction, 1890–1891, Nueces County file, box 4–23/198, SDE, TSA.

30. Zamora O'Shea, "Ranches of Southwest Texas."

31. Fitzsimmons, "Annual Report," 1881–1882, 1885–1886, 1889–1890, Nueces County file, box 4–23/198, SDE, TSA.

32. George D. Fitzsimmons stated on his passport application that his father arrived in the United States around 1845, but Fitzsimmons's own Declaration of Citizenship states 1848. Military records indicate that he enlisted from New York. Joseph Fitzsimmons, Declaration of Citizenship, September 21, 1853, Nueces County Clerk's Office, Nueces County, TX; George D. Fitzsimmons, US Passport Applications, 1795–1925, National Archives and Records Administration, Ancestry (ancestry.com), accessed August 13, 2018; Joseph Fitzsimmons, July 29, 1848, US Army, Register of Enlistments, 1798–1914, Records of the Adjutant General's Office, 1780–1917, Record Group 94, National Archives, Washington,

DC, Ancestry (ancestry.com), accessed August 13, 2018.

33. Joseph Fitzsimmons, Declaration of Citizenship, September 21, 1853.

34. Joseph Fitzsimmons, Civil War Muster Rolls Index Cards, November 22, 1859, and August 11, 1861, Texas Adjutant General's Department, Texas State Library and Archives Commission, Ancestry (ancestry.com), accessed August 13, 2018.

35. Joseph Fitzsimmons, "Declaration of Survivor of Indian War," August 16, 1902, Record Group 15, Records of the Department of Veterans Affairs, 1773–2007, National Archives.

36. This interpretation is based on the fact that he fought against Native Americans on the Texas frontier and joined the Confederate Army five months after Lincoln issued the Emancipation Proclamation, despite his own Unionist sentiments.

37. See Paul S. Taylor, *An American-Mexican Frontier;* and Carlos K. Blanton, "Race, Labor, and the Limits of Progressive Reform."

38. In the following sentence, she credits J. T. Canales (whom she refers to as J. C. Canales because of his multiple last names) as helping her attend the Southwest Texas Normal in San Marcos. Zamora O'Shea, "Ranches of Southwest Texas."

39. After Marsh died, his wife filed to receive a pension as his widow. The form stated that he joined the military under the alias "Robert Belt" and that he had served from 1860 to 1865. The US Army Register of Enlistments' record for "Robert Belt," which has the same birth year and place of birth as Richard Marsh, states that he enlisted in June 1869 and deserted in March 1870. Richard A. Marsh (Robert Belt, alias), Civil War Pension Index: General Index to Pension Files, 1861–1943, Record Group no. 15, Series no. T288, National Archives, Washington, DC, Ancestry (ancestry.com), accessed November 22, 2018; Robert Belt, US Army, Register of Enlistments, 1798–1914, Record Group 94, National Archives, Ancestry (ancestry.com), accessed November 22, 2018.

40. "Richard Alvis Marsh," Texas State Historical Marker no. 4259, Brush Wood Cemetery, Edinburg, "Texas Historic Sites Atlas," accessed November 7, 2018, https://atlas.thc.state.tx.us/Map.

41. Marsh was born between 1842 and 1844, and Virginia Johnson was born in 1873. Marsh died in 1917, and shortly thereafter, his wife moved to San Antonio with two of their children. On the 1940 census, she stated that the highest level of education she completed was seventh grade. 1920 US Census, Bexar County, Texas, population schedule, Justice Precinct No. I, p. 3 B, dwelling 60, family 89, Virginia Marsh, digital image, Ancestry (ancestry.com), accessed November 22, 2017; 1940 US Census, Bexar County, Texas, population schedule, Los Angeles Heights, Justice Precinct No. 2, p. 6 A, dwelling 1221, family 131, Virginia Marsh, digital image, Ancestry (ancestry.com), accessed November 22, 2017.

42. R. A. Marsh, "General Report," unpublished report to the superintendent of public instruction, 1902–1903, Hidalgo County file, box 4–23/269, SDE, TSA. 1900 US Census, Hidalgo County, Texas, population schedule, Precinct No. 6, p. 266 A (stamped), dwelling 33, family 33, Richard A. Marsh, digital image, Ancestry (ancestry.com), accessed November 22, 2017; "Richard Alvis Marsh," Historical Marker 5215004259, "Texas Historic Sites Atlas," accessed January 3, 2019, https://atlas.thc.state.tx.us/. The THC's historical marker states that Marsh moved to Rio Grande City in 1880. It is possible that this date is correct; however, in the summer of 1880, Marsh, in his 30s, was living in Kentucky with his aging parents and working as a "Bill Poster." 1880 US Census, Fayette County,

population schedule, Ward 1, p. 66 D, dwelling 647, family 656, Richard Marsh, digital image, Ancestry (ancestry.com), accessed November 22, 2017.

43. 1880 US Census, Hidalgo County, Texas, population schedule, Hidalgo, p. 222, dwelling 267, family 267, Virginia Marsh and dwelling 266, family 266, J. Sergio Hinojosa, digital image, Ancestry (ancestry.com), accessed November 22, 2017.

44. Marsh died eighteen years before Zamora O'Shea published *El Mesquite*. Hidalgo County, Texas, Death Certificate for Richard Alvis Marsh, August 17, 1917, registered no. 8, Texas Department of Health, Bureau of Vital Statistics, Mercedes, digital image, Ancestry (ancestry.com), accessed January 3, 2019.

45. Zamora O'Shea, "Ranches of Southwest Texas."

46. 1880 US Census, Hidalgo County, Texas, population schedule, La Noria Cardeneña Rancho, p. 257 D (stamped), dwelling 407, family 407, Jose Maria Casada, digital image, Ancestry (ancestry.com), accessed August 13, 2018. Casada and his son boarded with the Chapa family, who owned a retail grocery store. Many children on the 1880 census for La Noria Cardeneña are listed as being "at school."

47. Andrés Tijerina, "Historical Introduction," xvii.

48. Zamora O'Shea, "Ranches of Southwest Texas."

49. Leticia M. Garza-Falcón, "Renewal through Language in Elena Zamora O'Shea's Novel *El Mesquite*," xxviii.

50. Zamora O'Shea, "Ranches of Southwest Texas." Italics in original.

51. Blanton, "Race, Labor and the Limits of Progressive Reform."

52. Zamora O'Shea, *El Mesquite*, 68.

53. González, *Border Renaissance*, 84.

54. See early correspondence between Zamora O'Shea and Castañeda in Carlos Castañeda Papers, box 32, folder 7, BLAC. For discussion of the politics of the archives and Zamora O'Shea and Castañeda's correspondence, see González, *Border Renaissance*, 85–86.

55. In multiple letters to Carlos Castañeda, she stated that she hoped her work would challenge the narrative of Anna J. Hardwicke Pennybacker's *A New History of Texas*, which Zamora O'Shea referred to as an "imaginary history of Texas." Students enrolled in elementary schools and colleges across Texas had been reading Pennybacker's "imaginary" version of Texas history since it was first published in 1888, and it remained a key text in the public school system for forty years. One of the many issues with Pennybacker's work was the argument that Texas history did not begin until Anglo American settlers arrived in 1824. Elena Zamora O'Shea to Carlos Castañeda, August 21, 1929, Carlos Castañeda Papers, box 32, folder 7, BLAC. Stacy A. Cordery, "Pennybacker, Anna J. Hardwicke," "Handbook of Texas Online," accessed September 13, 2018, http://www. tshaonline.org/handbook/online/articles/fpe30. For a discussion of Pennybacker and Zamora O'Shea, see González, *Border Renaissance*, 81–87. For a discussion of racism and the construction of Texas history, see Laura Lyons McLemore, *Inventing Texas*.

56. Zamora O'Shea, "Ranches of Southwest Texas."

57. 1930 US Census, Falls County, Texas, population schedule, Marlin City, Precinct 1, p. 12 B (stamped), dwelling 275, family 275, Marjorie Rogers, digital image, Ancestry (ancestry.com), accessed September 7, 2018.

58. Marjorie Rogers, "Mystery of Angel of Goliad Never Been Solved," *Dallas Morning News*, February 9, 1936.
59. Ibid.
60. Ibid.
61. Panchita Alavez did not make it into Davenport's address for the Texan Centennial dedication of the memorial for the Goliad Massacre. Harbert Davenport, "The Men of Goliad: Dedicatory Address."
62. There are multiple folders in the Harbert Davenport Papers related to the Angel of Goliad. See folders "The Angel of Goliad" and "Literary Effort: Davenport, Harbert, 'The Angel of Goliad,'" box 2-23/177, Harbert Davenport Papers, TSA.
63. Ibid.
64. Marjorie Rogers, "Mystery of Angel of Goliad," *Dallas Morning News*, February 9, 1936.
65. Elena Zamora O'Shea, "Sequel to the Angel of Goliad," *Dallas Morning News*, March 15, 1936.
66. See note 496.
67. Zamora O'Shea, "Sequel to the Angel of Goliad."
68. Ibid.
69. "Note by Father Joseph G. O'Donohoe," folder "Literary Effort: Davenport, Harbert, 'The Angel of Goliad,'" Harbert Davenport Papers, TSA, Austin, TX.
70. Garza-Falcón, "Renewal through Language in Elena Zamora O'Shea's novel *El Mesquite*," xxiv.
71. Interestingly, her son Daniel Patrick O'Shea's 1913 birth certificate lists Zamora O'Shea's occupation as "Housewife," though it was not filed until 1942. Birth Certificate for Daniel Patrick Ernest Leo O'Shea, 13 May 1913, Jim Wells County, Texas, Texas Department of Health, Bureau of Vital Statistics, Ancestry (ancestry. com), accessed January 3, 2019.
72. I will continue to refer to Jovita González as "González," as other scholars have also done, rather than by her married name "González Mireles." In various archival papers dated after 1935, she continued to use her maiden name. I do so here, especially for clarity when discussing the married couple's work that they did together.
73. Jovita González, no. 59, 1897, Baptismal Records, Vol. 9, 1891-1902, Our Lady of Refuge Church, Roma, TX, Catholic Archives of Texas, Austin. Leticia Garza-Falcón noted the discrepancy in her birthday between the Texas Folklore Society records, which lists her year of birth as 1899, and other publications, which list it as 1904. Garza-Falcón used 1899. Garza-Falcón, *Gente Decente*, 269, n. 2, and appendix B.
74. González also left her birthday out of her short autobiography, which was published in the collection *Dew on the Thorn*, edited by José Limón.
75. In making a case for her ability to take on the project, González stated, "I was born thirty-two years ago, just as the first Americans were pushing into what is now the Rio Grande Valley." Saint Mary's Hall, 1934-1936, RG 1.1, Series 200 R, folder 3332, box 279, Rockefeller Foundation, Rockefeller Archive Center.
76. She stuck to 1904 for the most part. In the 1940 census, she reported that she was thirty-three years old, born in 1907. 1940 United States Census, Nueces County, Texas, population schedule, Corpus Christi, p. 4 B (stamped), house number 402, family 92, Jovita G. de Mireles, digital image, Ancestry (ancestry.com), accessed June 23, 2018.

77. E. E. Mireles, Petition for Naturalization, 23 January 1937, no. 5600, Texas Naturalization Records, Records of District Courts of the United States, Record Group 21, National Archives of Fort Worth, Texas, digital image, Ancestry (ancestry.com), accessed June 23, 2018.

78. Starr County clerk's office confirmed this was why she needed two witnesses. Birth Certificate for Jovita González, January 18, 1904, issued February 10, 1951, vol. 14, p. 233, in Starr County Clerk's Office, Starr County, TX. A copy of her birth certificate is located in box 3, folder 11, Jovita González Mireles Papers, Wittliff Collections, Albert B. Alkek Library, Texas State University, San Marcos. In her autobiography, González states that her mother's parents were Francisco Guerra Guerra and Josefa Barrera Barrera. Francisco and Josefa Guerra were her family's neighbors in the 1900 census, and Patricia was their daughter. Other neighbors were Jesus González Guerra and Manuela B. Guerra, whose son was Roque Guerra. I believe either Jesus or Manuela were siblings of González's mother, which would make Roque her cousin. 1900 US Census, Starr County, Texas, population schedule, Justice's Precinct No. Four, p. 141 A (stamped), dwelling 43, family 54, Jovita Gonzalez; dwelling 45, family 57, Roque Guerra; dwelling 42, family 52, Patricia Guerra, digital image, Ancestry (ancestry.com), accessed June 23, 2018. Jovita González, "Early Life and Education," *Dew on the Thorn*, ix.

79. In the 1900 census, González was four years old and Patricia Guerra was sixteen. Guerra listed her age as twenty in both the 1900 and 1910 censuses. In the 1920 census, taken after her marriage to Encarnación Salinas, she listed her age as forty-seven. 1910 US Census, Starr County, Texas, population schedule, Precinct No. 4, p. 12 B, dwelling 4, family 4, Patricia Guerra [Patricia Guena], digital image, Ancestry (ancestry.com), accessed January 3, 2019; 1920 US Census, Starr County, Texas, population schedule, Justice Precinct No. 1, p. 13 A, dwelling 252, family 270, Patricia G. Salinas, digital image, Ancestry (ancestry.com), accessed January 6, 2019.

80. Scholars also have paid much attention to González's relationship with J. Frank Dobie and her folklore and literary writings. See José Limón, *Dancing with the Devil*, chap. 3; "Introduction," *Dew on the Thorn*; and "Introduction," *Caballero: A Historical Novel*. See also María Eugenia Cotera, "Jovita González Mireles; Cotera, *Native Speakers*, chaps. 3 and 6; Cotera, "A Woman of the Borderlands"; Nicole Guidotti-Hernández, *Unspeakable Violence*, chap. 3;. Garza-Falcón, *Gente Decente*, chap. 3; Louis Gerard Mendoza, *Historia*, chap. 1; González, *Border Renaissance*, chap. 5; Donna M. Kabalen de Bichara, *Telling Border Life Stories*; and Karen R. Roybal, *Archives of Dispossession*, chap. 3.

81. In 1934, González received a Rockefeller Foundation grant. Taylor wrote her a recommendation letter, along with J. Frank Dobie and Eugene C. Barker. Saint Mary's Hall, RAC.

82. Jovita González, "Early Life and Education," *Dew on the Thorn*.

83. 1900 US Census; González, "Early Life and Education," x.

84. "Los Ciudadanos Mexicanos Visitan al Cónsul Fernández," *La Prensa*, April 3, 1913.

85. San Antonio City Directories, 1910, 1913, 1914, 1915, 1916, 1917, 1918, 1919, 1921, 1924, 1929; Texana Room, San Antonio Public Library Special Collections;

"Falleció el Sr. Jacobo González," *La Prensa* August 27, 1930.

86. "Los Estudiantes de Español de la High School Organizaron un Club," *La Prensa*, November 29, 1914.

87. "Graduates of Class," *San Antonio Express*, June 2, 1915, p. 12.

88. "Una Mexicana que Triunfa," *La Prensa*, August 25, 1915.

89. "La Asociación 'Guillermo Prieto' de Moore, Tex," *La Prensa*, October 18, 1916. Jovita González is listed as a teacher in Frio County's Annual Report of School Funds from 1916 to 1917, Annual Report of School Funds, CSD, 1911–1938, microfilm reel 47, Texas Education Agency, TSA, Austin.

90. "La Asociación 'Guillermo Prieto' de Moore, Tex," *La Prensa*, October 18, 1916. Though González was credited with the idea and effort to organize Asociación Guillermo Prieto, she was not an officer. All the officers were men who, most likely, were business owners or otherwise prominent members of the community.

91. Ibid.

92. Ibid.

93. "Un Brillante Fiesta Escolar," *La Prensa*, May 16, 1917. *La Prensa* included the names of the teachers of the public school. González is the only one with a Spanish surname.

94. González, *Life along the Border*, 88.

95. Ibid., 91.

96. The only source González cites for this particular section of her thesis is an article from *El Nacional*, a newspaper published in Piedras Negras, Coahuila, Mexico, that praised the work of el Colegio Altamirano.

97. San Antonio City Directory, 1926. González appears in the city directory as a schoolteacher in 1916–1919, 1921–1922, and 1924. From 1926 to 1934, she's listed as a teacher at Saint Mary's Hall, with the exception of 1931. Texana Room, San Antonio Public Library; *La Reata*, 1929–1935, Marrs and Verna McLean Library, Special Collections, Saint Mary's Hall, San Antonio.

98. Quoted in González, *Life Along the Border*, 113.

99. Ibid., 113–114.

100. González, *Life Along the Border*, 116.

101. Saint Mary's Hall, 1934–1936, RG 1.1, Series 200 R, folder 3332, box 279, Rockefeller Foundation, Rockefeller Archive Center.

102. "The Spanish Club," in *La Reata*, 1929, Marrs and Verna McLean Library, Special Collections, Saint Mary's Hall, San Antonio.

103. Ibid. Cotera makes the same argument in her analysis of González's thesis. See "A Woman of the Borderlands," 17.

104. The songs that González sang with her students at St. Mary's Hall were "La Huer Janita," "El Padrecito," "La Puerta Está Quebrada," "Santo Domingo," "Salió un Coyote," "Yo Solita," "Do Re Mi, Do Re Fa," "Me Gustan Todas," "Cuando los Pastores," and "Naranja Dulce." John Lomax Southern States Collection, American Folklife Center, Library of Congress, Washington, DC.

105. Saint Mary's Hall, 1934–1936, RG 1.1, Series 200 R, folder 3332, box 279, Rockefeller Foundation, Rockefeller Archive Center.

106. Officer: David H. Stevens, "Diary, 1932–1934," Rockefeller Foundation Records, Officers' Diaries, RG 12, S-Z (FA394), online collections and catalog of Rockefeller Archive Center, accessed June 30, 2018, http://dimes.rockarch.org/a3097ba4-fa3b-496f-ab31-2704f1627619.

107. Ibid.

108. Saint Mary's Hall, 1934–1936, RG 1.1, Series 200 R, folder 3332, box 279, Rockefeller Foundation, Rockefeller Archive Center.

109. Stevens's officer diary, 1932–1934.

110. Saint Mary's Hall, 1934–1936, RG 1.1, Series 200 R, folder 3332, box 279, Rockefeller Foundation.

111. "Se Casa la Señorita Jovita González," *La Prensa*, July 14, 1935.

112. Limón, "Introduction," *Dew on the Thorn*, xxv.

113. *La Reata*, 1934–1935, Marrs and Verna McLean Library, Special Collections, Saint Mary's Hall, San Antonio.

114. If she considered her Rockefeller Foundation–funded research as work toward a PhD, this would explain why she pursued doctoral programs in folklore, as opposed to history, especially since her MA was in history. UT Graduate School Records, box/vol/serial no. 4P188, University of Texas at Austin; Student Directories, 1930–1935, Briscoe Center for American History. In his recommendation for González to the Rockefeller Foundation, Dobie noted her work during the summer of 1932 at the "University of Mexico." Saint Mary's Hall, 1934–1936, RG 1.1, Series 200 R, folder 3332, box 279, Rockefeller Foundation, Rockefeller Archive Center.

115. She asked Paul Taylor and Ruth Coit, the Head of School for Saint Mary's Hall, to write letters on her behalf. Monica Donovan to Ruth Coit, October 6, 1938, box 1, folder 8; Ruth Coit to Jovita González Mireles, October 18, 1938, box 1, folder 8; González de Mireles to Rudolph Schevill, April 25, 1939, box 1, folder 9, E. E. Mireles and Jovita González Mireles Papers, Mary and Jeff Bell Library, Special Collections and Archives, Texas A&M University, Corpus Christi. Limón states in his introduction to *Dew on the Thorn* that González looked into three different PhD programs: Stanford, Berkeley, and the University of New Mexico. However, I only found evidence of Stanford and Berkeley in González's personal papers.

116. Castañeda to Maverick, August 14, 1939, box 1, folder 9, E. E. Mireles and Jovita González Mireles Papers, Mary and Jeff Bell Library, Special Collections and Archives, Texas A&M University, Corpus Christi.

117. Maverick to Castañeda, August 30, 1939, box 28, folder 9, Carlos E. Castañeda Papers, BLAC.

118. Castañeda sent Maverick a report just before the city began its work and attended the various functions celebrating the project's progress. Castañeda and Maverick correspondence, box 28, folder 9, Carlos E. Castañeda Papers, BLAC. A city ordinance passed on October 12, 1939, allowed for the restoration of the downtown historical area. Lydia Magruder, "La Villita," "Handbook of Texas Online," accessed March 25, 2015, http://www.tshaonline.org/handbook/online/articles/hpl01.

119. Eve Raleigh was a pseudonym for Margaret Eimer. Both *Dew on the Thorn* and *Caballero* were published posthumously by Arte Público Press and Texas A&M Press, respectively.

120. For a discussion of the Good Neighbor Policy and education in Texas, see Blanton, *Strange Career*, 96–102.

121. Blanton, *Strange Career*, 101–102.

122. "W. S. Benson Company, E. E. Mireles' Royalty Report," August 1, 1952–July 31, 1953, box 20, folder 11. E. E. Mireles and Jovita González Mireles Papers, Mary

and Jeff Bell Library, Special Collections and Archives, Texas A&M University, Corpus Christi, Texas.

123. In the E. E. Mireles and Jovita González Mireles Papers at Texas A&M-Corpus Christi, the original handwritten manuscript for *El Español Elemental: Quinto Libro* survives. All of the historical readings are written in González's handwriting.

124. García, *Mexican Americans*, 248-249. The notion of friendly relations that stem from a shared past among North American countries began in 1890 with the founding of the Commercial Bureau of the American Republics at the First International Americans Conference. By the Fourth International Americans Conference, held in Buenos Aires in 1910, the name of the organization changed to the Pan American Union. "Pan American Union: Resolution Adopted by the Fourth International American Conference at Buenos Aires," Treaties and Other Agreements of the United States of America, Law Library of Congress, Washington, DC.

125. Pan American Round Table vertical file, Dolph Briscoe Center for American History, University of Texas at Austin; Texas and Pan American Round Table of San Antonio Records, 1909-2006, University of Texas at San Antonio Libraries Special Collections, University of Texas at San Antonio.

126. E. E. Mireles and Jovita G. Mireles, *Mi Libro Español: Libro Tres*, 87-88.

127. Ibid., 90-91.

128. E. E. Mireles and Jovita G. Mireles, *El Español Elemental: Sexto Libro*, 31-32.

129. Ibid., 34-35.

130. W. S. Benson to E. E. Mireles, July 19, 1949, box 20, folder 11, E. E. Mireles and Jovita González Mireles Papers, Mary and Jeff Bell Library, Special Collections and Archives, Texas A&M University, Corpus Christi. Between the late 1940s and 1967, when the publisher ceased publication of the texts, orders dropped steadily. González and Mireles bought the 1,300 complete sets of *El Español Elemental* that the publisher had left for $1,950 in 1968. W. S. Benson & Company Invoice, January 30, 1968, in ibid.

131. This is the same escuelita that García's sister, Clotilde, and Rolando Hinojosa-Smith's sibling attended. For more information, see chap. 4.

132. George I. Sánchez to Hector P. García, September 27, 1954, box 4, folder 10, George I. Sánchez Papers, BLAC.

133. LULAC founder M. C. González was an attorney and advisor to the Mexican Consul General in San Antonio. Because of the segregation that was taking place in Guadalupe County, and because of the superintendent's insistence that it was necessary pedagogically, the Consul General asked González to contact Sánchez for his professional opinion. George I. Sánchez to M. C. González, March 7, 1942, box 17, folder 11, George I. Sánchez Papers, BLAC.

134. Ibid.

135. Blanton, *George I. Sánchez*, 227.

136. George I. Sánchez to M. C. González, January 6, 1942, box 17, folder 11, George I. Sánchez Papers, BLAC.

137. Sánchez to García, September 27, 1954, George I. Sánchez Papers, BLAC.

138. This argument was also a central factor in Mexican American–initiated desegregation court cases. See Valencia, *Chicano Students and the Courts*.

139. González and Mireles's series *Mi Libro Español* was supposed to be part of this

Inter-American series, but Mireles decided to publish with a local publisher without giving Sánchez notice. For information on the Inter-American series, see Sánchez's correspondence with Macmillan editors, box 23, folders 3–13, and box 24, folders, 1–4. See also Blanton, *George I. Sánchez*, 74–75. For information on *Mi Libro Español* and the Inter-American series, see above and folder 4.5, E. E. Mireles and Jovita González Papers, Texas A&M University–Corpus Christi.

140. "Spanish-Speaking Children Start English at Beginning," *Corpus Christi Caller-Times*, July 12, 1959.

141. The thesis is written in English. "The Teaching of Spanish in Texas Schools," Summer 1952, box 1, folder 5. Jovita González Mireles Papers, 1921–1993. Southwestern Writers Collection, Witliff Collections, Texas State University, San Marcos.

142. Lipski, *Varieties of Spanish in the United States*, 75.

143. Ibid, 71.

144. Ibid., 88.

145. Mireles, "The Teaching of Spanish in Texas Schools."

146. Kreneck, *Mexican American Odyssey*. Kreneck does not discuss Tijerina's work within the framework of escuelita history, but he does contrast his political views with those of Henry B. González, who understood the Mexican American experience in the United States as that of minorities fighting discrimination and demanding their rights. See pp. 222–224 and 241.

147. Ibid., chap. 1.

148. Ibid., 21.

149. Ibid., chap. 1. See also San Miguel, *"Let All of Them Take Heed,"* chap. 6; and Barrera, "The Little Schools in Texas, 1897–1965." San Miguel and Barrera do not agree on the connection between escuelitas and the Little Schools of the 400. While Barrera sees a strong connection, San Miguel does not.

150. Kreneck, *Mexican American Odyssey*, chap. 8; San Miguel, *"Let All of Them Take Heed,"* chap. 6; and Barrera, "The Little Schools in Texas."

151. Ibid.

152. Kreneck, *Mexican American Odyssey*, 200.

153. Ceremony dedicating the organizing of "The Little School of the 400," 1958, box 1, folder 16, Felix Tijerina, Sr., Family Papers, series "Little School of the 400," Houston Metropolitan Research Center.

154. "Remarks of Gov. Price Daniel," in ibid.

155. Ibid.

156. Once the board of directors "determined that an adequate measure of accomplishment has been established" with the preschool program, as the organization's bylaws explained, the LULAC Educational Fund would begin awarding college scholarships. LULAC Educational Fund, Constitution and Bylaws, 1957, box 1, folder 18, Felix Tijerina Papers. See also, Kreneck, *Mexican American Odyssey*, 213–218.

157. Tijerina, "A Personal Message to Farsighted Texans," LULAC Education Fund pamphlet, no date, box 1, folder 17, Felix Tijerina Papers.

158. Ibid. Ellipsis in original.

159. Letter to Board of Directors, LULAC Educational Fund, Inc., September 23, 1958, box 1, folder 19, Felix Tijerina Papers. See also Kreneck, *Mexican American Odyssey*, 232–233.

160. See Preschool Instructional Program, "Correspondence, Mailouts, Statistics, 1957–1906," box 2, folder 2, Felix Tijerina Papers; and Kreneck, *Mexican American Odyssey*, 244–249. In his presentation, Tijerina included information on other English language–instruction preschools that operated independently of LULAC's Little Schools of the 400 program, such as the one E. E. Mireles oversaw in Corpus Christi. Mireles was a regular donor to the Little Schools of the 400 program.

161. It also gained corporate sponsorship as Gulf Oil became its largest donor, giving $9,175 in 1960. LULAC Educational Fund, "Finances, 1957–1963," box 1, folder 19, Felix Tijerina Papers.

162. Egon R. Tausch to Felix Tijerina, July 7, 1961, box 2, folder 3, Felix Tijerina Papers.

163. Ibid.

164. Louis Alexander, "Texas Helps Her Little Latins," *Saturday Evening Post*, August 5, 1961.

165. Ibid.

166. George I. Sánchez, "History, Culture, Education," 17.

167. Ibid., 23.

168. Herschel T. Manuel, *Spanish-Speaking Children of the Southwest*, 191.

169. For work on the dissension within LULAC, see Kreneck, *Mexican American Odyssey*, 214 and 267–268.

170. Ibid., 307–310.

171. Ibid., 308–309.

172. "My School Day Autobiography," 1942–1946. Each student had a small "autobiography" book in which, at the end of each school year, students and teachers wrote messages to each other. The only message written in English in Rosa Lidia Vásquez Peña's book is from Miss A. E. Salinas, her English teacher. Vásquez Peña states, however, that she could not speak any English when she left el Colegio Altamirano. Rosa Lidia Vásquez, interview, July 3, 2018, San Antonio, TX.

173. "Convocatoria" flyer, November 1955, Hebbronville, TX, Personal Papers of Rosa Lidia Vásquez Peña.

174. Emilia Dávila, Petition for Naturalization, October 26, 1972, no. 5789, Texas Naturalization Records, Records of District Courts of the United States, Record Group 21, National Archives of Fort Worth, Texas, digital image, Ancestry (ancestry.com), accessed February 7, 2018.

CONCLUSION. THE CONTESTED LEGACY OF ESCUELITAS IN AMERICAN CULTURE

1. For information on the controversial HB 2281, see Nicholas B. Lundholm, "Cutting Class: Why Arizona's Ethnic Studies Ban Won't Ban Ethnic Studies"; and "Arizona's Ethnic Studies Ban Goes to Trial," NPR, "All Things Considered," July 14, 2017, http://www.npr.org/2017/07/14/537291234/arizonas-ethnic-studies-ban-in-public-schools-goes-to-trial.

2. Velia Jiménez Morelos, interview with author, August 3, 2012, Tucson, AZ.

3. Ibid.

4. Quoted in James Barrera, "The 1968 San Antonio School Walkouts." See also Ignacio M. García, "'The Best Bargain . . . Ever Received': The 1968 Commission on Civil Rights Hearing in San Antonio, Texas."

5. For a fuller discussion of these alternative schools that emerged during the Chicano Movement, see San Miguel's *Brown, Not White*, 92–93 and 98–103; and *Chicana/o Struggles for Education*, chap. 5. San Miguel interprets these huelga schools as being part of the longer escuelita tradition.

6. Michael Soldatenko, *Chicano Studies*, 6.

7. Ibid.

8. Emilio Zamora's 1978 conference paper "Las Escuelitas: A Texas-Mexican Search for Educational Excellence" calls escuelitas "concrete examples of Mexicano self-determination and resistance and the earliest precursors of modern Mexicano colleges and bilingual-bicultural instruction" (74). Francisco Hernández, who wrote the escuelita-focused seminar paper "Schools for Mexicans" and interviewed José Limón about his escuelita experience in 1980, was the director of Casa de la Raza, a Chicano alternative school in Berkeley, CA. Francisco Hernández, telephone interview with author, April 8, 2013.

9. Lundholm, "Cutting Class." See also "Arizona's Ethnic Studies Ban Goes to Trial," NPR, "All Things Considered," July 14, 2017, http://www.npr.org/2017/07/14/537291234/arizonas-ethnic-studies-ban-in-public-schools-goes-to-trial.

10. J. Weston Phippen, "The Textbook that Calls Mexicans Lazy," *The Atlantic*, September 9, 2016, accessed July 14, 2017, https://www.theatlantic.com/news/archive/2016/09/mexican-american-studies-texas/498947/.

11. "Grassroots, Civil Rights, Education Groups Announce Coalition Opposed to Offensive Mexican American Heritage Textbook Proposed for Texas Schools," *Responsible Ethnic Studies Textbook Coalition*, July 18, 2016, accessed July 14, 2017, http://www.masfortexas.org/pressrelease.

12. "Federal Judge Tells Arizona It Can't Ban Mexican American Studies," *Washington Post*, December 28, 2017.

13. Vicki Ruiz, "Nuestra América: Latino History as United States History," 655, 656.

14. Ibid., 672. Italics in original.

15. Lozano, *An American Language*, 17.

BIBLIOGRAPHY

ARCHIVAL ABBREVIATIONS

BLAC   Benson Latin American Collection
SRE   Secretaría de Relaciones Exteriores, Archivo de la Embajada de México en los Estados Unidos de América
TSA   Texas State Archives

ARCHIVAL AND PERSONAL COLLECTIONS

American Folklife Center, Library of Congress, Washington, DC
    Lomax, John, Southern States Collection
Bancroft Library, University of California, Berkeley
    Taylor, Paul S., Papers
Benson Latin American Collection, University of Texas, Austin
    Castañeda, Carlos, Papers
    González Mireles, Jovita, Papers
    Idar, Clemente, Papers
    Order of Sons of America (Council 5) Records
    Rodriguez, Jacob, Collection
    Sánchez, George I., Papers
Blagg-Huey Library, Texas Woman's University, Denton
    Escuelita Vertical File
    Idar, Jovita, Vertical File
    Villarreal, María, Vertical File
Briscoe Center for American History, University of Texas, Austin
    Maverick, Sr., Maury, Papers
    Pan American Round Tables Vertical File
    Sutton, W. S., Papers
    University of Texas Graduate School Records
Catholic Archives of Texas, Texas Catholic Conference of Bishops, Austin
    Our Lady of Refuge Church Baptismal Records
Daughters of the Republic of Texas Library, San Antonio
    Oheim, George Frederic, Papers
DeGolyer Library, Southern Methodist University, Dallas
    Jones III, Lawrence T., Texas Photograph Collection
House of Neighborly Services, San Antonio
    Preschool Education Collection
Houston Metropolitan Research Center
    Little Schools of the 400 Collection
    Tijerina, Felix, Papers
Institute of Texan Cultures, San Antonio
    Idar, Jovita, Vertical File
    La Villita Vertical File

Ligarde, Honore, Vertical File
Marrs and Verna McLean Library, Saint Mary's Hall, San Antonio
    La Reata Collection
Mary and Jeff Bell Library, Texas A&M University, Corpus Christi
    García, Clotilde P., Papers
    García, Hector P., Papers
    Mireles, E. E., and Jovita González Mireles Papers
Museum Foundation of Hebbronville, Hebbronville
    Colegio Altamirano Collection
Museum of South Texas History, Edinburg
    Closner Ramsey Collection
    Hidalgo County Judges Photograph Collection
Nueces County Clerk's Office, Corpus Christi
    Declaration of Citizenship Records
Rockefeller Archive Center, Sleepy Hollow, New York
    Officer Diaries
    Record Group 1.1: Saint Mary's Hall
San Antonio Public Library, Texana Room
    San Antonio City Directories
Secretaría de Relaciones Exteriores, Archivo de la Embajada de México en los Estados
    Unidos de América, Mexico City
Starr County Clerk's Office, Rio Grande City
    Vital Records
Texas State Archives, Austin
    Harbert Davenport Papers
    State Department of Education Files
        Bexar County
        Brownsville
        Cameron County
        Duval County
        Eagle Pass
        El Paso County
        Hidalgo County
        Laredo
        Maverick County
        Nueces County
        San Antonio
        San Diego
        Starr County
        Webb County
        Zapata County
    Texas Education Agency Annual Reports
        Frio County
        Hidalgo County
University of Houston Library
    Perales, Alonso S., Papers
    Villegas de Magnón, Leonor, Papers

University of Texas at El Paso Library
    C. L. Sonnichsen Special Collections
    Institute of Oral History
University of Texas at San Antonio Libraries Special Collections
    Pan American Round Table of San Antonio Records, 1909–2006
Vásquez Peña, Rosa Lidia, Personal Papers, San Antonio
    Colegio Altamirano Collection
Webb County Heritage Foundation, Laredo
    Holding Institute Vertical File
    Mexican Revolution Vertical File
    Smith, Leonor M., Collection
Witliff Collection, Texas State University, San Marcos
    González Mireles, Jovita, Papers

NEWSPAPERS

Brownsville Herald
Dallas Morning News
El Aldeano
El Comercio
El Democrata Fronterizo
El Paso Herald
Houston Post
La Crónica
La Prensa
Laredo Times
Laredo Weekly Times
New York Herald
Oakland Tribune
Port Arthur News
San Antonio Evening News
San Antonio Express-News
Saturday Evening Post

INTERVIEWS

Alvarez, Becky. Interview by author, September 14, 2018, digital recording, House of
    Neighborly Service, San Antonio, Texas.
Cantú, Norma. Interview by author, October 3, 2018, digital recording, Mama's
    Kitchen Restaurant, San Antonio, Texas.
Dávila, Idalia. Interview by author, May 31, 2018, digital recording, Museum
    Foundation of Hebbronville, Hebbronville, Texas.
Flores, Adelina. Interview by author, May 17, 2013, digital recording, residence, San
    Antonio, Texas.
Flores, Belisario. Interview by author, May 17, 2013, digital recording, residence, San
    Antonio, Texas.
Garza, Sergio. Interview by author, May 31, 2018, digital recording, Garza Furniture
    Store, Hebbronville, Texas.
Gutiérrez, José. Interview by author, May 31, 2018, digital recording, Museum
    Foundation of Hebbronville, Hebbronville, Texas.

Hinojosa-Smith, Rolando. Interview by author, February 4, 2013, digital recording, University of Texas, Austin.

Jiménez Morelos, Velia. Interview by author, August 3, 2012, digital recording, residence, Tucson, Arizona.

Limón, José. Interview by Francisco Hernández, June 30, 1980, cassette tape recording, Berkeley, California.

Lopez, Ramona Lydia. Interview by author, August 3, 2012, digital recording, residence, Tucson, Arizona.

Marín, Manuel. Interview by author, August 3, 2012, digital recording, residence, Tucson, Arizona.

Nora, Amaury. Interview by author, December 7, 2018, digital recording, Panera Bread, San Antonio, Texas.

Ramírez, Gilda E. Interview by author, May 11, 2018, digital recording, Texas A&M University–Corpus Christi.

Rendón, Laura. Interview by author, December 7, 2018, digital recording, Panera Bread, San Antonio, Texas.

Vásquez Peña, Rosa Lidia. Interview by author, July 3, 2018, digital recording, residence, San Antonio, Texas.

GOVERNMENT DOCUMENTS, UNITED STATES AND MEXICO

Registro Civil del Estado de Durango, Mexico

Registro Civil del Estado de Tamaulipas, Mexico

Texas Birth and Death Certificate Records

Texas Naturalization Records

United States Army Register of Enlistments Records

United States Census Records

United States Civil War Muster Roll Records

United States Civil War Pension Records

United States Passport Applications

UNPUBLISHED PAPERS, THESES, AND DISSERTATIONS

Cameron, James W. "The History of Mexican Public Education in Los Angeles, 1910–1930." PhD dissertation, University of Southern California, 1976.

Chávez Leyva, Yolanda. "'Que Son Los Niños?' Mexican Children Along the U.S.-Mexico Border, 1880–1930." PhD dissertation, University of Arizona, 1999.

Dabney, Edgar R. "The Settlement of New Braunfels and the History of Its Earlier Schools." MA thesis, University of Texas, 1927.

Hernández, Francisco. "Schools for Mexicans." Seminar paper, Stanford University, n.d.

Lipski, John M. "The Impact of the Mexican Revolution on Spanish in the United States." Paper presented at the Festival of International Books and Arts (FESTIBA). University of Texas Pan American, March 24, 2010.

Muñoz, Laura. "The Historical Restoration of the Mexican American Teacher in South Texas."

Valerio-Jiménez, Omar. "Refuting History Tales: Collective Memories, Mexican Texans, and Texas History." Trinity-UTSA-TAMUSA History Research Workshop, October 26, 2018. San Antonio, Texas.

Ziegler, Vanessa Michelle. "The Revolt of the 'Ever-Faithful Isle': The Ten Years' War in Cuba, 1868–1878." PhD dissertation, University of California, Santa Barbara, 2007.

PUBLISHED SOURCES

Acuna, Rodolfo. *Occupied America: The Chicano's Struggle Toward Liberation*. San Francisco: Canfield, 1972.

Adams, David Wallace. *Education for Extinction: American Indians and the Boarding School Experience, 1875–1928*. Lawrence: University of Kansas Press, 1995.

Albarrán, Elena Jackson. *Seen and Heard in Mexico: Children and Revolutionary Cultural Nationalism*. Lincoln: University of Nebraska Press, 2014.

Allsup, Carl. *The American G.I. Forum: Origins and Evolution*. Austin, TX: Center for Mexican American Studies, 1982.

——. "Education is Our Freedom: The American G.I. Forum and Mexican American School Segregation in Texas, 1948–1957." *Aztlán* 8 (Fall 1977): 27–50.

Almaráz, Felix. *Knight without Armor: Carlos Eduardo Castañeda, 1896–1958*. College Station: Texas A&M University Press, 1999.

Annual Report of the President of Stanford University for the Thirtieth Academic Year Ending August 31, 1921. Stanford University, California, 1921.

Anzaldúa, Gloria. *Borderlands/La Frontera: The New Mestiza*. San Francisco: Aunt Lute Books, 1987.

Araiza, Margarita. "On a Historical Note: March Exhibit Focuses on Notable Laredoan." *LareDOS: A Journal of the Borderlands* (February 1998): 44–45.

Baker, Benjamin M. *Fifth Biennial Report of the Superintendent of Public Instruction for the Scholastic Years August 31, 1885, and August 31, 1886*. Austin, TX: State Printing Office, 1886.

Balderamma, Francisco. *In Defense of La Raza: The Los Angeles Mexican Consulate and the Mexican Community, 1929–1936*. Tucson: University of Arizona Press, 1982.

Barragán Goetz, Philis M., and Carlos K. Blanton. "The World of Education among Mexican Immigrants and Mexican Americans in J. T. Canales' South Texas." In *Reverberations of Racial Violence: Critical Reflections on U.S. History*, edited by Sonia Hernández and John M. González. Austin: University of Texas Press, forthcoming.

Barrera, Aida. "The 'Little Schools' in Texas, 1897–1965." *American Educational History Journal* 33, no. 2 (2006): 35–45.

Barrera, James. "The 1968 San Antonio School Walkouts: The Beginning of the Chicano Student Movement in South Texas." *Journal of South Texas* 21, no. 1 (Spring 2008): 39–61.

Bazant de Saldaña, Mílada. *Historia de la Educación Durante el Porfiriato*. 1993. Reprint, Mexico City: El Colegio de México, Centro de Estudios Históricos, 2006.

Berman, Marshall. *All That Is Solid Melts into Air: The Experience of Modernity*. New York: Simon and Schuster, 1982.

Biographical Catalogue of the Chancellors, Professors, and Graduates of the Department of Arts and Sciences of the University of the City of New York. New York: Alumni Association, 1894.

Blanton, Annie Webb. "The Foreign Problem in Texas and the Need of an Illiteracy Commission." In *A Hand Book of Information as to Education in Texas*,

1918-1922. Austin, TX: Department of Education, 1923, 22–25.

Blanton, Carlos Kevin. "From Intellectual Deficiency to Cultural Deficiency: Mexican Americans, Testing, and Public School Policy in the American Southwest, 1920–1940." *Pacific Historical Review* 72, no. 1 (February 2003): 39–62.

———. *George I. Sánchez: The Long Fight for Mexican American Integration*. New Haven: Yale University Press, 2015.

———. "Race, Labor, and the Limits of Progressive Reform: A Preliminary Analysis of the Enforcement of Compulsory Attendance in South Texas during the 1920s." *Journal of South Texas* 13, no. 2 (Fall 2000): 207–219.

———. *The Strange Career of Bilingual Education in Texas, 1836–1981*. College Station: Texas A&M University Press, 2004.

Bogardus, Emory. *Essentials of Americanization*. Los Angeles: University of Southern California Press, 1919. Rev. ed., 1920.

———. "The Mexican Immigrant." *Journal of Applied Sociology* 11, no. 5 (1927): 470–488.

Bralley, F. M., *Seventeenth Biennial Report of the State Department of Education for the Years Ending August 31, 1909, and August 31, 1910*. Austin, TX: Austin Printing Co., Printers, 1911.

Brown, Norman D. *Hood, Bonnet, and Little Brown Jug: Texas Politics, 1921–1928*. College Station: Texas A&M University Press, 1984.

Bushnell, David. *The Making of Modern Colombia: A Nation in Spite of Itself*. Berkeley: University of California Press, 1993.

Calcagno, Francisco. *Biográfico Cubano*. New York: Imprinta y Libreria de N. Ponce De Leon, 1878.

Calderón, Roberto R. *Mexican Coal Mining Labor in Texas and Coahuila, 1880–1930*. College Station: Texas A&M University Press, 2000.

Camarillo, Alberto. *Chicanos in a Changing Society: From Mexican Pueblos to American Barrios in Santa Barbara and Southern California, 1848–1930*. Cambridge, MA: Harvard University Press, 1979.

Carlisle, J. M. *Eighth Biennial Report of the State Superintendent of Public Instruction for the Scholastic Years Ending August 31, 1891, and August 31, 1892*. Austin, TX: Ben C. Jones & Co., State Printers, 1893.

———. *Eleventh Biennial Report of the State Superintendent of Public Instruction for the Scholastic Years Ending August 31, 1897, and August 31, 1898*. Austin, TX: Ben C. Jones & Co., State Printers, 1898.

Católogo Oficial de las Exhibiciones de los Estados Unidos Mexicanos. Comisión Nacional Mexicana: Exposición Internacional de St. Louis, 1904.

Chávez, Ernesto. *The U.S. War with Mexico: A Brief History with Documents*. Boston: Bedford/St. Martin's Press, 2008.

Child, Brenda. *Boarding School Seasons: American Indian Families, 1900–1940*. Lincoln: University of Nebraska Press, 1998.

Child, Brenda, Margaret Archuleta, and Tsianina Lomawaima. *Away from Home: American Indian Boarding School Experiences, 1879–2000*. Phoenix: Heard Museum, 2000.

Christopher, Frank, dir. *The Lemon Grove Incident*. Produced by Paul Espinosa. Documentary. 58 min. Cinema Guild, 1985.

Coleman, Michael C. *American Indian Children at School, 1850–1930*. Jackson: University of Mississippi Press, 1991.

Conway, Christopher. "Ignacio Altamirano and the Contradictions of Autobiographical Indianism." *Latin American Literary Review* 34, no. 67 (January–June 2006): 34–49.

———. *Nineteenth-Century Spanish America: A Cultural History*. Nashville: Vanderbilt University Press, 2015.

Cook, Howard Scott. *Mexican Brick Culture in the Building of Texas, 1800s–1980s*. College Station, TX: Texas A&M University Press, 1998.

Cotera, María Eugenia. "Jovita González Mireles: A Sense of History and Homeland." In *Latina Legacies: Identity, Biography, and Community*. Edited by Vicki Ruiz and Virginia Sánchez Korrol. New York: Oxford University Press, 2005.

———. *Native Speakers: Ella Deloria, Zora Neale Hurston, Jovita González, and the Poetics of Culture*. Austin: University of Texas Press, 2008.

———. "A Woman of the Borderlands: 'Social Life in Cameron, Starr, and Zapata Counties' and the Origins of Borderlands Discourse." In *Life along the Border: A Landmark Tejana Thesis*, by Jovita González. Edited by María Eugenia Cotera. College Station: Texas A&M University Press, 2006.

Cottrell, Debbie Mauldin. *Pioneer Woman Educator in Texas: The Progressive Spirit of Annie Webb Blanton*. College Station: Texas A&M University Press, 1993.

Cremin, Lawrence T. *The Transformation of the School: Progressivism in American Education, 1876–1957*. New York: Alfred A. Knopf, 1961.

Davenport, Harbert. "The Men of Goliad: Dedicatory Address at the Unveiling of the Monument Erected by the Texas Centennial Commission at the Grave of Fannin's Men." *Southwestern Historical Quarterly* 43, no. 1 (July 1939): 1–41.

DeJong, David H. *Promises of the Past: A History of Indian Education in the United States*. Golden, CO: North American Press, 1993.

De la Cova, Antonio. "Cuban Exiles in Key West during the Ten Years' War, 1868–1878." *Florida Historical Quarterly* 89, no. 3 (Winter 2011): 287–319.

De León, Arnoldo. "Blowout 1910 Style: A Chicano School Boycott in West Texas." *Texana* 12, no. 2 (1974): 124–140.

———. *Ethnicity in the Sun Belt: Mexican Americans in Houston*. College Station: Texas A&M University Press, 2001.

———. *The Tejano Community, 1836–1900*. Albuquerque: New Mexico Press, 1982.

———, ed. *War Along the Border: The Mexican Revolution and Tejano Communities*. College Station: Texas A&M University Press, 2012.

Dewey, Alicia Marion. *Pesos and Dollars: Entrepreneurs in the Texas-Mexico Borderlands, 1880–1940*. College Station: Texas A&M University Press, 2014.

Eby, Frederick. *The Development of Education in Texas*. New York: Macmillan, 1925.

Enoch, Jessica. *Refiguring Rhetorical Education: Women Teaching African American, Native American, and Chicano/a Students, 1865–1911*. Carbondale: Southern Illinois University Press, 2008.

Espinosa, Felipe Ávila. *Entre el Porfiriato y la Revolución: El Gobierno Interino de Francisco León de la Barra*. Mexico City: Universidad Nacional Autónoma de México, Instituto de Investigaciones Históricas, 2012.

Falvella, James W. *Souvenir Album of Laredo, the Gateway to Mexico: Told in Pictures, Historical and Descriptive Write-ups, Also a History of Webb County and Its Great Resources*. Laredo, TX: J. W. Falvella, 1917.

Felski, Rita. *The Gender of Modernity*. Boston: Harvard University Press, 1995.

Fernández Aceves, María Teresa. "Imagined Communities: Women's History and the

History of Gender in Mexico." *Journal of Women's History* 19, no. 1 (Spring 2007): 200–205.

———. *Mujeres: En el Cambio Social en el Siglo XX Mexicano* México: CIESAS, Siglo XXI, 2014.

Flores, María Eva. "What a Difference a War Makes!" In *Mexican Americans and World War II*, edited by Maggie Rivas-Rodriguez. Austin: University of Texas Press, 2005.

Flores, Richard R. *Remembering the Alamo: Memory, Modernity, and the Master Symbol*. Austin: University of Texas Press, 2002.

Flores, Ruben. *Backroads Pragmatists: Mexico's Melting Pot and Civil Rights in the United States*. Philadelphia: University of Pennsylvania Press, 2014.

Foley, Neil. "Becoming Hispanic: Mexican Americans and the Faustian Pact with Whiteness." *Reflexiones 1997: New Directions in Mexican American Studies*. Austin: Center for Mexican American Studies of the University of Texas, 1998.

———. *The Quest for Equality: The Failed Promise of Black-Brown Solidarity*. Cambridge: Harvard University Press, 2010.

———, ed. *Reflexiones 1997: New Directions in Mexican American Studies*. Austin: Center for Mexican American Studies of the University of Texas, 1998.

———. *The White Scourge: Mexicans, Blacks, and Poor Whites in Texas Cotton Culture*. Berkeley: University of California Press, 1997.

Fox, Cybelle. *Three Worlds of Relief: Race, Immigration, and the American Welfare State from the Progressive Era to the New Deal*. Princeton, NJ: Princeton University Press, 2012.

Gamio, Manuel. *The Life Story of the Mexican Immigrant*. Chicago: University of Chicago Press, 1931.

———. *Mexican Immigration to the United States: A Study of Human Migration and Adjustment*. New York: Arno, 1969.

García, Ignacio M. "'The Best Bargain . . . Ever Received': The 1968 Commission on Civil Rights Hearing in San Antonio, Texas." *Southwestern Historical Quarterly* 122, no. 3 (January 2019): 246–276.

García, Juan Ramon. *Operation Wetback: The Mass Deportation of Mexican Undocumented Workers in 1954*. Westport, CT: Praeger, 1980.

García, Mario. *Desert Immigrants: The Mexicans of El Paso, 1880–1920*. New Haven: Yale University Press, 1981.

———. *Mexican Americans*. New Haven: Yale University Press, 1989.

García, Richard A. *Rise of the Mexican American Middle Class: San Antonio, 1929–1941*. College Station: Texas A&M University Press, 1991.

Garza-Falcón, Leticia. *Gente Decente: A Borderlands Response to the Rhetoric of Dominance*. Austin: University of Texas Press, 1998.

———. "Renewal through Language in Elena Zamora O'Shea's Novel *El Mesquite*." In *El Mesquite*, by Elena Zamora O'Shea. College Station: Texas A&M University Press, 2000.

Getz, Lynne Marie. *Schools of Their Own: The Education of Hispanos in New Mexico, 1850–1940*. Albuquerque: University of New Mexico Press, 1997.

Gilmore, Glenda. *Gender and Jim Crow: Women and the Politics of White Supremacy in North Carolina, 1896–1920*. Chapel Hill: University of North Carolina Press, 1996.

Gonzales, Michael J. *The Mexican Revolution, 1910–1940*. Albuquerque: University of New Mexico Press, 2002.

Gonzalez, Gabriela. "Carolina Munguía and Emma Tenayuca: The Politics of Benevolence and Radical Reform, 1930s." In *Gender on the Borderlands: The Frontier Reader*, edited by Antonio Castañeda, Susan H. Armitage, Patricia Hart, and Karen Weatheron, pp. 200–229. Lincoln: University of Nebraska Press, 2007.

———. "Jovita Idar." In *Texas Women: Their Histories, Their Lives*, edited by Elizabeth Hayes Turner, Stephanie Cole, and Rebecca Sharpless, pp. 225–248. Athens: University of Georgia Press, 2015.

———. *Redeeming La Raza: Transborder Modernity, Race, Respectability, and Rights*. New York: Oxford University Press, 2018.

González, Gilbert G. *Chicano Education in the Era of Segregation*. Philadelphia: Balch Institute Press, 1990.

———. *Mexican Consuls and Labor Organizing: Imperial Politics in the American Southwest, 1920–1940*. Austin: University of Texas Press, 1999.

———. "Segregation and the Education of Mexican Children, 1900–1940." In *The Elusive Quest for Equality: 150 Years of Chicano/Chicana Education*, edited by José Moreno. Cambridge, MA: Harvard Educational Review, 1999.

González, Gilbert G., and Raúl Fernández. "Chicano History: Transcending Cultural Models." *Pacific Historical Review* 63, no. 4 (November 1994): 469–497.

González, John Morán. *Border Renaissance: The Texas Centennial and the Emergence of Mexican American Literature*. Austin: University of Texas Press, 2009.

González, Jovita. *Dew on the Thorn*. Houston: Arte Público, 1997.

———. *Life Along the Border*. Edited by María Eugenia Cotera. College Station: Texas A&M University Press, 2006.

Gould, Lewis L. *Progressives and Prohibitionists: Texas Democrats in the Wilson Era*. Austin: University of Texas Press, 1973.

Grantham, Dewey W. *Southern Progressivism: The Reconciliation of Progress and Tradition*. Knoxville: University of Tennessee Press, 1983.

Gross, Ariel J. *What Blood Won't Tell: A History of Race on Trial in America*. Cambridge: Harvard University Press, 2008.

Guidotti-Hernández, Nicole. *Unspeakable Violence: Remapping U.S. and Mexican National Imaginaries*. Durham, NC: Duke University Press, 2011.

Gutiérrez, David G. *Walls and Mirrors: Mexican Americans, Mexican Immigrants, and the Politics of Ethnicity*. Berkeley: University of California Press, 1995.

"Handbook of Texas Online." *Texas State Historical Association website*, http://www.tshaonline.org/handbook/online.

Harper Ho, Virginia. "Noncitizen Voting Rights: The History, the Law, and Current Prospects for Change." *Law & Inequality: A Journal of Theory and Practice* 18, no. 2 (2000): 271–322.

Hart, John Mason. *Empire and Revolution: The Americans in Mexico since the Civil War*. Berkeley: University of California Press, 2002.

Hayduk, Ron. *Democracy for All: Restoring Immigrant Voting Rights in the U.S.* New York: Routledge, 2006.

Heldt, Antonio Barbosa. *Como Enseñar a Leer y Escribir*. Mexico City: Editorial Pax Mexico, Libreria Carlos Césarman, 1971.

Hernández, José Angel. *Mexican American Colonization during the Nineteenth Century*. New York: Cambridge University Press, 2012.

Hernández, Sonia. "Chicanas in the U.S.-Mexican Borderlands: Transborder Conversations of Feminism and Anarchism, 1905-1938." In *A Promising Problem: The New Chicana/o History*. Edited by Carlos K. Blanton. Austin: University of Texas Press, 2016: 135-160.

Hinojosa, Felipe. "*¡Medicina Sí Muerte No!*: Race, Public Health, and the 'Long War on Poverty' in Mathis, Texas, 1948-1971." *Western Historical Quarterly* 44, no. 4 (Winter 2013): 437-458.

Hinojosa-Smith, Rolando. "*La Prensa*: A Lifelong Influence of Hispanics in Texas." *The Americas Review* 17, no. 3 and 4 (Fall/Winter 1989): 125-129.

Horsman, Reginald. *Race and Manifest Destiny: The Origins of American Racial Anglo-Saxonism*. Cambridge, MA: Harvard University Press, 1981.

Investigation of Mexican Affairs, Preliminary Report and Hearings of the Committee on Foreign Relations, United States Senate, vol. 1. Washington, DC: Government Printing Office, 1920.

Isbell, Frances W. "El Capote Ranch." In *Hidalgo County Ranch Histories*. Edinburg, TX: Hidalgo County Historical Society and Hidalgo County Historical Commission, 1994.

Jacobs, Margaret D. *White Mother to a Dark Race: Settler Colonialism, Maternalism, and the Removal of Indigenous Children in the American West and Australia, 1880-1940*. Lincoln: University of Nebraska Press, 2009.

Kabalen de Bichara, Donna M. *Telling Border Life Stories: Four Mexican American Women Writers*. College Station: Texas A&M University Press, 2013.

Kanellos, Nicolás. *Hispanic Literature of the United States: A Comprehensive Reference*. Westport, CT: Greenwood, 2003.

Knepper, Kate, and Sarah S. Donaldson. "Women in Radiation Oncology and Radiation Physics." In *A History of the Radiological Sciences, edited by* Raymond Gagliardi. Reston, VA: Radiology Centennial, Inc., 1996.

Kreneck, Thomas H. *Del Pueblo: A Pictorial History of Houston's Hispanic Community*. College Station: Texas A&M University Press, 2012.

———. *Mexican American Odyssey: Felix Tijerina, Entrepreneur and Civic Leader, 1905-1965*. College Station: Texas A&M University Press, 2001.

Limón, José. *Dancing with the Devil: Society and Cultural Poetics in Mexican-American South Texas*. Madison: University of Wisconsin Press, 1994.

———. "Introduction." In *Caballero: A Historical Novel* by Jovita González, edited by José Limón and María Eugenia Cotera. College Station: Texas A&M University Press, 1997.

———. "Introduction." In *Dew on the Thorn*, by Jovita González. Houston: Arte Público, 1997.

———. "El Primer Congreso Mexicanista de 1911: A Precursor to Contemporary Chicanismo." *Aztlan* 5, nos. 1 and 2 (Spring and Fall 1974): 85-117.

Lindheim, Bessie. *Story of Laredo*, No. 16: *Leonor Villegas Magnon and the Mexican Revolution*. Edited by Stan Green. Laredo, TX: Texas A&M International University, 1991.

Link, William A. *The Paradox of Southern Progressivism, 1880-1930*. Chapel Hill: University of North Carolina Press, 1992.

Lipski, John M. *Varieties of Spanish in the United States*. Washington, DC: Georgetown University Press, 2008.

Lomas, Clara. "Introduction: Revolutionary Women and the Alternative Press in the

Borderlands." In *The Rebel*, by Leonor Villegas de Magnón; edited by Clara Lomas. Houston: Arte Público, 1994.

———. "Transborder Discourse: The Articulation of Gender in the Borderlands in the Early Twentieth Century." In *Gender on the Borderlands: The Frontier Reader*, edited by Antonio Castañeda, Susan H. Armitage, Patricia Hart, and Karen Weatheron. Lincoln: University of Nebraska Press, 2007.

Lozano, Rosina. *An American Language: The History of Spanish in the United States.* Oakland: University of California Press, 2018.

Lundholm, Nicholas B. "Cutting Class: Why Arizona's Ethnic Studies Ban Won't Ban Ethnic Studies." *Arizona Law Review* 53, no. 3 (2011): 1042–1088.

MacDonald, Victoria-María. "Demanding Their Rights: The Latino Struggle for Educational Access and Equity." "American Latino Theme Study: Education." National Park Service website, https://www.nps.gov/articles/latinothemeeducation.htm.

Macías, Anna. *Against All Odds: The Feminist Movement in Mexico to 1940.* Westport, CT: Greenwood, 1982.

Mantilla, Luis F. *Libro de Lectura No. 1.* New York: Ivison, Phinney, Blakeman and Company, 1876.

Manuel, Herschel T. *The Education of the Mexican and Spanish-Speaking Children in Texas.* Austin: Fund for Research in Social Sciences, University of Texas, 1930.

———. *Spanish-Speaking Children of the Southwest.* Austin: University of Texas Press, 1965.

Marrs, S. M. N., and Mary Nash. "History and the Status of the Teaching of Spanish in Texas." *Texas Outlook* 14 (February 1930): 3–4.

Martínez, George A. "Legal Indeterminacy, Judicial Discretion and the Mexican-American Litigation Experience, 1930–1980." *UC Davis Law Review* 27, no. 3 (1994): 555–618.

Martinez, Monica Muñoz. *The Injustice Never Leaves You: Anti-Mexican Violence in Texas.* Cambridge, MA: Harvard University Press, 2018.

McCluskey, Audrey Thomas. *A Forgotten Sisterhood: Pioneering Black Women Educators and Activists in the Jim Crow South.* New York: Rowman & Littlefield, 2014.

McCluskey, Audrey Thomas, and Elaine M. Smith, eds. *Mary McLeod Bethune: Building a Better World, Essay and Selected Documents.* Bloomington: Indiana University Press, 1999.

McDonald, David R. *José Antonio Navarro: In Search of the American Dream in Nineteenth-Century Texas.* Austin: Texas State Historical Association, 2010.

McKinstry, H. E. "The American Language in Mexico." *American Mercury* (March 1930): 336–338.

McLemore, Laura Lyons. *Inventing Texas: Early Historians of the Lone Star State.* College Station: Texas A&M University Press, 2004.

Mello, Renato González. "Manuel Gamio, Diego Rivera, and the Politics of Mexican Anthropology." *RES: Anthropology and Aesthetics* no. 45 (Spring 2004): 161–185.

Menchaca, Martha. *Naturalizing Mexican Immigrants: A Texas History.* Austin: University of Texas Press, 2011.

Mendoza, Louis Gerard. *Historia: The Literary Making of Chicana and Chicano History.* College Station: Texas A&M University Press, 2001.

Mickenberg, Julia. *Learning from the Left: Children's Literature, the Cold War, and Radical Politics in the United States.* New York: Oxford University Press, 2006.

Mireles, E. E., R. B Fisher, and Jovita G. Mireles. *Mi Libro Español: Libro Uno.* Austin, TX: W. S. Benson and Company, 1941.

———. *Mi Libro Español: Libro Dos.* Austin, TX: W. S. Benson and Company, 1941.

Mireles, E. E., and Jovita G. Mireles. *El Español Elemental: Primer, Segundo, Tercer, Cuarto, Quinto, Sexto Libros.* Austin, TX: W. S. Benson, 1949.

———. *Mi Libro Español: Libro Tres.* Austin, TX: W. S. Benson and Company, 1943.

Montejano, David. *Anglos and Mexicans in the Making of Texas, 1836–1986.* Austin: University of Texas Press, 1987.

———. "The Demise of 'Jim Crow' for Texas Mexicans, 1940–1970." *Aztlán* 16, no. 1–2 (1985): 27–69.

Ngai, Mae M. *Impossible Subjects: Illegal Aliens and the Making of Modern America.* Princeton, NJ: Princeton University Press, 2004.

Olcott, Jocelyn. *Revolutionary Women in Postrevolutionary Mexico.* Durham, NC: Duke University Press, 2005.

Ontiveros, Randy J. *In the Spirit of a New People: The Cultural Politics of the Chicano Movement.* New York: New York University Press, 2013.

Orozco, Aurora E. "Mexican Blood Runs through My Veins." In *Speaking Chicana: Voice, Power, and Identity,* edited by D. Letticia Galindo and María Dolores Gonzales. Tucson: University of Arizona Press, 1999.

Orozco, Cynthia E. *No Mexicans, Women, or Dogs Allowed: The Rise of the Mexican American Civil Rights Movement.* Austin: University of Texas Press, 2009.

Papers Relating to the Foreign Relations of the United States, Transmitted to Congress with the Annual Message of the President, December 4, 1871. Washington, DC: Government Printing Office, 1871.

Paredes, Américo. *With His Pistol in His Hand: The Ballad of Gregorio Cortez.* Austin: University of Texas Press, 1958.

Pavlenko, Aneta. "'We Have Room for but One Language Here': Language and National Identity in the U.S. at the Turn of the 20th Century." *Multilingua* 21, nos. 2/3 (August 2002): 163–196.

Perales, Monica. *Smeltertown: Making and Remembering a Southwest Border Community.* Chapel Hill: University of North Carolina Press, 2010.

Ramírez, Rafael. *Thoughts and Sentiments of Hebbronville.* Bloomington, IN: Xlibris, 2011.

Ramos, Raúl. "Understanding Greater Revolutionary Mexico: The Case for a Transnational Border History." In *War along the Border: The Mexican Revolution and Tejano Communities,* edited by Arnoldo De León. College Station: Texas A&M University Press, 2012.

Ramsdell, Charles W. *Reconstruction in Texas.* New York: Columbia University Press, 1910.

Rangel, S. C., and C. M. Alcala. "Project Report: De Jure Segregation of Chicanos in Texas Schools." *Harvard Civil Rights—Civil Liberties Law Review* 7, no. 2 (March 1972): 307–391.

Report and Hearings of the Committee on Foreign Relations, United States Senate, vol. 1. Washington, DC: Government Printing Office, 1920.

Restall, Matthew. *Seven Myths of the Spanish Conquest.* New York: Oxford University Press, 2003.

Reyhner, John, and Jeanne Eder. *American Indian Education: A History.* Norman: University of Oklahoma Press, 2004.

Rodriguez, Norma Longoria. "La Escuelita: Antonio's Legacy." *La Voz* 27, no. 9 (November 2014): 18.

Roosevelt, Theodore. *Fear God and Take Your Own.* New York: George H. Doran Company, 1916.

Rosales, F. Arturo. *¡Pobre Raza!: Violence, Justice, and Mobilization among México Lindo Immigrants.* Austin: University of Texas Press, 1999.

Roybal, Karen R. *Archives of Dispossession: Recovering the Testimonios of Mexican American Herederas, 1848-1960.* Chapel Hill: University of North Carolina Press, 2017.

Ruiz, Vicki. *From Out of the Shadows: Mexican Women in Twentieth-Century America.* New York: Oxford University Press, 1998.

———. "Nuestra América: Latino History as United States History." *Journal of American History* 93, no. 3 (December 2006): 655-672.

Saldívar, Ramón. *The Borderlands of Culture: Américo Paredes and the Transnational Imaginary.* Durham: Duke University Press, 2006.

Salinas, Cinthia. "El Colegio Altamirano (1897-1958): New Histories of Chicano Education in the Southwest." *Educational Forum* 65, no. 1 (Fall 2000): 80-86.

Samaniego López, Marco Antonio. "El Norte Revolucionario: Diferencias Regionales y Sus Paradojas en la Relación con Estados Unidos." *Historia Mexicana* 60, no. 2 (October–December 2010): 961-1018.

Sánchez, George I. "History, Culture, Education." In *La Raza: Forgotten Americans,* edited by Julian Samora, 1-26. Notre Dame, IN: University of Notre Dame Press, 1966.

Sánchez, George J. *Becoming Mexican American: Ethnicity, Culture, and Identity in Chicano Los Angeles, 1900-1945.* New York: Oxford University Press, 1993.

Sánchez, Gerardo, ed. *Cartas de José Martí a Néstor Ponce de León.* CreateSpace Independence Publishing Platform, 2013.

Sánchez-Eppler, Karen. "Childhood." In *Keywords for Children's Literature,* edited by Philip Nel and Lissa Paul. New York: New York University Press, 2011.

———. *Dependent States: The Child's Part in Nineteenth-Century American Culture.* Chicago: University of Chicago Press, 2005.

San Miguel, Jr., Guadalupe. *Brown, Not White: School Integration and the Chicano Movement in Houston.* College Station: Texas A&M University Press, 2001.

———. *Chicana/o Struggles for Education: Activism in the Community.* College Station: Texas A&M University Press, 2013.

———. "Culture and Education in the American Southwest: Towards an Explanation of Chicano School Attendance, 1850-1940." *Journal of American Ethnic History* 7 (Spring 1998): 5-21.

———. *"Let All of Them Take Heed": Mexican Americans and the Campaign for Educational Equality in Texas, 1910-1981.* Austin: University of Texas Press, 1987.

San Miguel, Jr., Guadalupe, and Rubén Donato. "Latino Education in Twentieth-Century America: A Brief History." In *Handbook of Latinos and Education: Theory, Research, and Practice,* edited by Enrique G. Murillo, Sofia A. Villenas et al. New York: Routledge, 2010.

San Miguel, Jr., Guadalupe, and Richard R. Valencia. "From the Treaty of Guadalupe Hidalgo to *Hopwood*: The Educational Plight and Struggle of Mexican Americans in the Southwest." *Harvard Educational Review* 68 (Fall 1998): 353-412.

Sierra, Christine, and Adaljiza Sosa Riddell. "Chicanas as Political Actors: Rare Literature, Complex Practice." *National Political Science Review* 4 (1994): 297–317.

Sinéctica, no. 28 (February–July 2006). https://sinectica.iteso.mx/index.php/ SINECTICA/issue/view/31.

Sklar, Kathryn Kish. *Catharine Beecher: A Study in American Domesticity*. New Haven: Yale University Press, 1973.

Smith, Katharine Capshaw. *Children's Literature of the Harlem Renaissance*. Bloomington: Indiana University Press, 2004.

Smith, Michael M. "The Mexican Immigrant Press Beyond the Borderlands: The Case of *El Cosmopolita*, 1914–1919." *Great Plains Quarterly* 10, no. 2 (Spring 1990):71–85.

———. "The Mexican Revolution in Kansas City: Jack Danciger Versus the Colonia Elite." *Kansas History* 14, no. 3 (August 1991): 206–218.

Smith, Michael M., and Jorge Durand. "'El Cosmopolita' de Kansas City (1914–1919): Un Periódico Para Mexicanos." *Frontera Norte* 13, no. 26 (July–December 2001): 7–30.

Soldatenko, Michael. *Chicano Studies: The Genesis of a Discipline*. Tucson: University of Arizona Press, 2009.

Sotero, Soria H. "A Gift of Literacy." In *Memories for Tomorrow: Mexican-American Recollections of Yesteryear*, edited by Margaret Beeson, Marjorie Adams, and Rosalie King. Detroit: Blaine Ethridge Books, 1983.

Szasz, Margaret Connell. *Education and the American Indian: The Road to Self-Determination, 1928–1973*. Albuquerque: University of New Mexico Press, 1974.

Taylor, Paul S. *An American-Mexican Frontier: Nueces County, Texas*. New York: Russell and Russell, 1934.

———. *Mexican Labor in the United States*, vol. 1. Berkeley: University of California Press, 1930.

———. *Mexican Labor in the United States*, vol. 2. Berkeley: University of California Press, 1932.

"Texas Historic Sites Atlas." *Texas Historical Commission website*, https://atlas.thc. state.tx.us/Map.

Tijerina, Andres. "Historical Introduction." In *El Mesquite*, by Elena Zamora O'Shea. College Station: Texas A&M University Press, 2000.

Tindall, George Brown. *The Emergence of the New South, 1913–1946*. Baton Rouge: Louisiana State University Press, 1967.

———. *The Ethnic Southerners*. Baton Rouge: Louisiana State University Press, 1976.

———. *A Twentieth-Century History of Southwest Texas*, vol. 2. Chicago: Lewis Publishing, 1907. WorldCat website, https://www.worldcat.org/title/ twentieth-century-history-of-southwest-texas/oclc/1941544.

Twenty-Seventh Annual Register, 1917–1918. Stanford University, Stanford, CA, February 1918.

Valencia, Richard R. *Chicano Students and the Courts: The Mexican American Legal Struggle for Educational Equality*. New York: New York University Press, 2008.

Valerio-Jiménez, Omar. *River of Hope: Forging Identity and Nation in the Rio Grande Borderlands*. Durham: Duke University Press, 2013.

Vaughan, Mary Kay. "Primary Education and Literacy in Nineteenth-Century Mexico: Research Trends, 1968–1988." *Latin American Research Review* 25, no. 1 (January 1, 1990): 42–43.

———. *The State, Education, and Social Class in Mexico, 1880–1928*. DeKalb: Northern Illinois University Press, 1982.

Villegas de Magnón, Leonor. *The Rebel*. Houston: Arte Público, 1994.

Washington, Anne Reed. "Judge Juan Manuel De la Viña." In *Roots by the River: A Story of a Texas Tropical Borderland*, edited by Valley By-Liners. Canyon, TX: Staked Plains Press, 1978.

Wasserman, Mark. "The Social Origins of the 1910 Revolution in Chihuahua." *Latin American Research Review* 15, no. 1 (1980): 15–38.

Weikle-Mills, Courtney. *Imaginary Citizens: Child Readers and the Limits of American Independence, 1640–1868*. Baltimore: Johns Hopkins University Press, 2013.

White, Alfred. *The Apperceptive Mass of Foreigners as Applied to Americanization: The Mexican Group*. San Francisco: R and E Research Associates, 1923.

Zamora, Emilio. "Las Escuelitas: A Texas-Mexican Search for Educational Excellence." In *Los Tejanos: Children of Two Cultures*. Published proceedings of the South Texas Head Start Bilingual-Bicultural Conference. Edinburg: South Texas Regional Training Office, 1978.

———. "Sara Estela Ramírez: Una Rosa en el Movimiento." In *Mexican Women in the United States: Struggles, Past and Present*, edited by Magdalena Mora and Adelaida del Castillo. Los Angeles: UCLA Chicano Studies Research Center Publications, 1980.

———. *The World of the Mexican Worker in Texas*. College Station: Texas A&M University Press, 2000.

———, ed. *The World War I Diary of José de la Luz Sáenz*. College Station: Texas A&M University Press, 2014.

Zamora O'Shea, Elena. *El Mesquite*. 1935. College Station: Texas A&M University Press, 2000.

———. "The Ranches of Southwest Texas as They Were in the '80s–'90s." In *El Mesquite*. College Station: Texas A&M University Press, 2000.

INDEX

CPSIA information can be obtained
at www.ICGtesting.com
Printed in the USA
LVHW100738081122
732593LV00002B/29